THE WOMEN POETS
IN ENGLISH

THE
WOMEN POETS
IN ENGLISH

AN ANTHOLOGY

Edited, with
an Introduction by
ANN STANFORD

A HERDER AND HERDER BOOK

McGraw-Hill Book Company

New York • St. Louis • San Francisco

123456789 BPBP 798765432

Library of Congress Cataloging in
Publication Data

Stanford, Ann, comp. The women poets
in English.

1. English poetry (Collections)
2. American poetry (Collections)
3. Women's writings, English.
4. Women's writings, American.
I. Title. PR1177.S8 821'.008 72-4145
ISBN 0-07-073223-X

CONTENTS

v

The Women Poets in English

The Women Poets in English

Part Two

The Women Poets in English

The Women Poets in English

ACKNOWLEDGMENTS

Note *Almost a decade and a half ago I began work on an anthology of women poets. At that time, there had not been an anthology based on the inclusion of women important historically or by virtue of their intrinsic merit during this century. The late Oscar Williams encouraged me in the project, though its time had not yet come round. To Kenneth Rexroth and Justus George Lawler I owe thanks for encouraging the revival of the long-planned collection.*

Many colleagues and friends have made suggestions for poets to be included and have lent books from their own libraries. Professors David Anderson, Robert apRoberts, and Richard Vogler of California State University, Northridge have been especially helpful, as has Professor Virginia Tufte of the University of Southern California, and Mr. Robert Baty. I have relied heavily on the collections in the Library of the University of California, Los Angeles, and am grateful for the help of the staff there, in particular that of Frances Rose, Graduate Reserve Librarian. The staff of the English Department, at California State University, Northridge, has given much patient help in the preparation of the manuscript. I owe a deep debt of appreciation to my friend, the poet and scholar, Dr. Robin Johnson, who has worked with me on the editing, who did much of the research for the biographies, and who translated "The Lay of the Honeysuckle" especially for this anthology.

Finally, I wish to thank those many poets who have been so generous in making their work available for inclusion here.

"Come Not Near My Songs," "Song of a Woman Abandoned by the Tribe," "Song for the Newborn," Pilgrimage Song" from *The American Rhythm*.

The Women Poets in English

INTRODUCTION

1

From the first sixteen centuries of our era only a few names of women who recited or wrote their poems have come down to us. But we may be sure that wherever poetry was part of a culture, some of its women were composing and helping to preserve its songs and legends. The women whose names are remembered suggest the presence of others unknown.

This collection begins with two anonymous poems from the Anglo-Saxon which several leading scholars believe were composed by women. Both use women as narrators. In "The Wife's Lament" (ca. 900), the speaker is friendless in a land far from her own, estranged from her husband through the machinations of his kinsmen. She mourns the loss:

> *I make this song   about me full sadly*
> *my own wayfaring.   I a woman tell*
> *what griefs I had   since I grew up*
> *new or old   never more than now.*

The poem ends with a curse on the man who caused her sorrow.

"Eadwacer" (ca. 800) is a more mysterious poem. In it, a woman yearns for the absent and perhaps outlawed Wulf and taunts the man beside her:

> *Do you hear, Eadwacer? . . .*
> *How easy for man to break what never was bound—*
> *   our song together.*

Two to three hundred years after the making of these laments, a woman became famous for her rhymed tales of romance derived from

Celtic and Breton lore. Marie de France, who wrote during the last half of the twelfth century, was connected with the court of the Norman king of England, Henry II. She composed her lays in Anglo-Norman, the language of the court. All during the Middle Ages, they were popular—so popular that a thirteenth-century chronicler, who obviously did not care for fiction, wrote thus of her: "Dame Marie, who turned into rhyme and made verses of 'Lays' which are not in the least true. For these she is much praised, and her rhyme is loved everywhere; for counts, barons, and knights greatly admire it, and hold it dear. And they love her writing so much and take such pleasure in it that they have it read and often copied. These Lays are wont to please ladies, who listen to them with delight, for they are after their own hearts."

In the dedication to her book, Dame Marie says of her tales: "Many a one, on many a day, the minstrel has chanted to my ear. I would not that they should perish, forgotten, by the roadside. In my turn, therefore, I have made of them a song." In making her book, Marie de France became the person who, almost alone, was to preserve the Breton lay as we know it today.

During the centuries after Marie de France, the contest between the two languages, Anglo-Saxon and Anglo-Norman, was resolved. Chaucer in the last part of the fourteenth century demonstrated the possibilities for sound and story in the new vernacular, and his work inspired a number of "Chaucerian" writers who told their tales in rhyme. Among the poems published by Speght in his edition of Chaucer and other poets in 1598 was a poem in which the narrator, a woman, watches from an arbor the songs, games, jousts, and other activities of the followers of the Leaf and the followers of the Flower —representing constancy and inconstancy. This little narrative of about six hundred lines is a work of grace, charm, and unity. Dryden believed it to be by Chaucer, and chose it as one of five pieces that he translated from that master. The subtitle of his translation is "The Lady in the Arbour," a name I have adapted in the text to identify the anonymous author herself.

From the last quarter of the fifteenth century comes another, somewhat longer, narrative, again from one of the Chaucerian collections, that of Thynne in 1528. "The Assembly of Ladies" is in the same rhyme royal, or Chaucerian stanza, and the author again identifies herself as a woman—in fact, as a "lady" of higher degree than the gentlewomen who also appear in the poem, one of them as her waiting woman. "The Assembly of Ladies" is a dream vision, in which the narrator falls asleep in an arbor. She dreams she is awakened by the lady Persèveraunce, who arranges for her to be guided to the palace of Pleasant Regard, presided over by the lady Loyalty. There the narrator and her friends are allowed to present their complaints about their treatment in love. The poem gives a good picture of a medieval court with its arrangements for caring for petitioners. I have called this author by the name, "The Lady of the Assembly."

As in the case of the above narrative poems, most of the Middle English lyrics, too, are anonymous. However, there are a few lines by an identifiable author in the correspondence preserved by the medieval Paston family. In February, 1477, young Margery Brews sent a letter to the man she hoped to marry, John Paston III. In the midst of her expressions of love, she bursts into rhyme. Apparently young Margery herself could not write, for this secret letter to her "Valentine" was set down for her by her father's clerk.

In 1486 the abbey of St. Albans brought out one of the first printed books in England, *The Treatyses Pertynyng to Hawkynge, Huntynge and Fisshyng with an Angle.* The section called *Boke of Huntyng* is by Dame Julians Barnes, who refers to herself through most of the poem as "your Dame." Her book instructs young aristocrats in the complicated vocabulary and ritual of the hunt. For the most part, it is a rhymed version of a French treatise. Of its author, nothing is known, though several spurious accounts have been given of her.

From around 1500 a poem is preserved attributed to Queen Elizabeth of York, the wife of Henry VII; it is a joyous and elaborate song, celebrating love, pleasure, beauty, and grace. Not again in the century do we have so exuberant a song from an Englishwoman, though other women of high rank were also writing—among them Lady Margaret Roper, Queen Catherine Parr, and Lady Jane Grey. They did translations or wrote prose pieces or verses in Latin, all outside the scope of this anthology, as are the poems of Mary, Queen of Scots, who wrote in French, and who, in prison, on the day before her execution composed and recited a prayer in Latin verse.

Likewise from prison came Anne Boleyn's denial of the reports of her misconduct, "Defiled is my name full sore" and the splendid lyric "O death! rock me asleep," often attributed to her. Anne Askew, the Protestant martyr, was another who wrote from prison. Daughter of a knight of Lincolnshire, she had been married against her will to a wealthy neighbor and in her unhappiness began to spend long hours reading the Bible. When her husband objected, she returned to her own family and later went, with her two children, to London. There she was acquainted with several of the ladies around Queen Catherine Parr and possibly with the Queen herself. Arrested by the Queen's enemies, ostensibly for her views on the sacrament, and tortured on the rack, Anne Askew would implicate no one else, nor would she recant. She was burned in July, 1546, thereby winning a place in Foxe's *Book of Martyrs*. Her own account of the trial, printed on the continent later the same year, contains "The Ballad Which Anne Askewe Made and Sang When She Was in Newgate."

Queen Elizabeth, too, wrote poems during her imprisonment at Woodstock in the reign of her sister Mary. They indicate her suspicions and thoughts of vengeance against her foes, themes expressed at length in the poem written about 1587 during the crisis over the presence of Mary, Queen of Scots, in the realm. Elizabeth threatens to "poll their tops" who support that "Daughter of Debate." The strong and involved syntax found in her few original poems is present also in the translations that Queen Elizabeth made from Horace, Plutarch, Seneca, and Boethius.

Elizabeth is also often credited with the poem which begins "I grieve and dare not show my discontent," supposedly written after she gave up the idea of marrying her French suitor. It is much smoother than her other poems, and it is possible that another poet wrote it and passed it off as the Queen's. The practice, common at the time, makes it difficult to know the actual author of many other poems as well. There is a sonnet attributed to the Queen in John Soowthern's *Pandora,* for example, which follows four other sonnets purporting to be by the Countess of Oxford mourning the death of a son. All five poems are in a form so peculiar to Soowthern that it must be assumed he wrote the whole series. The number of attributions of poems to women does indicate, however, that it was not unusual for women to be writing poetry at the time. Many women in Elizabeth's day were well educated, and a part of education was not only to translate from the classics, but to write poems in Latin as well.

Nevertheless, during the whole sixteenth century, there are only three books of poetry in English by women. Two are by a single author, a gentlewoman named Isabella Whitney. Her first book, published in 1567, bore the title *The Copie of a Letter, lately written in Meeter by a yonge gentilwoman to her unconstant lover* and was signed by the initials, "Is. W." The young gentlewoman actually fills only half the book with her jogging rhythm; the other half is taken by the gentleman's reply. Six years later, in 1573, the same author, this time identified by her full name, followed her *Letter* with *A Sweet Nosgay, or pleasant Posye containing a hundred and ten Phylosophicall Flowers.* A few flowers from the *Nosgay* have been included here.

In 1592 the third book appeared—Mary Sidney Herbert's *The Tragedie of Antonie Done into English by the Countess of Pembroke.* It was a translation of Garnier's play written in the classic style—long verse monologues interspersed with choruses—and it was popular enough to be republished in 1595. The Countess was a generous patron of poets, by whom her work was much praised. One of them, Gabriel Harvey, wrote: "And what if she can publish more works in a month than Nash hath published in his whole life; or the pregnantest of our inspired Heliconists can equal?" If such vast production ever existed, little of it has survived. It was not the fashion then for poets of noble families to appear in print; they wrote primarily for the pleasure of themselves and their friends. The only lyrics traceable to Mary Herbert are the "Dialogue between Two Shepherds," written to honor the visit of the Queen to the Countess's house, and a lament for her brother Sir Philip Sidney, attributed to the Countess in Bartlet's *Book of Ayres.*

The Countess's most important poetical work, however, was not published until the nineteenth century—her *Psalms of David.* Her brother, Sir Philip, had at the time of his death translated the first forty-three; the Countess continued the translation, completing the other 128. Most scholars agree with Grosart's comment that the Countess's are "infinitely in advance of her brother's in thought, epithet and melody." The whole work is a remarkable one.

When the Sidneys undertook the translation, the most commonly known versions of the Psalms were the undistinguished ballad stanzas of Sternhold and Hopkins then regularly sung in the Church of England. The Sidneys attempted to create a fresh combination of meter and rhyme suited to the mood and content of each of the hymns. They succeeded so well that only one pair in their whole collection has the same pattern. At times the Countess expanded and clarified her text in terms suggested by such commentators as John Calvin. The work remains a monument to the skill, intelligence, and devotion of the translators, particularly the Lady Mary.

The Women Poets in English

Meanwhile in Scotland the Reformation had gone on apace, and from Edinburgh in 1603 came a small book which reflected the gloomy views of the Scottish Reformers. The book was *Ane Godlie Dreame,* and in it Elizabeth Melvill, Lady Culross, gave a gruesome depiction of hell, where "poor damned souls, tormented sore for sin in flaming fire, were frying wondrous fast." The work proved popular. Originally printed in the Scots dialect, it came out in an Anglicized edition shortly after, and there were four editions in all by 1606. Elizabeth Melvill's book was doubtless popular because of its embodiment of Calvinistic theology, for the controversy between Catholicism and the various forms of Protestantism was intense among all classes of people. Otherwise, *Ane Godlie Dreame* might have remained in manuscript along with Mary Herbert's *Psalms* and the work of many other poets. Lucy Harington, Countess of Bedford, for example, was a patron of poets, among them John Donne, and among the poems formerly attributed to him is one that was in fact written by the Countess. It begins "Death, be not proud," just as does Donne's famous sonnet, but it proceeds as an elegy. Since manuscripts circulated freely then, it is not now possible to discern which of the two poets used the opening phrase first.

Another woman sometimes mentioned as a patron is Lady Elizabeth Carey, who had been tutored by the poet John Davies of Hereford. In 1613, her own large work was published, identified only by the inttials E. C. It was *The Tragedie of Mariam, the Faire Queene of Jewry,* the first original play by a woman in England.

Another member of the remarkable Sidney family, Mary Sidney Wroth, the niece of the Countess of Pembroke, appeared in print in 1621 with a long prose romance, *The Countess of Montgomerie's Urania,* the first prose fiction by a woman in English. Like Sir Philip's *Arcadia,* upon which it was modeled, the *Urania* was liberally interspersed with poems in a variety of forms. For all Mary Wroth's impressive aristocratic and literary pedigree, spelled out in full on the title page, the *Urania* was a pot-boiler, and its author gains a place as the first in a long line of women forced to take up the pen to stave off creditors. The Lady Mary's attempt at professional authorship did not turn out well; the amours of the shepherds and shepherdesses, princes and princesses of the mythical country of Urania resembled too closely —some even claimed they reflected—the scandals of Jacobean society, and Lady Mary was forced to withdraw her book from sale.

In the same year as the publication of the *Urania,* Rachel Speght, of whom little is known, had two long poems published in a little book titled *Mortalitie's Memorandum, with a Dreame Prefixed, imaginarie in manner, reall in matter.* The author includes a stanza defending the right of women to be considered as whole persons, with mind, will, and power. She had come to the defense of women once before, in 1617, with *A Mouzell for Melastomus, the Cynicall Bayter of, and foule mouthed Barker against Evahs Sex. Or an Apologeticall Answere to that Irreligious and Illiterate Pamphlet made by Jo. Sw. . . . The Arraignement of Women.* Apparently she was criticized for her "muzzle"; part of her "Dreame" is an agitated account of the reaction to it, and "Mortalitie's Memorandum" seems to be an attempt to show that her views on religion, at least, are orthodox. Thus the work of this early poet is marred by the pervading consciousness of opposition.

In 1630 there appeared a small book called *A Chaine of Pearle; or, a Memoriall of the Peerless Graces and heroick vertues of Queene Elizabeth.* The book was "composed by the Noble Lady Diana Primrose," and contained a commendatory poem on its author by another woman, Dorothy Berry. In reciting the virtues of the late Queen under the headings of Religion, Chastity, Temperance, etc., Lady Diane reveals the high points of Elizabeth's reign as it appeared to her subjects. By this time the kingdom had had almost a quarter century of rule by the Stuart kings, a rule which more and more of the populace found oppressive. In 1629, the year before Lady Diana's pamphlet was published, Charles I had dissolved Parliament, which was the last hope of many for relief from the arbitrariness of the King and the slow movement of the Church back toward Catholicism. A pamphlet in praise of the late Queen thus had political overtones. In showing the glories of her reign, it silently remarked the iniquities of her successors. Moreover, the fifty-year reign of the intelligent Queen, looked back on now as a golden age, could not but be an inspiration to women. As Anne Bradstreet wrote in 1643:

> *Now say, have women worth? or have they none?*
> *Or had they some, but with our Queen is't gone?*
> *Nay masculines, you have thus taxed us long,*
> *But she, though dead, will vindicate our wrong.*
> *Let such as say our sex is void of reason,*
> *Know 'tis a slander now but once was treason.*

Yet, despite the example of the late Queen and others, opposition to the publication of books by women remained. Evidences of the condemnation of women who wrote, or even read too much, are found all through this, and even succeeding, periods. In New England, Governor Winthrop wrote thus in his journal for 1645:

> *Mr. Hopkins, the governor of Hartford upon Connecticut, came to Boston, and brought his wife with him . . . who was fallen into a sad infirmity, the loss of her understanding and reason, which had been growing upon her divers years, by occasion of her giving herself wholly to reading and writing, and had written many books. Her husband, being very loving and tender of her, was loath to grieve her; but he saw his error, when it was too late. For if she had attended her household affairs, and such things as belong to women, and not gone out of her way and calling to meddle in such things as are proper for men, whose minds are stronger, etc., she had kept her wits, and might have improved them usefully and honorably in the place God had set her.*

Even as he wrote this, the Governor had within his own colony another woman who had taken up the pen and was composing long poems on history, physiology, and current events, as well as elegies and poems about her own experiences and family. This was Anne Bradstreet, the first dedicated writer of poetry in the English colonies. In 1650 Mistress Bradstreet's brother-in-law took her poems to London, where they were printed without her knowledge. The little book did not bear her name, but was called *The Tenth Muse Lately Sprung Up in America . . . By a Gentlewoman in those parts.* The preface to the reader carefully explained that the author of the poems had not neglected her household duties while writing but had taken the time from "sleep and other refreshments." A second edition was published in Boston in 1678, under the title *Several Poems.* It was the first book of belles-lettres published in the English colonies. Though it came out after Anne Bradstreet's death, many of the passages had been revised for publication by the author herself, and the edition included personal poems not present in the earlier book. The freshness and life of Anne Bradstreet's writing still impresses us today. Here is a real woman speaking, in phrases that found echoes later in the Romantic period of the early nineteenth century. We can respond to her pictures of a mother trying to quiet a restless baby, a woman who fears she may die in childbirth, a woman expressing in homely imagery her love for her husband and children. Anne Bradstreet was conscious of criticism of herself as a woman writer:

> I am obnoxious [oblivious] to each carping tongue
> Who says my hand a needle better fits.
> A poet's pen all scorn I should thus wrong,
> For such despite they cast on female wits:
> If what I do prove well, it won't advance,
> They'll say it's stol'n, or else it was by chance.

But she was encouraged by her husband, her father, and other relatives and went on writing throughout her life.

Margaret Cavendish, the Duchess of Newcastle, also was warmly supported in her writing by her husband. Beginning with her *Poems and Fancies* in 1653, she produced twelve volumes of plays, verses, and essays. For her pains, she was criticized and called "mad," a term by which she is still often described. "Sure the poore woman is a little distracted, shee could never bee so rediculous else as to venture at writeing book's, and in verse too," a female contemporary wrote to a friend. The Duke shared the criticism directed at his wife. Pepys called him "an ass to suffer her to write what she does to him and of him." When we read her own account of her life, we cannot but be attracted to this energetic woman with her untrained natural gifts and her ardent desire for fame. She attempted a tremendous range of projects, and she has left a few very pleasant lyrics.

Much more sober and restrained are the *Divine Songs* of Anne Collins also published in 1653. The Preface is careful to explain that its author was kept, apparently by illness, from "bodily employments"; the poems themselves show that Anne Collins was a Puritan who had little help in her avocation of poetry other than her own reading.

More fortunate in her associates was Katherine Philips, known as "the matchless Orinda." She was the center of a literary circle devoted to neo-Platonism, which had among its members the poets Henry Vaughan and Abraham Cowley, and that master of prose, Jeremy Taylor. Her poems are thoughtful and poised, seriously concerned with philosophy, friendship, the joys of simplicity. Country life is praised for its emphasis on true values; passionate love is cast out with the words "Hence, Cupid, with your cheating toys." The poems of Orinda circulated widely in manuscript and were published in a pirated edition in 1664. A corrected edition appeared in 1667.

Katherine Philips was the favorite of an esoteric coterie. But in the early 1670s a woman destined to participate boldly in popular literature and the drama burst upon the London literary scene. Aphra Behn, "the incomparable Astraea," was a woman of colorful background and incredible vigor. She spent part of her youth in the South American colony of British Guiana and was married briefly to a British merchant of Dutch extraction. After his death, she became a spy for Charles II in the Netherlands and later was thrown into debtors' prison. Upon her release, she turned to writing for a livelihood, becoming the first Englishwoman to earn her living by the pen. In the two decades after 1671, Mrs. Behn produced seventeen clever and lively plays, twelve novels, and a sizeable body of verse. Her novels contain character studies important to the development of that then new genre. One of them, *Oroonoko, or The Royal Slave*, was the first to express sympathy for the slaves and outrage against the cruelties of slave traders. Most of her poems are lyrics that were to be sung during the production of her plays. Skillful, witty, light in tone, they are among the most famous songs of the Restoration theater.

Another playwright, John Dryden, in 1686 wrote one of his most celebrated odes to the "Pious Memory of the Accomplisht Young Lady Mrs. Anne Killigrew Excellent in the Two Sister-Arts of Poesie and Painting." In life, however, Anne Killigrew encountered some of the same problems as did Anne Bradstreet. Her poem titled "Upon the Saying That My Verses Were Made by Another," contains the lines:

> *Like Esop's painted jay, I seem'd to all,*
> *Adorn'd in plumes, I not my own could call:*
> *Rifled like her, each one my feathers tore,*
> *And, as they thought, unto the owner bore.*

And, in truth, Dryden was not so much celebrating her work as using her death as the occasion for a poem on poetry itself.

Mary Lee, Lady Chudleigh, responded to social pressures by satire. Like Rachel Speght in the sixteenth century, she spoke out on the subject of women's place. Her poem "To the Ladies" begins "Wife and servant are the same," and in 1709 she published a lively piece, *The Ladies Defence: or, The Bride-Woman's Counsellor Answered: A Poem in Dialogue Between Sir John Brute, Sir Wm. Loveall, Melissa, and a Parson*, unfortunately too long to be represented here.

Mary Lee's contemporary, and the most talented woman poet of this period, was Anne Finch, Countess of Winchelsea. She did not write her poems for publication, the reason being revealed in one of them:

> *Alas! a woman that attempts the pen,*
> *Such a presumptuous creature is esteemed,*
> *The fault can by no virtue be redeemed.*
> *They tell us we mistake our sex and way.*

Her *Miscellany Poems* were, nevertheless, published in 1713, and her love of nature marks her as another forerunner of the Romantic period that was to come almost a century later.

Satire on the foibles of society continued to be important in the eighteenth century, as exemplified in the writing of Jane Brerton, Constantia Grierson, Laetitia Pilkington, Ann Murry, and especially Lady Mary Wortley Montagu. The latter's *Town Eclogues,* written jointly with Alexander Pope and John Gay, depict the sorrows of women who grew old or lost their looks in a society which emphasized beauty and beaux.

In America for more than a century there were no successors to Anne Bradstreet. Then in 1761 a young black girl was brought from her home in Africa and sold as a servant to the Wheatley family of Boston. The girl, named Phillis Wheatley, was well treated and soon showed an aptitude for learning. She began to write in the neo-classic style of her day, addressing her poems to a wide variety of persons, including General Washington and the students at Harvard University. Her poems were published in 1773, the first book by a black American. For a time she was a celebrity, but after the death of her patron family and desertion by her husband, she fell into poverty and obscurity and died at an early age. Her poetry was as good as most written in America at that time, all of it echoing the English neo-classical writers. Unfortunately, she never wrote of her African experience or the realities of being transported as a slave.

Besides satire and formal poetry, popular ballads based on current happenings or older tales were popular throughout the eighteenth century. Many of the older ballads were in Scots dialect, for the Scots had kept up the tradition of oral poetry and ballad singing, particularly among the women of the so-called "singing families." One of these women, Anna Gordon Brown of Falkland, became known for her large repertoire of the ancient songs. Over a period of years, at the request of collectors, she wrote down thirty-three ballads in fifty-one

variant versions. David C. Fowler, who has made a study of the de-
velopment of her techniques as a ballad singer, has also commented
on the high quality of her versions, pointing out that Child in his
famous collection chooses hers as the best in twenty-four out of her
thirty-three ballads. Fowler's study records many instances in which
she made new versions or revisions particularly pertinent to women's
interests. For example, her "Willie of Douglas Dale," based on the
older ballad, "Child Waters," devotes six stanzas to the choice of a
nursemaid for the baby; moreover, at the time of the baby's birth in
the greenwood, Willie is much more solicitous for the comfort and
welfare of mother and child than is the original Lord John in "Child
Waters." Fowler also points out that, in Mrs. Brown's own version of
"Child Waters," Lord John is "modified in the direction of Willie,
and Burd Ellen tends to show more spirit than fair Ellen, her medieval
predecessor in the Percy folio version." The reworking of ballad
material, the putting of ballads into the singer's own style, goes on
even today among American folk-ballad singers who still use the
old frameworks. Mrs. Brown was an exceedingly skillful singer, re-
working and recombining the best elements of the stories she in-
herited. A few of her pieces were her own inventions, or were based
on older ballads now lost. One of these is the romance "The Gay
Goshawk" (Child's Number 96A) reproduced here.

Though no one contributed as much as Mrs. Brown to the preserva-
tion of older pieces, other women in Scotland became known for their
ballads during the eighteenth and nineteenth centuries. These are
represented here by Jane Elliot, Lady Anne Lindsay, Lady Carolina
Nairne, Joanna Baillie, and Lady John Scott. Many times the older
songs were refined in the later versions, by taking out uncouth or
bawdy references. Such polite revision was not confined to women;
Robert Burns so revised the ballads when he worked with them, and
one of Mrs. Falkland's editors took a sexually suggestive reference
out of one of hers.

The ballads used simple language, their stories were romantic—
tales of love or adventure, and often of the supernatural. These sub-
jects, together with an emphasis on the healing power of nature and
attention to the life of simple people, were to become important in-
gredients of nineteenth-century poetry.

One of the earliest women to display these characteristics was
Charlotte Smith. Like Aphra Behn, she turned to writing from neces-
sity. Early in life she had been persuaded to marry a young man with

whom she had little in common; over the protests of Charlotte, he spent foolishly and ended in debtor's prison. His wife was imprisoned with him for a time. Upon her release, striving to make a living for him and her nine children, she tried to sell the poems she had been writing at odd hours. Several publishers refused them, and in 1784 she had the sixteen *Elegiac Sonnets* printed at her own expense. They were an immediate success, and a second edition came out that same year. To each edition Mrs. Smith added more poems, until by the tenth edition of 1811 there were ninety-two sonnets. Mrs. Smith was innovative in taking her stanza form from Shakespeare, an author then much out of fashion. She was criticized, particularly by Anna Seward, for her "formlessness." In fact, she was perhaps the most influential figure in returning the sonnet to a form more suited to the English language. Moreover, she helped to turn the attention of her contemporaries back to the great Elizabethan. Despite the success of her sonnets, Charlotte Smith's lot was a hard one, and her poems often reveal melancholy thoughts and exclamations of despair. Some give faithful renderings of the country things around her, especially flowers; while others pick out wild and lurid scenes of nature clothed in darkness. Pastoral, gloomy, and Gothic, Mrs. Smith's poems are characteristic of her age, as well as precursors of what was soon to come.

Though she was essentially a poet, Charlotte Smith was forced by poverty to become a novelist. Her first novel, *Emmeline,* published in 1788, was admired by Sir Walter Scott, who later wrote a biography of its author. Two novels, totalling seven volumes, appeared in 1792, and thereafter, Mrs. Smith published a voluminous novel a year until her health failed in 1799. Her tremendous output perhaps had a vitiating effect upon the quality of her novels; nevertheless she stands as the important woman novelist between Fanny Burney and Anne Radcliffe. It was the latter whose novels established the vogue for the Gothic romance, a genre still much in the hands of women. The atmosphere created by wild and untamed aspects of nature are to be found in Anne Radcliffe's poetry as well as in her novels. Like Charlotte Smith's, her landscapes reflect the mood of the observer.

The work of the eighteenth-century novelists—Austen, Burney, Smith, Radcliffe, and others—smoothed the way for publication by women in the nineteenth century. Felicia Hemans wrote a vast quantity of poems, many of them romantic narratives. They had a musical quality and quick movement that made them popular in her day. Some of them, such as "The Homes of England" and "The Landing of the Pilgrim Fathers in New England," are familiar still.

Much more serious as a poet is Elizabeth Barrett Browning, whom Gilbert Chesterton called "the most European of all the English poets" of the Victorian age. Her concern with the affairs of Europe was intense, though she is best known for her *Sonnets from the Portuguese,* written during the courtship of Robert Browning. She had no intention of publishing these, but when her husband discovered them, he insisted on their being given to the public. They were highly regarded in their time, though it has become fashionable to criticize them. Mrs. Browning had an active intellect which often focussed upon contemporary problems, as in her poems against child labor and the forced drafting of soldiers in Europe. In her long poem "Curse for a Nation" she denounced the practice of slavery in America.

Quite the opposite of the broad European experience of Elizabeth Barrett Browning was that of the three Brontë sisters, who spent most of their brief lives in their father's rectory at Haworth. Charlotte, the eldest, having failed to impress Southey with her manuscripts, turned to teaching school as a supplement to the family's income. In 1845, the three sisters published a book of poems at their own expense; but only two copies were sold. Later Charlotte explained their choosing to publish their books under the names of Currer, Ellis, and Acton Bell. "We did not like to declare ourselves women, because—without at that time suspecting that our mode of writing and thinking was not what is called 'feminine'—we had a vague impression that authoresses are liable to be looked on with prejudice; we had noticed how critics sometimes use for their chastisement the weapon of personality, and for their reward, a flattery, which is not true praise." Their novels did indeed shock their Victorian contemporaries by showing women as passionate beings, not merely objects to be loved. Their poetry was more conventional, though in form and language it shows a directness and simplicity that was to remain the mode for many lyricists far into the future.

The simple form and diction of the Brontës was used also by Christina Rossetti and Emily Dickinson later in the century. All of these poets were, in the eyes of the world, lacking in experience. Yet the very quietness and seclusion of their lives may have aided their probing so effectively into deeper layers of being. Christina Rossetti's religious vision and Dickinson's descriptions of eternity bring vast panoramas into simple forms and homely images. Dickinson's combination of the large statement with the small and detailed object and her stunning use of metaphor have made her one of the major voices in American poetry.

From the middle of the nineteenth century, much of the energy of women poets was directed into humanitarian causes. Abolition of slavery, woman suffrage, improving the condition of working women and the poor, all claimed the attention of leading women. Julia Ward Howe, active in many such causes, was most famous for her "Battle Hymn of the Republic" published in *The Atlantic* in 1862. Though she wrote books of travel, essays, and poetry, it was mainly the authorship of the "Hymn" that resulted in her election to the American Academy of Arts and Letters—the first woman member.

At mid-century, Emma Lazarus was born into a wealthy Jewish family whose ancestors had been in America for generations. Her early poems showed great promise and brought the praise and friendship of Emerson; she was better known, however, for her poetic translations of Goethe and Heine. Though she had always been interested in her background as a descendant of the Sephardic Jews of Spain, the terrible pogroms in Russia in the early 1880s turned her into one of the leading opponents of anti-Semitism. Her prose and poetry in the cause of rights for the Jewish minorities and for all human beings were known on two continents. Her last work was a series of "Little Poems in Prose" called *By the Waters of Babylon*. These poems are experimental, going beyond the extended line of Whitman, whose work she, of course, knew. Like his, they depend in part on the ancient rhythms of Hebrew poetry. But they are innovative in the direction of Amy Lowell's later experiments in "polyphonic prose," which they precede by over a quarter of a century. Emma Lazarus is now mostly remembered for the few moving lines on the base of the Statue of Liberty; her work as a whole has not yet received the careful attention of scholars.

At the end of the nineteenth century poets in England, too, were taking part in humanitarian causes. Alice Meynell, who worked as a journalist to help support her large family, often appeared on platforms and in demonstrations which sought for women the right to vote and to advance in the professions. Her two major poetic periods bracket this active life, occurring before her marriage and in her later years. Mary Elizabeth Coleridge, an accomplished writer of prose and verse, did not feel a professional urgency about her poetry; in fact, deferred publication of her poems out of fear of not living up to her famous name. She devoted much of her time to helping working women and teaching literature in the Working-Women's College. Her best poems open avenues of romantic escape, having a haunting otherworldly quality.

In 1884 the first book of lyrics by Michael Field appeared in England, and lavish praise was heaped on "Mr. Field" by the reviewers. Michael Field, it turned out, was actually two women, Katharine Bradley and Edith Cooper, aunt and niece. For whatever reason, the twenty-seven tragedies and eight volumes of lyrics they published over the years after the revelation of their unique collaboration received little public notice. Nevertheless, for over thirty years the two maintained an unusual harmony of insight, especially in their plays, and, as Michael put it, "the work is perfect mosaic." Only at the very end of their lives, in their religious lyrics, did they write separately, though even these last volumes bear their common name.

Consciousness of a world beyond permeates much of the poetry of Charlotte Mew, who first began publishing in *The Yellow Book* during the 1890s. In her constant awareness of other levels of experience and in what has been called her "devastating simplicity of statement," Mew has been compared to Emily Dickinson. In her character studies, irony, occasional use of country dialect, and revelation of the harshness of country life, she is also akin to Thomas Hardy, who greatly admired her poetry. She was an exacting critic of her own work and saved little of it, but her two small volumes contain a high percentage of exceptionally fine poems. Charlotte Mew was the victim of a Victorian upbringing which did not provide daughters with any training for self-support. Confined to genteel poverty, she was never able to rate herself at her true value, and at last died by her own hand, her life a tragic example of the repression wrought by a restricting society on an artist of great ability.

2

In the autumn of 1912 a young American, Hilda Doolittle, brought to Ezra Pound in London a group of poems based on the ancient Greek lyrics. Pound thereupon coined the word, "Les Imagistes," and arranged for the publication of three poems by "H. D., Imagiste" in the January, 1913, issue of Harriet Monroe's magazine *Poetry*. The poems were "Hermes of the Ways," "Priapus" (later retitled "Orchard"), and "Epigram." With "Oread," published the following year in *The Egoist*, these have been called "the defining works of the second, decisive phase of Imagism," and H. D., especially in the poems gathered in *Sea Garden* (1925), has remained the example of the "perfect imagist."

Amy Lowell, hearing of the new group of poets in England, went there to meet them. Taking command of the imagist movement, she gave wide publicity to the canons of verse originally set forth by Ezra Pound, which called for concreteness of language and image, restraint, suggestion rather than statement or moral, care in the selection of each word—rules which continue to be basic to much modern poetry. Amy Lowell, a commanding figure in American poetry for many years, did not confine herself to imagism, but moved to other kinds of verse. Notable among these were her translations and adaptations of Chinese poetry and her experiments with what she called "polyphonic prose," a form in which the line as a unit is abandoned, but the other qualities of poetry remain, that is, recurrent patterns of sound and rhythm, repetition of syntactical units, strong and colorful images. One of her finest pieces is "The Basket," the first example of polyphonic prose in English. It contains passages of surrealism and others of sexual symbolism which are modern enough to have been written today.

Meanwhile in France, Mina Loy was writing her free verse poems of outspoken eroticism, influenced by some of the same impulses that moved the imagists. Her work also reflects the theories then current in French art, especially those of the Dadaists. Adelaide Crapsey, who studied in Rome and traveled in France before returning to America to work on her long essay on metrics, was influenced by the Japanese haiku and tanka. During the last year of her life (1914) she wrote the small volume of poems which contain most notably her "cinquains," based on those brief forms. Her book appeared in 1915, and her poems were later published in the magazine *Others*, which also introduced Mina Loy to the American avant-garde.

In 1915 too, Marianne Moore was at the beginning of her long career as poet and editor. Even her earliest work that year in *Poetry* showed qualities that have remained her trademarks—intricate stanzas based on a count of syllables, the inclusion of quotations and blocks of esoteric knowledge. She pushed the image in the direction of concrete and full detail.

The Women Poets in English

Edith Sitwell was another poet who felt the need for change during those years. Later, she described her feelings: "At the time I began to write, a change in the direction, imagery and rhythms in poetry had become necessary, owing to the rhythmical flaccidity, the verbal deadness, the dead and expected patterns, of some of the poetry immediately preceding us." In escaping from "expected patterns," however, Sitwell did not follow the imagists in their emphasis on precision. She was drawn to the shadowy and musical forms of the French symbolists, and under their influence developed her unique and elaborate style.

While these modern classicists were working out their rhythms and forms under European influences, others, in America, were working at a more indigenous rhythm, based on the tradition of Whitman, his development of an open form and his concern with the details of the lives of working men and women. One such poet was Lola Ridge, born in Ireland and raised in Australia, who came to the United States in 1907. Part of her long poem "The Ghetto," based on her own experience, was published in *The New Republic* in 1918, and her book by that name came out the same year. Her second book, *Sun-Up*, was concerned with the organization of the working classes in the labor movement; her third contained poems sympathetic with workers in China and Russia. Her poems remain surprisingly contemporary, and a revival of her name in literary histories and anthologies is in order.

The new freedom in verse form was given further impetus in the United States through a study of the songs of the native Americans. Frances Densmore has been probably the greatest collector of these songs; but her translations, gathered from native informants, stand outside the scope of this anthology. It remained for Mary Austin, a school teacher living at the edge of the California desert, to attempt consciously to bring what she called the "natural" rhythms of the native Americans into poetry in English. Her book *The American Rhythm*, (1923), contained a long essay on the subject as well as her own adaptations of the songs of various tribes of the Southwest. About the same time Beatrice Ravenel was incorporating the lore of the Yemassees of the Southeast in her poems, and Constance Lindsay Skinner had created an imaginary village based on the culture of the Northwest tribes in her *Songs of the Coast Dwellers*.

Other poets were keeping closer to the older traditions. In England, Elizabeth Daryush, with her father Robert Bridges, experimented with syllabics, but her poetry remains largely traditional. In 1920 Ruth Pitter's long and substantial career began with *First Poems,* and in 1926 Victoria Sackville-West celebrated English country life in *The Land.* In the United States Edna St. Vincent Millay, whose career was launched with "Renascence" in 1912, became the best known lyricist of the twenties, representing the buoyant spirit of the years following World War I. Elinor Wylie, too, was, in her life as in her intense poetry, a vivid representative of the period, bringing out four volumes before her death in 1928. From this decade also came the first of Dorothy Parker's satiric verse and two volumes of Léonie Adams' elaborate and superbly controlled poems. From Elizabeth Madox Roberts, better known as a novelist, came *Under the Tree,* poems ostensibly for children, though the subtleties of the simple verse can best be appreciated by adults. In 1923 the first of Louise Bogan's lyrics appeared. There are only 105 in her final collection. Precise, intelligent, in the tradition of the late Elizabethan writers such as Jonson, she promises to remain one of the finest lyricists of this century.

The new verse in America, flowing from imagism, the Whitmanian influence, and the interest in Indian songs, was given a public through such little magazines as *Poetry, Others, The Little Review, The Measure,* and *The Dial* as a second wave of poets writing in free verse became visible in the early twenties. Notable among them was Babette Deutsch, long one of the foremost among this country's men and women of letters, whose intelligent and urbane voice has been a continuing influence in American poetry.

In the thirties Marya Zaturenska began to publish poetry which, with its subtle half tones, created a mythology of its own. Muriel Rukeyser's first book came in 1935; its title *Theory of Flight* suggests the awareness of scientific and social realities for which she has since been known. In the same decade, Phyllis McGinley brought out the first of her satires on suburbia, Josephine Miles began to use her succinct and witty verse against all forms of pomposity, and the English poet Stevie Smith published *A Good Time Was Had by All,* the first of her serio-comic works. Kay Boyle, who had then lived in Europe for ten years, appeared with the first of several books based on her international experience.

Early in the forties, Hildegarde Flanner, who had been writing for many years, brought out her most significant book, *If There Is Time,* infused with the Quaker outcry against any violation of life, and Marguerite Young's *Moderate Fable,* the second of her imaginative volumes, appeared. From the end of World War II the number of poets has continued to grow. Many have followed the imagists' demand for the use of concrete images and have made their impact by focussing on objects and detail until the objects themselves become significant of the poem's larger meanings. In the work of Maxine Kumin and Mary Oliver attended to literal detail is so skillfully joined with traditional form that the result is a new order of poetry. Constance Carrier, also working in controlled forms, dwells on the minutiae of a scene with the eye of a camera. May Swenson in *Iconographs* has pushed the perception of the object so far that in many of her poems the shape of the lines themselves become visual symbols of the object.

Women poets have retained their interest in social causes, including now the movement for peace. In 1938 Robin Hyde, a New Zealand journalist, described the tragedies she saw among the peasants during the war in China; her poems seem to be descriptions of the current Indo-China war. Muriel Rukeyser and Denise Levertov are strong advocates of peace, both through their writing and in public actions. Gwendolyn Brooks and Lucille Clifton are among those who have written realistically of the experience of being black. Carolyn Kizer, in "Pro Femina" and other poems, was one of the first to write of what is now "women's liberation."

Other poets have pushed into the area of the subconscious, of dreams, or of surrealism. Such is the work of Barbara Guest, a poet and painter of the New York school, and of Diane Wakoski and the young Canadian, Margaret Atwood.

Anne Sexton and Sylvia Plath are generally considered representatives of the confessional poets, who pursue the inquiry into their suffering as far as it can go, to the verge of suicide or, in Plath's case, beyond. Closest to the confessional attitude in England is Elizabeth Jennings, with the account of the mental hospital in her recent books.

Australia and New Zealand have produced poets of especial strength. In some ways, particularly in the strong emphasis on region, they are similar to the poets of the American mid-west and west. Gwen Harwood and Nancy Cato write vivid descriptions of the dramatic Australian landscape. So does Judith Wright, one of the major voices of the century, who manages to project the landscape, making it symbolic of interior realities.

Few moderns still claim the poet's vatic role, that of transmitter of the oracle or prophetic voice. But Kathleen Raine, a native of

England, in many of her finest poems reminds us of this voice, as in "Invocation":

Let my body sweat
let snakes torment my breast
my eyes be blind, ears deaf, hands distraught

. . . . . .

if only the lips may speak
if only the god will come.

Miss Raine's background is in science, and her study, the symbolism of William Blake. She combines the physical with the mystical and her poems rest as marvelously poised as the hawk in her "Envoi" which "against the weight in the bone . . . hangs perfect in mid-air."

One area in which poetry by women has moved toward a new tradition in this century is in poetry about love. Contemporary poets have worked out several ways of writing about this oldest of subjects. Jean Garrigue's poems are symbolic, yet sensuous, and extensive. Denise Levertov and Caroline Kizer are direct, often brief. Ruth Herschberger uses startling metaphors. Anne Sexton confesses all, with a clinical probing for the deepest effects of the experience. Other younger poets are writing about love forcefully and naturally and sometimes aggressively as well.

Women have become confident that their experiences are a valid subject for poetry. They are contributing to poetry's mainstream in every part of the English-speaking world. Doubtless some are writing verse that will outlive the century; others are enriching the poetry of their own regions—so many, in fact, that a single volume cannot include all who might well be represented. What a poet does, finally, depends on talent, and on energy, encouragement, and opportunity. And what she is able to do now depends, too, on those who went before. It is the purpose of this anthology to bring together the work of the women poets, from the anonymous voices of the Anglo-Saxon past to the present, when women are writing forcefully and freely out of anger, vision, and love.

PART ONE

Anonymous

Eadwacer

To my people it's as though he gave them a sacrifice:
They will destroy him if he comes among them.
   It is otherwise with us.

Wulf is on one island, I on another.
A fastness is that island, rung round with fens.
Fierce men are there on the island.
They will destroy him if he comes among them.
   It is otherwise with us.

I thought of my Wulf's far wanderings
when it was rainy weather and I sat weeping
when the war-chief caught me in his arms—
it was joy then, yet it was also hateful.

Wulf, my Wulf! Waiting for you
has made me ill, your seldom coming,
this sorrowing mood—not lack of meat.

Do you hear, Eadwacer? Our poor whelp
a wolf bears off to the wood.

How easy for man to break what never was bound—
   our song together.

The Wife's Lament

I make this song   about me full sadly
my own wayfaring.   I a woman tell
what griefs I had   since I grew up

3

new or old   never more than now.
Ever I know   the dark of my exile.

First my lord went out   away from his people
over the wave-tumult.   I grieved each dawn
wondered where my lord   my first on earth might be.
Then I went forth   a friendless exile
to seek service   in my sorrow's need.
My man's kinsmen   began to plot
by darkened thought   to divide us two
so we most widely   in the world's kingdom
lived wretchedly   and I suffered longing.

My lord commanded me   to move my dwelling here.
I had few loved ones   in this land
or faithful friends.   For this my heart grieves:
that I should find the man   well matched to me
hard of fortune   mournful of mind
hiding his mood   thinking of murder.

Blithe was our bearing   often we vowed
that but death alone   would part us two
naught else.   But this is turned round
now . . .   as if it never were
our friendship.   I must far and near
bear the anger   of my beloved.
The man sent me out   to live in the woods
under an oak tree   in this den in the earth.
Ancient this earth hall.   I am all longing.

The valleys are dark   the hills high
the yard overgrown   bitter with briars
a joyless dwelling.   Full oft the lack of my lord
seizes me cruelly here.   Friends there are on earth
living beloved   lying in bed
while I at dawn   am walking alone
under the oak tree   through these earth halls.
There I may sit   the summerlong day
there I can weep   over my exile
my many hardships.   Hence I may not rest
from this care of heart   which belongs to me ever
nor all this longing   that has caught me in this life.

May that young man   be sad-minded always
hard his heart's thought   while he must wear
a blithe bearing   with care in the breast
a crowd of sorrows.   May on himself depend
all his world's joy.   Be he outlawed far
in a strange folk-land—   that my beloved sits
under a rocky cliff   rimed with frost
a lord dreary in spirit   drenched with water
in a ruined hall.   My lord endures
much care of mind.   He remembers too often
a happier dwelling.   Woe be to them
that for a loved one   must wait in longing.

Marie de France

The Lay of the Honeysuckle

Pleased am I, and more than willing
To recount the lay called *Honeysuckle,*
And the truth of all that is sung,
And of all that happened to them, and where.
Heard are many versions, some recited,
And many now are found in writing
Of Tristram and Queen Isolt
Whose joy was in their surpassing love
Which brought them also sadness, pain,
And judgment of death on the same day.

    King Mark increased in wrath, anger
Against his nephew, rash young Tristram,
And banished him beyond the realm
For love that smoldered for the Queen.
To his homeland he returned,
To South Wales, the land of his birth,
An exile there, one year entire,
Exposing himself, betraying himself
To a life of death, of destruction.
Be in no way amazed at that,
        For if ever a lover truly loves

Grieved and leaden-hearted he'll be
When he is kept from his desire.
Tristram, pensive with suffering,
Left once more from his native land,
Went, more direct than arrows, to Cornwall
For there, in Cornwall, lived his Queen.

Alone he hid by day in the forest
Unwilling any soul might betray him.
At twilight he came forth, near evening,
The time all mortals must find shelter.
Among the poor, among the serfs,
He searched for a place to spend the night.
He asked them all for news of the court,
Of the King, his life, of his plans.
Each rumor heard, they shared with Tristram:
Every baron has been called
To Tintagel, at King Mark's wish
To hold his court on Whitsuntide;
Each baron in the realm must come;
Each will travel, soon arrive
For pleasure, celebration, sport,
And, ah! the Queen will be there too!
When Tristram heard, he laughed for joy.
Hardly could Isolt ride by
To Tintagel, unseen by him.

King Mark set out on the appointed day,
And near a byway on the road
The King's whole retinue must pass,
Tristram hid in a wooded thicket.
He severed a branch from a hazel-tree
And sharply squared its tip;
He peeled and trimmed the hazel-wand,
Then, with his dagger, carved his name.
If Queen Isolt should see this stick,
(For which, covertly, she may watch—
It had occurred, at other times,
That she had known him by this sign—)
If she detects his whittled branch,
She will know her lover is near.
The meaning of his message, the gist

Of the word he sent to her, is this:
    A long time he has been standing here,
    Lingering, lying in wait,
    Anticipating some way to see her,
    For in no wise can he live without her;
    Because we two are bound together
    As the honeysuckle vine
    To the hazel-tree must cling
    As it seizes and entwines itself,
    As it wreaths and winds itself round the wood,
    Well-able, together, to endure.
    But if ever they are wrenched apart
    The hazel-tree will quickly die,
    And death claims, too, the honeysuckle.
    "Beloved, so it is with us:
    No life without you, nor yours without me!"

    The Queen at last came riding by
Scanning the slopes beside the way
And glimpsed the blazoned hazel-wand,
Saw letters known so well by heart.
She ordered all her train to halt,
Everyone, from her escort knights
To those who wander at their side.
She wished now to dismount, to rest.
As she commanded, so they did.
        She moved apart from her countrymen
        And called to her side her serving maid,
        Brangwyn, worthy of her trust.
They moved a distance up the path;
Within the woods she found her Tristram,
Who loved her beyond all mortal beings.
Great was their joy at coming together.
All his pent-up words flowed freely,
All quick thoughts she shared with ease:
        How she brooded, how she schemed
        To find a way to appease the King;
        How her grief had grown, and regret
        For accusations Mark believed,
        The cause of Tristram's banishment.
The time approached to depart from her love;

But when their separation came,
They both knew many tears.
Tristram returned again to Wales
Until his uncle might summon him.

Because of the feeling of joy he knew
After gazing so long on his love,
And because of the word he sent to her,
And because the Queen instructed him
To commit their words to memory,
Tristram, skilled at playing the harp,
Sang of it all in a new lay;
Briefly will I give you its name:
 Goat-leaf it is called, in English,
 And in French called *Honeysuckle*.
 Now I have told all the truth in it,
 Of this lay I related to you.

Translated by Robin Johnson

The Lady of the Arbour

From *The Flower and the Leaf**

And at the last I cast my mine eye aside,
And was ware of a lusty company
That came, roaming out of the field wide,
Hand in hand, a knight and a lady;
The ladies all in surcoats, that richly
Purfled were with many a rich stone;
And every knight of green wore mantles on,

Embroidered well, so as the surcoats were,
And each one had a chapelet on her head;
Which did right well upon the shining hair,
Made of goodly flowers, white and red.

---

* In this and the two following fifteenth-century poems the
plural *es* and the final *ed* of the past forms of the verbs
should be pronounced as separate syllables.

The knightes eke, that they in hand led,
In suit of them, wore chapelets every one
And them before went minstrels many a one,

As harpes, pipes, lutes, and psalt'ry,
All in green; and on their heades bore
Of divers flowers, made full craftily
All in a suit, goodly chapelets they wore
And so, dancing, into the mead they fare,
In-mid the which they found a tuft that was
All overspread with flowers in compass.

Whereunto they inclined every one
With great reverence, and that full humblely
And, at the laste, there began anon
A lady for to sing right womanly
A bargaret in praising the daisy;
For, as me thought, among her notes sweet,
She said, *Si douce est la Marguerite.*

Then they all answered her infere
So passingly well, and so pleasantly,
That it was a blissful noise to hear.
But I not how, it happed suddenly,
As, about noon, the sun so fervently
Wax'd hot, that all the pretty tender flowers
Had lost the beauty of their fresh coloures,

For-shrunk with heat; the ladies eke to-burnt,
That they ne wist where they them might bestow.
The knightes swelt, for lack of shade nigh shent;
And after that, within a little throw,
The wind began so sturdily to blow,
That down goeth all the flowers every one
So that in all the mead there left not one,

Save such as succored were, among the leaves,
From every storm, that might them assail,
Growing under hedges and thick groves;
And after that, there came a storm of hail
And rain in-fere, so that, withouten fail,
The ladies nor the knightes had one thread
Dry upon them, so dripping was their weed.

And when the storm was clean passed away,
Those clad in white, that stood under the tree,
They felt nothing of the great affray,
That they in green without had in y-be.
To them they went for ruth and pity,
Them to comfort after their great dis-ease;
So fain they were the helpless for to ease.

Then was I ware how one of them in green
Had on a crowne, rich and well sitting;
Wherefore I deemed well she was a queen,
And those in green on her were awaiting.
The ladies then in white that were coming
Towardes them, and the knightes in-fere
Began to comfort them and make them cheer.

The queen in white, that was of great beauty,
Took by the hand the queen that was in green,
And said, "Sister, I have right great pity
Of your annoy, and of the troublous teen
Wherein ye and your company have been
So long, alas! and, if that it you please
To go with me, I shall do you the ease

In all the pleasure that I can or may."
Whereof the tother, humbly as she might,
Thanked her; for in right ill array
She was, with storm and heat, I you behight.
And every lady then, anon-right,
That were in white, one of them took in green
By the hand; which when the knightes had seen,

In like wise, each of them took a knight
Clad in green, and forth with them they fare
Unto an hedge, where they, anon-right,
To make their joustes, lo! they would not spare
Boughes to hew down, and eke trees square,
Wherewith they made them stately fires great
To dry their clothes that were wringing wet.

And after that, of herbes that there grew,
They made, for blisters of the sun burning,

Very good and wholesome ointments new,
Where that they went, the sick fast anointing;
And after that, they went about gathering
Pleasant salades, which they made them eat,
For to refresh their great unkindly heat.

The lady of the Leaf then gan to pray
Her of the Flower, (for so to my seeming
They shoulde be, as by their quaint array),
To sup with her; and eke, for any thing,
That she should with her all her people bring.
And she again, in right goodly manner,
Thanketh her of her most friendly cheer,

Saying plainly, that she would obey
With all her heart all her commandement.
And then anon, without longer delay,
The lady of the Leaf hath one y-sent
For a palfrey, as after her intent,
Arrayed well and fair in harness of gold,
For nothing lacked that to him long should.

And after that, to all her company
She made to purvey horses and every thing
That they needed; and then, full lustily,
Even by the arbor where I was sitting
They passed all, so pleasantly singing
That it would have comforted any wight;
But then I saw a passing wondrous sight:

For then the nightingale, that all the day
Had in the laurel sat, and did her might
The whole service to sing longing to May,
All suddenly began to take her flight;
And to the lady of the Leaf forthright
She flew, and set her on her hand softly,
Which was a thing I marveled of greatly.

The goldfinch eke, that from the medlar-tree
Was fled, for heat, into the bushes cold,
Unto the lady of the Flower gan flee,
And on her hand he set him, as he would,

And pleasantly his winges gan to fold.
And for to sing they pained them both as sore
As they had done of all the day before.

.   .   .   .   .   .

The Lady of the Assembly

From *The Assembly of Ladies*

The Palace of Pleasant Regard

We followed her unto the chamber-door,
"Sisters," quoth she, "come ye in after me."
But wit ye well, there was a paved floor,
The goodliest that any wight might see
And furthermore, about then looked we
On each corner, and upon every wall,
The which was made of beryl and crystal;

Wherein was graven of stories many a one;
First how Phyllis, of womanly pity,
Died piteously, for love of Demophon.
Next after was the story of Thisbe,
How she slew herself under a tree.
Yet saw I more, how in right piteous case
For Anthony was slain Cleopatras.

The other side was, how Melusine the sheen
Untruly was deceived in her bain.
There was also Anelida the queen,
Upon Arcite how sore she did complain.
All these stories were graved there, certain;
And many more than I rehearse you here;
It were too long to tell you all in-fere.

And because the walles shone so bright,
With fine umple they were all overspread,
To that intent, folk should not hurt their sight;
And thorough [*sic*] it the stories might be read.
Then furthermore I went, as I was led;

And there I saw, withouten any fail,
A chaire set, with full rich apparail.

And five stages it was set from the ground,
Of chalcedony full curiously wrought;
With four pommels of gold, and very round,
Set with sapphires, as good as could be thought;
That, wot ye what, if it were thorough sought
As I suppose, from this country to Inde,
Another such it were right far to find!

For, wit ye well, I was right near that,
So as I durst, beholding by and by;
Above there was a rich cloth of estate,
Wrought with the needle full strangely,
Her word thereon; and thus it said truly
A endurer, to tell you in wordes few,
With great letters, the better I them knew.

Thus as we stood, a door opened anon;
A gentlewoman, seemly of stature,
Bearing a mace, came out, herself alone;
Soothly, me thought, a goodly creature!
She spoke nothing too loud, I you ensure,
Nor hastily, but with goodly warning:
"Make room," quoth she, "my lady is coming!"

With that anon I saw Perséverance,
How she held up the tapet in her hand.
I saw also, in right good ordinance,
This great lady within the tapet stand,
Coming outward, I will ye understand;
And after her a noble company,
I could not tell the number certainly.

·   ·   ·   ·   ·   ·

Julians Barnes

From *Book of Hunting*

Wheresoever ye fare by frith or by fell,
My dear child, take heed how Tristram doth you tell

How many manner beastes of venery there were.
Listen to your dame, and she shall you lere.
Four manner beastes of venery there are,
The first of them is the hart, the second is the hare,
    The boar is one of tho,
    The wolf, and not one mo.

And where that ye come in plain or in place,
I shall you tell which be beastes of enchase.
One of them is the buck, another is the doe,
The fox and the marten and the wild roe.
And ye shall, my dear child, other beastes all,
Where so ye them find, rascal ye shall them call
    In frith or in fell
    Or in forest, I you tell.

And for to speak of the hart, if ye will it lere,
Ye shall him a calf call at the first year,
The second year a brocket, so shall ye him call,
The third year a spayade, learneth thus all,
The fourth year a stag call him by any way,
The fifth year a great stag, your dame bid you say,
    The sixth year call ye him an hart.
    Doeth so, my child, if ye will be in quart.

    .   .   .   .   .

When ye hunt at the roe, then shall ye see there:
He crosses and treasons your houndes before.
A great roebuck ye call him not so
But a fair roebuck and a fair roe.
With the bowels and with the blood
Reward ye your houndes, my sonnes so good
And each foot ye shall cut in four, I you ken.
Take the bowels and the blood and do all together then
Giveth it then to your houndes so,
And much the gladder then they will go.
That to your houndes a reward is called,
For it is eaten on the ground and on the skin dealt.
The roe shall be hurdled by venery, I ween,
The two forther legges the head laid between,
And take one hinder leg up, I you pray,
And that other leg, right as I you say,

Upon the other forther leg both ye them put
And with that other forther leg up ye them knit.
On this manner thus when ye have wrought,
All whole to the kitchen then it shall be brought,
   Save that your houndes eat
   The bowels and the feet.

   .   .   .   .   .   .

Time of grease beginneth at Midsummer day
And till Holy-rood day lasteth, as I you say.
The season of the fox from the Nativity
Till the Annunciation of Our Lady free.
Season of the roebuck at Easter shall begin
And till Michaelmas lasteth nigh or she blynne.
The season of the roe beginneth at Michaelmas,
And it shall endure and last until Candlemas.
At Michaelmas beginneth hunting of the hare
And lasteth till Midsummer, there will no man it spare.
The season of the wolf is in each country
At the season of the fox and evermore shall be.
The season of the boar is from the Nativity
Till the Purification of Our Lady so free,
For at the Nativity of Our Lady sweet
He may find, where he goeth, under his feet
Both in woods and fields corn and other fruit
When he after food maketh any suit,
Crabbes and acornes and nuttes, there they grow,
Hawes and hippes and other things enow
That till the Purification lastes, as ye see,
And maketh the boar in season to be,
   For, while that fruit may last,
   His time is never past.

   .   .   .   .   .   .

Margery Brews

Unto My Valentine

Unto my right well-beloved Valentine, John Paston, Esq., be this bill delivered, etc.

   Right reverend and worshipful and my right well-beloved Valentine, I recommend me unto you, full heartily desiring to hear of your welfare, which I beseech Almighty God long for to perserve unto His pleasure and your heart's desire. And if it please you to hear of my welfare, I am not in good health of body nor of heart, nor shall be till I hear from you.

> For there wotteth no creature what pain that I endure,
> And, for to be dead, I dare it not discure.

And my lady, my mother, hath labored the matter to my father full diligently, but she can no more get than ye know of, for the which God knoweth I am full sorry. But if ye love me, as I trust verily that ye do, ye will not leave me therefor. For if ye had not half the livelihood that ye have, for to do the greatest labor that any woman alive might, I would not forsake you.

> And if ye command me to keep me true wherever I go,
> Ywis I will do all my might you to love, and never no mo.
> And if my friends say that I do amiss,
> They shall not me let so for to do.
> Mine heart me bids evermore to love you
> Truly over all earthly thing,
> And if they be never so wroth,
> I trust it shall be better in time coming.

No more to you at this time, but the Holy Trinity have you in keeping; and I beseech you that this bill be not seen of none earthly creature save only yourself, etc. And this letter was endited at Topcroft, with full heavy heart, etc.

> *By your own,*
> *Margery Brews*

Queen Elizabeth of York

My Heart Is Set Upon a Lusty Pin

My heart is set upon a lusty pin.
I pray to Venus of good continuance,
For I rejoice the case that I am in,
Delivered from sorrow, annexed to pleasance,

Of all comfort having abundance.
This joy and I, I trust, shall never twin—
My heart is set upon a lusty pin.

I pray to Venus of good continuance
Since she hath set me in the way of ease;
My hearty service with my attendance
So to continue it ever I may please;
Thus voiding from all pensful disease,
Now stand I whole far from all grievance—
I pray to Venus of good continuance.

For I rejoice the case that I am in,
My gladness is such that giveth me no pain,
And so to sorrow never shall I blynne,
And though I would I may not me refrain;
My heart and I so set 'tis certain
We shall never slake, but ever new begin—
For I rejoice the case that I am in.

Delivered from sorrow, annexed to pleasance,
That all my joy I set as aught of right,
To please as after my simple suffisance
To me the goodliest, most beauteous in sight;
A very lantern to all other light,
Most to my comfort on her remembrance—
Delivered from sorrow, annexed to pleasance.

Of all comfort having abundance,
As when that I think that goodlihead
Of that most feminine and meek countenance
Very mirror and star of woman head;
Whose right good fame so large abroad doth spread,
Full glad for me to have recognisance—
Of all comfort having abundance.

This joy and I, I trust, shall never twin,
So that I am so far forth in the trace,
My joys be double where others' are but thin,
For I am stably set in such a place,
Where beauty 'creaseth and ever willeth grace,
Which is full famous and born of noble kin—
This joy and I, I trust, shall never twin.

Queen Anne Boleyn (?)

Defiled Is My Name Full Sore

Defiled is my name full sore
  Through cruel spite and false report,
That I may say for evermore,
  Farewell, my joy! adieu comfort!
For wrongfully ye judge of me
  Unto my fame a mortal wound,
Say what ye list, it will not be,
  Ye seek for that can not be found.

O Death, Rock Me Asleep

O Death, rock me asleep,
  Bring me to quiet rest,
Let pass my weary guiltless ghost
  Out of my careful breast.
Toll on, thou passing bell;
Ring out my doleful knell;
Let thy sound my death tell.
  Death doth draw nigh;
  There is no remedy.

My pains who can express?
  Alas, they are so strong;
My dolour will not suffer strength
  My life for to prolong.
Toll on, thou passing bell;
Ring out my doleful knell;
Let thy sound my death tell.
  Death doth draw nigh;
  There is no remedy.

Alone in prison strong
  I wait my destiny.
Woe worth this cruel hap that I
  Should taste this misery!

Toll on, thou passing bell;
Ring out my doleful knell;
Let thy sound my death tell.
  Death doth draw nigh;
  There is no remedy.

Farewell, my pleasures past,
  Welcome, my present pain!
I feel my torments so increase
  That life cannot remain.
Cease now, thou passing bell;
Rung is my doleful knell;
For the sound my death doth tell.
  Death doth draw nigh;
  There is no remedy.

Anne Askew

The Ballad Which Anne Askew Made and Sang When She Was in Newgate

Like as the armed knight
Appointed to the field,
With this world will I fight,
And faith shall be my shield.

Faith is that weapon strong
Which will not fail at need.
My foes therefore among
Therewith will I proceed.

As it is had in strength
And force of Christ's way,
It will prevail at length,
Though all the devils say nay.

Faith in the fathers old
Obtained righteousness,
Which make me very bold
To fear no world's distress.

I now rejoice in heart,
And hope bid me do so,
For Christ will take my part,
And ease me of my woe.

Thou say'st, Lord, whoso knock,
To them wilt thou attend.
Undo therefore the lock,
And thy strong power send.

More enemies now I have
Than hairs upon my head.
Let them not me deprave,
But fight thou in my stead.

On thee my care I cast,
For all their cruel spite,
I set not by their haste,
For thou art my delight.

I am not she that list
My anchor to let fall,
For every drizzling mist,
My ship substantial.

Not oft use I to write
In prose nor yet in rhyme;
Yet will I show one sight
That I saw in my time.

I saw a royal throne
Where justice should have sit,
But in her stead was one
Of moody cruel wit.

Absorbed was righteousness
As of the raging flood.
Satan in his excess
Sucked up the guiltless blood.

Then thought I, Jesus, Lord,
When thou shalt judge us all,
Hard is it to record
On these men what will fall.

Yet, Lord, I thee desire
For that they do to me,
Let them not taste the hire
Of their iniquity.

Queen Elizabeth I

Written With a Diamond
on Her Window
at Woodstock

Much suspected by me,
Nothing proved can be,
　Quoth Elizabeth prisoner.

Written on a Wall
at Woodstock

Oh fortune, thy wresting wavering state
Hath fraught with cares my troubled wit,
Whose witness this present prison late
Could bear, where once was joy's loan quit.
Thou causedst the guilty to be loosed
From bands where innocents were inclosed,
And caused the guiltless to be reserved,
And freed those that death had well deserved.
But all herein can be nothing wrought,
So God send to my foes all they have thought.

Written in Her
French Psalter

No crooked leg, no bleared eye,
　No part deformed out of kind,
Nor yet so ugly half can be
　As is the inward suspicious mind.

The Doubt of Future Foes

The doubt of future foes exiles my present joy,
And wit me warns to shun such snares as threaten mine annoy;
For falsehood now doth flow, and subjects' faith doth ebb,
Which should not be if reason ruled or wisdom weaved the web.
But clouds of joys untried do cloak aspiring minds,
Which turn to rain of late repent by changed course of winds.
The top of hope supposed the root upreared shall be,
And fruitless all their grafted guile, as shortly ye shall see.
The dazzled eyes with pride, which great ambition blinds,
Shall be unsealed by worthy wights whose foresight falsehood finds.
The daughter of debate that discord aye doth sow
Shall reap no gain where former rule still peace hath taught to know.
No foreign banished wight shall anchor in this port;
Our realm brooks not seditious sects, let them elsewhere resort.
My rusty sword through rest shall first his edge employ
To poll their tops that seek such change or gape for future joy.

On Fortune

Never think you fortune can bear the sway
Where virtue's force can cause her to obey.

On Monsieur's Departure

I grieve and dare not show my discontent,
I love and yet am forced to seem to hate,
I do, yet dare not say I ever meant,
I seem stark mute but inwardly do prate.
    I am and not, I freeze and yet am burned,
    Since from myself another self I turned.

My care is like my shadow in the sun,
Follows me flying, flies when I pursue it,
Stands and lies by me, doth what I have done.
His too familiar care doth make me rue it.
    No means I find to rid him from my breast,
    Till by the end of things it be supprest.

Some gentler passion slide into my mind,
For I am soft and made of melting snow;
Or be more cruel, love, and so be kind.

Let me or float or sink, be high or low.
   Or let me live with some more sweet content,
   Or die and so forget what love ere meant.

Isabella Whitney

From *A Sweet Nosegay or Pleasant Posy*

The 61. Flower

In loving, each one hath free choice,
   or ever they begin,
But in their power it lieth not
   to end when they are in.

The 85. Flower

The present day we cannot spend
   as we the same should do
Except to count it as our last
   we frame our selves unto.

The 94.

Do not account that for thine own
   which may from thee be take:
But much esteem such treasure, as
   will never thee forsake.

The 102.

A little gold in law will make,
   the matter better speed
Than if thou broughtest of love as much
   as might in kindness breed.

The 103.

Gold savours well, though it be got
   with occupations vile:
If thou hast gold, thou welcome art,
   though virtue thou exile.

23

The 104.
Such poor folk as to law do go
  are driven oft to curse:
But in mean while, the Lawyer thrives,
  the money in his purse.

The 108.
Seek not man to please, for that
  is more than God bids do:
Please thou the best and never care,
  what wicked say thereto.

A sovereign receipt
The Juice of all these Flowers take
  and make thee a conserve:
And use it first and last: and it
  will safely thee preserve.

Anne Howard, Duchess of Arundel

Elegy on the Death of Her Husband

In sad and ashy weeds I sigh,
  I groan, I pine, I mourn;
My oaten yellow reeds
  I all to jet and ebon turn.
My wat'ry eyes, like winter's skies,
  My furrowed cheeks o'erflow.
All heavens know why men mourn as I,
  And who can blame my woe?

In sable robes of night my days
  Of joy consumed be;
My sorrow sees no light;
  My lights through sorrow nothing see:
For now my sun his course hath run,
  And from his sphere doth go,

To endless bed of soldered lead,
    And who can blame my woe?

My flocks I now forsake, that so
    My sheep my grief may know;
The lilies loath to take
    That since his death presum'd to grow.
I envy air because it dare
    Still breathe, and he not so;
Hate earth, that doth entomb his youth,
    And who can blame my woe?

Not I, poor I alone—(alone
    How can this sorrow be?)
Not only men make moan, but
    More than men make moan with me:
The gods of greens, the mountain queens,
    The fairy circles row,
The muses nine, and powers divine,
    Do all condole my woe.

Mary Sidney Herbert,
Countess of Pembroke

If Ever Hapless Woman
Had a Cause

If ever hapless woman had a cause
    To breathe her plaints into the open air,
And never suffer inward grief to pause,
    Or seek her sorrow-shaken soul's repair:
Then I, for I have lost my only brother,
Whose like this age can scarcely yield another.

Come therefore, mournful Muses, and lament;
    Forsake all wanton pleasing motions;
Bedew your cheeks. Still shall my tears be spent,
    Yet still increased with inundations.
For I must weep, since I have lost my brother,
Whose like this age can scarcely yield another.

The cruel hand of murder cloyed with blood
   Lewdly deprived him of his mortal life.
Woe the death-attended blades that stood
   In opposition 'gainst him in the strife
Wherein he fell, and where I lost a brother,
Whose like this age can scarcely yield another.

Then unto Grief let me a temple make,
   And, mourning, daily enter Sorrow's ports,
Knock on my breast, sweet brother, for thy sake.
   Nature and love will both be my consorts,
And help me aye to wail my only brother,
Whose like this age can scarcely yield another.

Psalm 55: *Exaudi, Deus*

My God most glad to look, most prone to hear,
   An open ear O let my prayer find,
And from my plaint turn not thy face away.
Behold my gestures, harken what I say
   While uttering moans with most tormented mind.
My body I no less torment and tear,
For lo, their fearful threatnings wound mine ear,
Who griefs on griefs on me still heaping lay,
   A mark to wrath and hate and wrong assigned;
   Therefore my heart hath all his force resigned
To trembling pants, Death's terrors on me pray,
I fear, nay shake, nay quiv'ring quake with fear.

Then say I, O might I but cut the wind,
   Borne on the wing the fearful dove doth bear:
Stay would I not, till I in rest might stay.
Far hence, O far, then would I take my way
   Unto the desert, and repose me there,
These storms of woe, these tempests left behind:
But swallow them, O Lord, in darkness blind,
Confound their councils, lead their tongues astray,
   That what they mean by words may not appear;
   For Mother Wrong within their town each where,
And daughter Strife their ensigns so display,
As if they only thither were confined.

These walk their city walls both night and day,
    Oppressions, tumults, guiles of ev'ry kind
Are burgesses and dwell the middle near;
About their streets his masking robes doth wear
    Mischief, clothed in deceit, with treason lined,
Where only he, he only bears the sway.
But not my foe with me this prank did play,
For then I would have borne with patient cheer
    An unkind part from whom I know unkind;
    Nor he whose forehead Envy's mark had signed,
His trophies on my ruins sought to rear,
From whom to fly I might have made assay.

But this to thee, to thee impute I may,
    My fellow, my companion, held most dear,
My soul, my other self, my inward friend:
Woe unto me, me unto whom did bind
    Exchanged secrets, who together were
God's temple wont to visit, there to pray.
O let a sudden death work their decay,
Who speaking fair, such cankered malice mind,
    Let them be buried breathing in their bier.
    But purple morn, black ev'n, and midday clear,
Shall see my praying voice to God inclined,
Rousing him up; and nought shall me dismay.

He ransomed me, he for my safety fined
    In fight where many sought my soul to slay;
He still, himself, (to no succeeding heir
Leaving his Empire) shall no more forbear:
    But, at my motion, all these Atheists pay,
By whom (still one) such mischiefs are designed;
Who but such caitiffs would have undermined,
Nay overthrown, from whom but kindness mere
    They never found? who would such trust betray?
    What butt'red words! yet war their hearts bewray;
Their speech more sharp than sharpest sword or spear
Yet softer flows than balm from wounded rind.

But, my o'erladen soul, thy self upcheer:
    Cast on God's shoulders what thee down doth weigh,

Long borne by thee with bearing pained and pined;
To care for thee he shall be ever kind.
By him the just, in safety held alway,
Changeless shall enter, live, and leave the year:
But, Lord, how long shall these men tarry here?
Fling them in pit of death where never shined
    The light of life; and while I make my stay
    On thee, let who their thirst with blood allay
Have their life-holding thread so weakly twined
That it, half spun, death may in sunder shear.

Psalm 58: Si Vere Utique

And call ye this to utter what is just,
    You that of justice hold the sov'reign throne?
And call ye this to yield, O sons of dust,
    To wronged brethren ev'ry man his own?
O no: it is your long malicious will
    Now to the world to make by practice known,
With whose oppression you the balance fill,
    Just to your selves, indiff'rent else to none.

But what could they, who ev'n in birth declined,
    From truth and right to lies and injuries?
To show the venom of their cank'red mind
    The adder's image scarcely can suffice;
Nay scarce the aspic may with them contend,
    On whom the charmer all in vain applies
His skillfull'st spells: aye missing of his end,
    While she self-deaf, and unaffected lies.

Lord crack their teeth, Lord crush these lion's jaws,
    So let them sink as water in the sand:
When deadly bow their aiming fury draws,
    Shiver the shaft ere past the shooter's hand.
So make them melt as the dishoused snail
    Or as the Embryo, whose vital band
Breaks ere it holds, and formless eyes do fail
    To see the sun, though brought to lightful land.

O let their brood, a brood of springing thorns,
    Be by untimely rooting overthrown

Ere bushes waxed, they push with pricking horns,
  As fruits yet green are oft by tempest blown.
The good with gladness this revenge shall see,
  And bathe his feet in blood of wicked one
While all shall say: the just rewarded be,
  There is a God that carves to each his own.

Psalm 139: Domine, Probasti

O Lord in me there lieth nought,
  But to thy search revealed lies:
    For when I sit
    Thou markest it:
  No less thou notest when I rise:
Yea closest closet of my thought
  Hath open windows to thine eyes.

Thou walkest with me when I walk,
  When to my bed for rest I go,
    I find thee there,
    And ev'ry where:
  Not youngest thought in me doth grow,
No not one word I cast to talk,
  But yet unutt'red thou dost know.

If forth I march, thou goest before,
  If back I turn, thou com'st behind:
    So forth nor back
    Thy guard I lack,
  Nay on me too, thy hand I find.
Well I thy wisdom may adore,
  But never reach with earthy mind.

To shun thy notice, leave thine eye,
  O whither might I take my way?
    To starry sphere?
    Thy throne is there.
  To dead men's undelightsome stay?
There is thy walk, and there to lie
  Unknown, in vain I should assay.

O Sun, whom light nor flight can match,
  Suppose thy lightful flightful wings

Thou lend to me,
And I could flee
As far as thee the ev'ning brings:
Ev'n led to West he would me catch,
    Nor should I lurk with western things.

Do thou thy best, O secret night,
    In sable veil to cover me:
        Thy sable veil
        Shall vainly fail:
    With day unmasked my night shall be,
For night is day, and darkness light,
    O father of all lights, to thee.

Each inmost piece in me is thine:
    While yet I in my mother dwelt,
        All that me clad
        From thee I had.
    Thou in my frame hast strangely dealt:
Needs in my praise thy works must shine
    So inly them my thoughts have felt.

Thou, how my back was beam-wise laid,
    And raft'ring of my ribs, dost know:
        Know'st ev'ry point
        Of bone and joint,
    How to this whole these parts did grow,
In brave embroid'ry fair arrayed,
    Though wrought in shop both dark and low.

Nay fashionless, ere form I took,
    Thy all and more beholding eye
        My shapeless shape
        Could not escape:
    All these time framed successively
Ere one had being, in the book
    Of thy foresight, enrolled did lie.

My God, how I these studies prize,
    That do thy hidden workings show!
        Whose sum is such,
        No sum so much:
    Nay summed as sand they sumless grow.

I lie to sleep, from sleep I rise,
    Yet still in thought with thee I go.

My God if thou but one wouldst kill,
    Then straight would leave my further chase
        This cursed brood
        Inured to blood:
    Whose graceless taunts at thy disgrace
Have aimed oft: and hating still
    Would with proud lies thy truth outface.

Hate not I them, who thee do hate?
    Thine, Lord, I will the censure be.
        Detest I not
        The cank'red knot,
    Whom I against thee banded see?
O Lord, thou know'st in highest rate
    I hate them all as foes to me.

Search me, my God, and prove my heart,
    Examine me, and try my thought:
        And mark in me
        If aught there be
    That hath with cause their anger wrought.
If not (as not) my life's each part,
    Lord safely guide from danger brought.

Elizabeth Melvill,
Lady Culross

From *A Godly Dream*

Then up I rose, and made no more delay,
My feeble arms about his neck I cast;
He went before, and still did guide the way,
Though I was weak, my spirit did follow fast.
Through moss and mire, through ditches deep we passed,
Through pricking thorns, through water and through fire,
Through dreadful dens which made my heart aghast,
He bare me up when I began to tire.

Sometime we clamb on craggy mountains high,
And sometimes stayed on ugly braes of sand:
They were so stay that wonder was to see,
But when I feared he held me by the hand.
Through thick and thin, through sea and eke through land,
Through great deserts we wand'red on our way.
When I was weak and had no strength to stand,
Yet with a look he did refresh me aye.

Through waters great we were compelled to wade,
Which was so deep that I was like to drown,
Sometime I sank, but yet my gracious guide
Did draw me up half dead and in a swoon.
In woods most wild, and far from any town,
We thirsted through, the briers together stack:
I was so weak their strength did beat me down,
That I was forced for fear to flee aback.

    .   .   .   .   .   .

Weary I was, and thought to sit at rest,
But he said no, thou may not sit nor stand;
Hold on thy course, and thou shalt find it best
If thou desirest to see that pleasant land.
Though I was weak, I rose at his command,
And held him fast; at length he let me see
That pleasant place that seemed to be at hand.
Take courage now, for thou art near, said he.

I looked up unto that Castle fair,
Glist'ring like gold and shining silver bright:
The stately towers did mount above the air;
They blinded me they cast so great a light.
My heart was glad to see that joyful sight.
My voyage then I thought was not in vain;
I him besought to guide me there aright,
With many vows never to tire again.

    .   .   .   .   .   .

I looked down and saw a pit most black,
Most full of smoke and flaming fire most fell;
That ugly sight made me to flee aback,
I feared to hear so many shout and yell.
I him besought that he the truth would tell;

Is this, said I, the Papists' purging place
Where they affirm that sely souls do dwell,
To purge their sin before they rest in peace?

.   .   .   .   .   .

This pit is Hell where through thou now must go,
There is the way that leads thee to thy land;
Now play the man, thou needst not tremble so,
For I shall help and hold thee by the hand.
Alas, said I, I have no force to stand,
For fear I faint to see that ugly sight.
How can I come amongst that baleful band?
Oh help me now, I have no force nor might.

.   .   .   .   .   .

Into that pit when I did enter in,
I saw a sight which made my heart aghast:
Poor damned souls tormented sore for sin,
In flaming fire were frying wonder fast,
And ugly spirits. And as I thought them passed
My heart grew faint, and I began to tire:
Ere I was ware one gripped me at last,
And held me high above a flaming fire.

The fire was great, the heat did pierce me sore,
My faith grew weak, my grip was wondrous small;
I trembled fast, my fear grew more and more,
My hands did shake that I him held withall.
At length they loosed, then I began to fall,
And cried aloud and caught him fast again:
Lord Jesus come and rid me out of thrall.
Courage, said he, now thou art past the pain.

With this great fear I started and awoke,
Crying aloud, Lord Jesus come again.
But after this no kind of rest I took,
I preesed to sleep, but it was all in vain.
I would have dreamed of pleasure after pain,
Because I know I shall it find at last.
God grant my guide may still with me remain;
It is to come that I believed was past.

.   .   .   .   .   .

33

Lucy Harington, Countess of Bedford

Elegy

Death be not proud, thy hand gave not this blow,
Sin was her captive, whence thy power doth flow;
The executioner of wrath thou art,
But to destroy the just is not thy part.
Thy coming, terror, anguish, grief denounce;
Her happy state, courage, ease, joy pronounce.
From out the crystal palace of her breast,
The clearer soul was called to endless rest,
(Not by the thundering voice, wherewith God threats,
But, as with crowned saints in heaven he treats,)
And, waited on by angels, home was brought,
To joy that it through many dangers sought;
The key of mercy gently did unlock
The doors 'twixt heaven and it, when life did knock.

Nor boast, the fairest frame was made thy prey,
Because to mortal eyes it did decay;
A better witness than thou art, assures,
That though dissolved, it yet a space endures;
No dram thereof shall want or loss sustain,
When her best soul inhabits it again.
Go then to people cursed before they were,
Their spoils in triumph of thy conquest wear.
Glory not thou thy self in these hot tears
Which our face, not for hers, but our harm wears,
The mourning livery given by Grace, not thee,
Which wills our souls in these streams washed should be,
And on our hearts, her memory's best tomb,
In this her epitaph doth write thy doom.
Blind were those eyes, saw not how bright did shine
Through flesh's misty veil the beams divine.
Deaf were the ears, not charmed with that sweet sound
Which did in the spirit-instructed voice abound.

Of flint the conscience, did not yield and melt,
At what in her last Act it saw, heard, felt.

Weep not, nor grudge then, to have lost her sight,
Taught thus, our after stay's but a short night:
But by all souls not by corruption choked
Let in high raised notes that power be invoked.
Calm the rough seas, by which she sails to rest,
From sorrows here, to a kingdom ever blest;
And teach this hymn of her with joy, and sing,
The grave no conquest gets, Death hath no sting.

Lady Elizabeth Carey

Chorus in Act III of Mariam

'Tis not enough for one that is a wife
    To keep her spotless from an act of ill;
But from suspicion she should free her life,
    And bare herself of power as well as will.
'Tis not so glorious for her to be free,
As by her proper self restrained to be.

When she hath spacious ground to walk upon,
    Why on the ridge should she desire to go?
It is no glory to forbear alone
    Those things that may her honour overthrow:
But 'tis thankworthy, if she will not take
All lawful liberties for honour's sake.

That wife her hand against her fame doth rear,
    That more than to her lord alone will give
A private word to any second ear;
    And though she may with reputation live,
Yet though most chaste, she doth her glory blot,
And wounds her honour, though she kills it not.

When to their husbands they themselves do bind,
    Do they not wholly give themselves away?
Or give they but their body, not their mind,

Reserving that, though best, for others' prey?
No, sure, their thoughts no more can be their own,
And therefore should to none but one be known.

Then she usurps upon another's right,
    That seeks to be by public language graced;
And though her thoughts reflect with purest light
    Her mind, if not peculiar, is not chaste.
For in a wife it is no worse to find
A common body, than a common mind.

And every mind, though free from thought of ill,
    That out of glory seeks a worth to show,
When any's ears but one therewith they fill,
    Doth in a sort her pureness overthrow.
Now Mariam had (but that to this she bent)
Been free from fear, as well as innocent.

Chorus in Act IV of Mariam

The fairest action of our human life
    Is scorning to revenge an injury;
For who forgives without a further strife,
    His adversary's heart to him doth tie.
And 'tis a firmer conquest truly said,
To win the heart, than overthrow the head.

If we a worthy enemy do find,
    To yield to worth it must be nobly done;
But if of baser metal be his mind,
    In base revenge there is no honour won.
Who would a worthy courage overthrow,
And who would wrestle with a worthless foe?

We say our hearts are great and cannot yield;
    Because they cannot yield, it proves them poor;
Great hearts are tasked beyond their power, but seld
    The weakest lion will the loudest roar.
Truth's school for certain doth this same allow,
High-heartedness doth sometimes teach to bow.

A noble heart doth teach a virtuous scorn,
    To scorn to owe a duty overlong;

To scorn to be for benefits forborne,
　　To scorn to lie, to scorn to do a wrong.
To scorn to bear an injury in mind,
To scorn a free-born heart slave-like to bind.

But if for wrongs we needs revenge must have,
　　Then be our vengeance of the noblest kind;
Do we his body from our fury save,
　　And let our hate prevail against our mind?
What can, gainst him a greater vengeance be,
Than make his foe more worthy far then he?

Had Mariam scorned to leave a due unpaid,
　　She would to Herod then have paid her love;
And not have been by sullen passion swayed.
　　To fix her thoughts all injury above
Is virtuous pride. Had Mariam thus been proud,
Long famous life to her had been allowed.

Mary Sidney Wroth,
Countess of Montgomery

From *Urania*

Morea's Sonnet

Bear part with me most straight and pleasant tree,
　　And imitate the torments of my smart
　　Which cruel love doth send into my heart,
　　Keep in thy skin this testament of me

Which love engraven hath with misery,
　　Cutting with grief the unresisting part,
　　Which would with pleasure soon have learned love's art,
　　But wounds still cureless, must my rulers be.

Thy sap doth weepingly bewray thy pain,
My heart-blood drops with storms it doth sustain,
　　Love senseless, neither good nor mercy knows
　　　　Pitiless I do wound thee, while that I
　　　　Unpitied, and unthought on, wounded cry:
　　Then out-live me, and testify my woes.

Pamphilia's Sonnet

Loss, my molester, at last patient be,
  And satisfied with thy cursed self, or move
  Thy mournful force thus oft on perjured love,
  To waste a life which lives by mischief's fee.

Who will behold true misery, view me,
  And find what wit hath feigned, I fully prove;
  A heaven-like blessing changed, thrown from above
  Into despair, whose worst ill I do see.

Had I not happy been, I had not known
  So great a loss; a king deposed feels most
  The torment of a throne-like-want when lost,
  And up must look to what late was his own.

Lucifer down cast, his loss doth grieve;
  My Paradise of joy gone, do I live?

Lindamira's Complaint

O Memory, could I but loose thee now,
  At least learn to forget as I did move
  My best and only thoughts to wait on love,
  And be as registers of my made vow.

Could I but let my mind to reason bow,
  Or see plain wrongs, neglects, and slightings prove
  In that dear Sphere, which as the heavens above
  I prized, and homage to it did allow.

Canst thou not turn as well a traitor too
  Since heaven-like powers teach thee what to do?
  Canst not thou quite forget thy pleasures past,

Those blessed hours, the only time of bliss,
  When we feared nothing but we time might miss
  Long enough to enjoy what's now off cast.

The Verses of the
Talkative Knight

Rise, rise from sluggishness, fly fast my dear,
  The early lark prevents the rising lights:
  The sun is risen and shines in the rights
  Of his bright glory, till your eyes appear.

Arise, and make your two suns so clear show
    As he for shame his beams call back again
    And drown them in the sea for sorrow's pain,
    That you, Commandress of the light may know.

The duty sun, and all, must yield to you
    Where richness of desert doth lie embraced,
    Night by your brightness wholly now defaced,
    And day alone left to you as lights due.

Yet be as weighty still in love to me,
    Press me with love, rather than lightly fly
    My passions like to women, made to tie
    Of purpose to unloose and oft be free.

Thus may your lightness showing ruin me;
    I cannot live if your affections die,
    Or leave off living in my constancy.
    Be light and heavy too, so we agree.

The Duke's Song

If a clear fountain still keeping a sad course
    Weep out her sorrows in drops, which like tears fall,
    Marvel not if I lament my misfortune,
        brought to the same call.

Who thought such fair eyes could shine, and dissemble?
    Who thought such sweet breath could poison love's shame?
    Who thought those chaste ears could so be defiled?
        hers be the sole blame.

While love deserved love, of mine still she failed not,
    Fool I to love still where mine was neglected,
    Yet faith and honor, both of me claimed it,
        although rejected.

Oft have I heard her vow, never sweet quiet
    Could once possess her while that I was else where,
    But words were breath then, and as breath they wasted
        into a lost air.

So soon is love lost, not in heart imprinted,
    Silly I, knew not the false power of changing,
    Love I expected, yet, ah, was deceived,
        more her fond ranging.

Infant Love tied me not to mistrust change,
  Vows kept me fearless, yet all those were broken:
  Love, faith, and friendship by her are dissolved,
    suffered unspoken.

Pamphilia to Amphilanthus

When every one to pleasing pastime hies,
  Some hunt, some hawk, some play while some delight
  In sweet discourse, and music shows joy's might:
  Yet I my thought do far above these prize.

The joy that I take is, that free from eyes
  I sit and wonder at this day-like night,
  So to dispose themselves as void of right
  And leave true pleasure for poor vanities.

When others hunt, my thoughts I have in chase;
  If hawk, my mind at wished end doth fly;
  Discourse, I with my spirit talk and cry;
  While others music choose as greatest grace.

O God, say I, can these fond pleasures move,
  Or music be but in sweet thoughts of love?

Rachel Speght

From *A Dream*

Upon a sudden, as I gazing stood,
Thought came to me and asked me of my state,
Inquiring what I was, and what I would,
And why I seemed as one disconsolate.
To whose demand, I thus again replied,
I as a stranger in this place abide.

   .   .   .   .   .   .

My grief, quoth I, is called Ignorance,
Which makes me differ little from a brute,
For animals are led by nature's lore;
Their seeming silence is but custom's fruit;

When they are hurt they have a sense of pain,
But want the sense to cure themselves again.

    .   .   .   .   .   .

Quoth she, I wish I could prescribe your help;
Your state I pity much and do bewail;
But for my part, though I am much employed,
Yet in my judgment I do often fail.
And therefore I'll commend unto your trial
Experience, of whom take no denial.

    .   .   .   .   .   .

I sought, I found, she asked me what I would.
Quoth I, your best direction I implore,
For I am troubled with an irksome grief,
Which, when I named, quoth she, declare no more,
For I can tell as much as you can say,
And for your cure I'll help you what I may.

The only medicine for your malady,
By which, and nothing else your help is wrought,
Is Knowledge, of the which there is two sorts,
The one is good, the other bad and nought;
The former sort by labour is attained,
The latter may without much toil be gained.

But 'tis the good which must effect your cure.
I prayed her then that she would further show
Where I might have it. That I will, quoth she.
In Erudition's garden it doth grow;
And in compassion of your woeful case,
Industry shall conduct you to the place.

Dissuasion hearing her assign my help
(And seeing that consent I did detect)
Did many remoras to me propose,
As dullness, and my memory's defect,
The difficulty of attaining lore,
My time, and sex, with many others more.

Which when I heard, my mind was much perplexed,
And as a horse new come into the field

Who with a harquebus at first doth start,
So did this shot make me recoil and yield.
But of my fear when some did notice take,
In my behalf, they this reply did make.

First, quoth Desire, Dissuasion, hold thy peace;
These oppositions come not from above.
Quoth Truth, they cannot spring from reason's root,
And therefore now thou shalt no victor prove.
No, quoth Industry, be assured this,
Her friends shall make thee of thy purpose miss.

For with my sickle I will cut away
All obstacles that in her way can grow,
And by the issue of her own attempt,
I'll make thee *labor omnia vincet* know.
Quoth Truth, and sith her sex thou dost object,
Thy folly I by reason will detect.

Both man and woman of three parts consist,
Which Paul doth body, soul, and spirit call,
And from the soul three faculties arise,
The mind, the will, the power; then wherefore shall
A woman have her intellect in vain,
Or not endeavor Knowledge to attain.

The talent God doth give must be employed,
His own with vantage he must have again;
All parts and faculties were made for use;
The God of Knowledge nothing gave in vain.
'Twas Mary's choice our Saviour did approve,
Because that she the better part did love.

.   .   .   .   .   .

Lady Diana Primrose

From *A Chain of Pearl*

The Fourth Pearl: Temperance

The golden bridle of Bellerephon
Is Temperance, by which our passion

And appetite we conquer and subdue
To reason regiment: else may we rue
Our yielding to men's Siren-blandishment,
Which are attended with so foul events.
This Pearl in her was so conspicuous
As that the King, her brother, still did use
To style her his sweet sister Temperance
By which her much admired self-governance
Her passions still she checked and still she made
The world astonished, that so undismayed
She did with equal tenor still proceed
In one fair course, not shaken as a reed,
But built upon the rock of Temperance.
Not dazed with fear, not mazed with any chance,
Not with vain hope (as with an empty spoon)
Fed or allured to cast beyond the moon,
Not with rash anger too precipitate,
Not fond to love, nor too, too prone to hate;
Not charmed with parasites' or Siren's songs,
Whose hearts are poisoned, though their sugared tongues
Swear, vow, and promise all fidelity
When they are brewing deepest villainy,
Not led to vain or too profuse expense,
Pretending thereby state magnificence,
Not spending on these momentary pleasures
Her precious time—but deeming her best treasures
Her subjects' love, which she so well preserved
By sweet and mild demeanor, as it served
To guard her surer than an army royal,
So true their loves were to her and so loyal.
O Golden Age! O blest and happy years!
O music sweeter than that of the Spheres!
When Prince and People mutually agree
In sacred concord and sweet symphony!

Anne Bradstreet

To My Dear and Loving Husband

If ever two were one, then surely we.
If ever man were loved by wife, then thee;
If ever wife was happy in a man,
Compare with me, ye women, if you can.
I prize thy love more than whole mines of gold
Or all the riches that the East doth hold.
My love is such that rivers cannot quench,
Nor ought but love from thee, give recompense.
Thy love is such I can no way repay,
The heavens reward thee manifold, I pray.
Then while we live, in love let's so persevere
That when we live no more, we may live ever.

A Letter to Her Husband Absent on Public Employment

"As Loving Hind"

As loving Hind that (Hartless) wants her Deer,
Scuds through the woods and fern with hark'ning ear,
Perplexed, in every bush and nook doth pry,
Her dearest Deer, might answer ear or eye;
So doth my anxious soul, which now doth miss,
A dearer Dear (far dearer Heart) than this,
Still wait with doubts, and hopes, and failing eye,
His voice to hear, or person to descry.
Or as the pensive Dove doth all alone
(On withered bough) most uncouthly bemoan
The absence of her Love, and loving Mate,
Whose loss hath made her so unfortunate:
Ev'n thus do I, with many a deep sad groan
Bewail my turtle true, who now is gone,
His presence and his safe return, still woos,
With thousand doleful sighs and mournful coos.
Or as the loving Mullet, that true Fish,

Her fellow lost, nor joy nor life do wish,
But launches on that shore, there for to die,
Where she her captive husband doth espy.
Mine being gone, I lead a joyless life,
I have a loving fere, yet seem no wife:
But worst of all, to him can't steer my course,
I here, he there, alas, both kept by force:
Return my Dear, my joy, my only Love,
Unto thy Hind, thy Mullet and thy Dove,
Who neither joys in pasture, house nor streams,
The substance gone, O me, these are but dreams.
Together at one tree, oh let us browse,
And like two Turtles roost within one house,
And like the Mullets in one river glide,
Let's still remain but one, till death divide.

    Thy loving Love and Dearest Dear,
    At home, abroad, and every where.

Before the Birth of One of Her Children

All things within this fading world hath end,
Adversity doth still our joys attend;
No ties so strong, no friends so dear and sweet,
But with death's parting blow is sure to meet.
The sentence past is most irrevocable,
A common thing, yet oh inevitable.
How soon, my Dear, death may my steps attend,
How soon't may be thy lot to lose thy friend,
We both are ignorant, yet love bids me
These farewell lines to recommend to thee,
That when that knot's untied that made us one,
I may seem thine, who in effect am none.
And if I see not half my days that's due,
What nature would, God grant to yours and you;
The many faults that well you know I have,
Let be interred in my oblivious grave;
If any worth or virtue were in me,
Let that live freshly in thy memory
And when thou feel'st no grief, as I no harms,

Yet love thy dead, who long lay in thine arms.
And when thy loss shall be repaid with gains
Look to my little babes, my dear remains.
And if thou love thyself, or loved'st me
These O protect from step-dame's injury.
And if chance to thine eyes shall bring this verse,
With some sad sighs honour my absent hearse;
And kiss this paper for thy love's dear sake,
Who with salt tears this last farewell did take.

The Prologue

To sing of wars, of captains, and of kings,
Of cities founded, commonwealths begun,
For my mean pen are too superior things:
Or how they all, or each their dates have run
Let poets and historians set these forth,
My obscure lines shall not so dim their worth.

But when my wond'ring eyes and envious heart
Great Bartas' sugared lines do but read o'er,
Fool I do grudge the Muses did not part
'Twixt him and me that overfluent store;
A Bartas can do what a Bartas will
But simple I according to my skill.

From schoolboy's tongue no rhet'ric we expect,
Nor yet a sweet consort from broken strings,
Nor perfect beauty where's a main defect:
My foolish, broken, blemished Muse so sings,
And this to mend, alas, no art is able,
'Cause nature made it so irreparable.

Nor can I, like that fluent sweet tongued Greek
Who lisped at first, in future times speak plain.
By art he gladly found what he did seek,
A full requital of his striving pain.
Art can do much, but this maxim's most sure:
A weak or wounded brain admits no cure.

I am obnoxious to each carping tongue
Who says my hand a needle better fits,
A poet's pen all scorn I should thus wrong,

For such despite they cast on female wits:
If what I do prove well, it won't advance,
They'll say it's stol'n, or else it was by chance.

But sure the antique Greeks were far more mild
Else of our sex, why feigned they those nine
And poesy made Calliope's own child;
So 'mongst the rest they placed the arts divine.
But this weak knot they will full soon untie,
The Greeks did nought, but play the fools and lie.

Let Greeks be Greeks, and women what they are
Men have precedency and still excel,
It is but vain unjustly to wage war;
Men can do best, and women know it well.
Preeminence in all and each is yours;
Yet grant some small acknowledgement of ours.

And oh ye high flown quills that soar the skies,
And ever with your prey still catch your praise,
If e'er you deign these lowly lines your eyes,
Give thyme or parsley wreath, I ask no bays;
This mean and unrefined ore of mine
Will make your glist'ring gold but more to shine.

Contemplations

Some time now past in the autumnal tide,
When Phoebus wanted but one hour to bed,
The trees all richly clad, yet void of pride,
Where gilded o'er by his rich golden head.
Their leaves and fruits seemed painted, but was true
Of green, of red, of yellow, mixed hue.
Rapt were my senses at this delectable view.

I wist not what to wish, yet sure thought I,
If so much excellence abide below
How excellent is he that dwells on high,
Whose power and beauty by his works we know!
Sure he is goodness, wisdom, glory, light,
That hath this under world so richly dight,
More heaven than earth was here, no winter and no night.

Then on a stately oak I cast mine eye,
Whose ruffling top the clouds seemed to aspire.
How long since thou wast in thine infancy?
Thy strength, and stature, more thy years admire,
Hath hundred winters passed since thou wast born?
Or thousand since thou brakest thy shell of horn?
If so, all these as nought, eternity doth scorn.

Then higher on the glistering sun I gazed,
Whose beams was shaded by the leavie tree;
The more I looked, the more I grew amazed,
And softly said, what glory's like to thee?
Soul of this world, this universe's eye,
No wonder some made thee a deity.
Had I not better known, (alas) the same had I.

Thou as a bridegroom from thy chamber rushes,
And as a strong man, joys to run a race;
The morn doth usher thee, with smiles and blushes,
The earth reflects her glances in thy face.
Birds, insects, animals with vegative,
Thy heat from death and dullness doth revive.
And in the darksome womb of fruitful nature dive.

Thy swift annual, and diurnal course,
Thy daily straight and yearly oblique path,
Thy pleasing fervor, and thy scorching force,
All mortals here the feeling knowledge hath.
Thy presence makes it day, thy absence night,
Quaternal seasons caused by thy might.
Hail creature, full of sweetness, beauty, and delight.

Art thou so full of glory, that no eye
Hath strength thy shining rays once to behold?
And is thy splendid throne erect so high
As to approach it, can no earthly mould?
How full of glory then must thy Creator be
Who gave this bright light luster unto thee?
Admired, adored for ever, be that Majesty.

Silent alone, where none or saw, or heard,
In pathless paths I lead my wand'ring feet,
My humble eyes to lofty skies I reared

To sing some song my mazed muse thought meet.
My great Creator I would magnify,
That nature had thus decked liberally.
But ah, and ah, again, my imbecility!

I heard the merry grasshopper then sing,
The black clad cricket bear a second part.
They kept one tune and played on the same string,
Seeming to glory in their little art.
Shall creatures abject thus their voices raise
And in their kind resound their maker's praise,
Whilst I as mute, can warble forth no higher lays?

 . . . . . .

When I behold the heavens as in their prime,
And then the earth (though old) still clad in green,
The stones and trees, insensible of time,
Nor age nor wrinkle on their front are seen;
If winter come, and greenness then do fade,
A spring returns, and they more youthful made.
But man grows old, lies down, remains where once he's laid.

By birth more noble than those creatures all,
Yet seems by nature and by custom cursed,
No sooner born, but grief and care makes fall
That state obliterate he had at first;
Nor youth, nor strength, nor wisdom spring again
Nor habitations long their names retain,
But in oblivion to the final day remain.

Shall I then praise the heavens, the trees, the earth
Because their beauty and their strength last longer?
Shall I wish there, or never to had birth,
Because they're bigger, and their bodies stronger?
Nay, they shall darken, perish, fade and die,
And when unmade, so ever shall they lie,
But man was made for endless immortality.

Under the cooling shadow of a stately elm
Close sat I by a goodly river's side,
Where gliding streams the rocks did overwhelm,
A lonely place, with pleasures dignified.
I once that loved the shady woods so well,

49

Now thought the rivers did the trees excel,
And if the sun would ever shine, there would I dwell.

While on the stealing stream I fixed mine eye,
Which to the longed-for ocean held its course,
I marked, nor crooks nor rubs that there did lie
Could hinder ought, but still augment its force.
O happy flood, quoth I, that holds thy race
Till thou arrive at thy beloved place,
Nor is it rocks or shoals that can obstruct thy pace.

Nor is't enough, that thou alone may'st slide,
But hundred brooks in thy clear waves do meet,
So hand in hand along with thee they glide
To Thetis' house, where all embrace and greet.
Thou emblem true, of what I count the best,
O could I lead my rivulets to rest,
So may we press to that vast mansion, ever blest.

Ye fish which in this liquid region 'bide,
That for each season have your habitation,
Now salt, now fresh where you think best to glide
To unknown coasts to give a visitation,
In lakes and ponds, you leave your numerous fry;
So nature taught, and yet you know not why,
You wat'ry folk that know not your felicity.

Look how the wantons frisk to taste the air,
Then to the colder bottom straight they dive,
Eftsoon to Neptune's glassy hall repair
To see what trade the great ones there do drive,
Who forage o'er the spacious sea-green field,
And take the trembling prey before it yield,
Whose armour is their scales, their spreading fins their shield.

While musing thus with contemplation fed,
And thousand fancies buzzing in my brain,
The sweet-tongued Philomel perched o'er my head,
And chanted forth a most melodious strain
Which rapt me so with wonder and delight,
I judged my hearing better than my sight,
And wished me wings with her a while to take my flight.

O merry bird (said I) that fears no snares,
That neither toils nor hoards up in thy barn,
Feels no sad thoughts, nor cruciating cares
To gain more good or shun what might thee harm
Thy clothes ne'er wear, thy meat is everywhere,
Thy bed a bough, thy drink the water clear,
Reminds not what is past, nor what's to come dost fear.

The dawning morn with songs thou dost prevent,
Sets hundred notes unto thy feathered crew,
So each one tunes his pretty instrument,
And warbling out the old, begin anew,
And thus they pass their youth in summer season,
Then follow thee into a better region,
Where winter's never felt by that sweet airy legion.

Man at the best a creature frail and vain,
In knowledge ignorant, in strength but weak,
Subject to sorrows, losses, sickness, pain,
Each storm his state, his mind, his body break,
From some of these he never finds cessation,
But day or night, within, without, vexation,
Troubles from foes, from friends, from dearest, near'st relation.

And yet this sinful creature, frail and vain,
This lump of wretchedness, of sin and sorrow,
This weather-beaten vessel wracked with pain,
Joys not in hope of an eternal morrow;
Nor all his losses, crosses and vexation,
In weight, in frequency and long duration
Can make him deeply groan for that divine translation.

The mariner that on smooth waves doth glide,
Sings merrily, and steers his barque with ease,
As if he had command of wind and tide,
And now become great master of the seas;
But suddenly a storm spoils all the sport,
And makes him long for a more quiet port,
Which 'gainst all adverse winds may serve for fort.

So he that saileth in this world of pleasure,
Feeding on sweets, that never bit of th' sour,

That's full of friends, of honour and of treasure,
Fond fool, he takes this earth ev'n for heav'n's bower.
But sad affliction comes and makes him see
Here's neither honour, wealth, nor safety;
Only above is found all with security.

O Time the fatal wrack of mortal things,
That draws oblivion's curtains over kings;
Their sumptuous monuments, men know them not,
Their names without a record are forgot,
Their parts, their ports, their pomp's all laid in th' dust
Nor wit nor gold, nor buildings 'scape time's rust;
But he whose name is graved in the white stone
Shall last and shine when all of these are gone.

Upon the Burning of Our House, July 10th, 1666

In silent night when rest I took
For sorrow near I did not look
I wakened was with thund'ring noise
And piteous shrieks of dreadful voice.
That fearful sound of *Fire!* and *Fire!*
Let no man know is my desire.
I, starting up, the light did spy,
And to my God my heart did cry
To strengthen me in my distress
And not to leave me succorless.
Then coming out, beheld a space
The flame consume my dwelling place.
And when I could no longer look,
I blest his name that gave and took,
That laid my goods now in the dust.
Yea so it was, and so 'twas just.
It was his own, it was not mine,
Far be it that I should repine;
He might of all justly bereft
But yet sufficient for us left.
When by the ruins oft I past
My sorrowing eyes aside did cast,

And here and there the places spy
Where oft I sat and long did lie:
Here stood that trunk, and there that chest,
There lay that store I counted best.
My pleasant things in ashes lie,
And them behold no more shall I.
Under thy roof no guest shall sit,
Nor at thy table eat a bit.
No pleasant tale shall e'er be told,
Nor things recounted done of old.
No candle e'er shall shine in thee,
Nor bridegroom's voice e'er heard shall be.
In silence ever shall thou lie,
Adieu, adieu, all's vanity.
Then straight I 'gin my heart to chide,
And did thy wealth on earth abide?
Didst fix thy hope on mold'ring dust?
The arm of flesh didst make thy trust?
Raise up thy thoughts above the sky
That dunghill mists away may fly.
Thou hast an house on high erect,
Framed by that mighty Architect,
With glory richly furnished,
Stands permanent though this be fled.
It's purchased and paid for too
By him who hath enough to do.
A price so vast as is unknown
Yet by his gift is made thine own;
There's wealth enough, I need no more,
Farewell, my pelf, farewell my store.
The world no longer let me love,
My hope and treasure lies above.

In Memory of My Dear Grandchild Elizabeth Bradstreet, who Deceased August, 1665

Farewell, dear babe, my heart's too much content,
Farewell sweet babe, the pleasure of mine eye,
Farewell fair flower that for a space was lent,

Then ta'en away unto eternity.
Blest babe, why should I once bewail thy fate,
Or sigh thy days so soon were terminate,
Sith thou art settled in an everlasting state.

By nature trees do rot when they are grown,
And plums and apples throughly ripe do fall,
And corn and grass are in their season mown,
And time brings down what is both strong and tall.
But plants new set to be eradicate,
And buds new blown to have so short a date,
Is by his hand alone that guides nature and fate.

Anne Collins

Song

My straying thoughts, reduced stay,
And so a while retired,
Such observations to survey
Which memory hath regist'red,
That were not in oblivion dead.

In which review of mental store,
One note affordeth comforts best,
Chiefly to be preferred therefore,
As in a cabinet or chest
One jewel may exceed the rest.

God is the Rock of his elect
In whom his grace is inchoate,
This note, my soul did most affect,
It doth such power intimate
To comfort and corroborate.

God is a Rock first in respect
He shadows his from hurtful heat,
Then in regard he doth protect
His servants still from dangers great
And so their enemies defeat.

In some dry desert lands (they say)
Are mighty rocks, which shadow make,
Where passengers that go that way,
May rest, and so refreshing take,
Their sweltish weariness to slake.

So in this world such violent
Occasions find we still to mourn,
That scorching heat of discontent
Would all into combustion turn
And soon our souls with anguish burn,

Did not our Rock preserve us still,
Whose spirit, ours animates,   /
That wind that bloweth where it will
Sweetly our souls refrigerates,
And so destructive heat abates.

From this our Rock proceeds likewise,
The saving streams, which graciously
Revives the soul which scorched lies,
Through sense of God's displeasure high, ·
Due to her for iniquity.

So this our Rock refreshing yields,
To those that unto him adhere,
Whom likewise mightily he shields,
So that they need not faint nor fear
Though all the world against them were.

.   .   .   .   .   .

Margaret Cavendish, Duchess of Newcastle

The Soul's Garment

Great Nature clothes the soul, which is but thin,
With fleshly garments, which the Fates do spin,
And when these garments are grown old and bare,
With sickness torn, Death takes them off with care,
And folds them up in peace and quiet rest,

And lays them safe within an earthly chest:
Then scours them well and makes them sweet and clean,
Fit for the soul to wear those clothes again.

From *The Convent of Pleasure*

Song

My cabinets are oyster-shells,
In which I keep my orient pearls;
To open them I use the tide,
As keys to locks, which opens wide
The oyster-shells; then out I take
Those orient pearls and crowns do make;
And modest coral I do wear,
Which blushes when it touches air.
On silver waves I sit and sing,
And then the fish lie listening:
Then sitting on a rocky stone
I comb my hair with fishes' bone;
The whilest Apollo with his beams
Doth dry my hair from watery streams.
His light doth glaze the water's face,
Make the large sea my looking-glass:
So when I swim on waters high,
I see myself as I glide by:
But when the sun begins to burn,
I back into my waters turn,
And dive into the bottom low:
Then on my head the waters flow
In curled waves and circles round,
And thus with waters am I crowned.

Mirth and Melancholy

As I was musing by myself alone,
My thoughts brought several things to work upon:
At last came two, which diversely were dressed,
One Melancholy, t'other Mirth expressed;
Here Melancholy stood in black array,
And Mirth was all in colours fresh and gay.

Mirth

Mirth laughing came, and running to me, flung
Her fat white arms about my neck, there hung,
Embraced and kissed me oft, and stroked my cheek,
Saying she would no other lover seek;
I'll sing you songs, and please you every day,
Invent new sports to pass the time away;
I'll keep your heart, and guard it from that thief,
Dull Melancholy, Care, or sadder Grief,
And make your eyes with Mirth to overflow;
With springing blood your cheeks soon fat shall grow;
Your legs shall nimble be, your body light,
And all your spirits like to birds in flight.
Mirth shall digest your meat, and make you strong,
Shall give you health, and your short days prolong;
Refuse me not, but take me to your wife;
For I shall make you happy all your life.
But Melancholy, she will make you lean,
Your cheeks shall hollow grow, your jaws be seen;
Your eyes shall buried be within your head,
And look as pale as if you were quite dead;
She'll make you start at every noise you hear,
And visions strange shall to your eyes appear;
Thus would it be, if you to her were wed.
Nay, better far it were that you were dead.
Her voice is low, and gives an hollow sound,
She hates the light, and is in darkness found;
Or sits with blinking lamps, or tapers small,
Which various shadows make against the wall.
She loves nought else but noise which discord makes,
As croaking frogs, whose dwelling is in lakes;
The raven's hoarse, the mandrake's hollow groan,
And shrieking owls, which fly i' th' night alone;
The tolling bell, which for the dead rings out;
A mill, where rushing waters run about;
The roaring winds, which shake the cedars tall,
Plough up the seas, and beat the rocks withal.
She loves to walk in the still moonshine night,
And in a thick dark grove she takes delight;
In hollow caves, thatched houses, and low cells,

She loves to live, and there alone she dwells,
Then leave her to herself alone to dwell,
Let you and I in Mirth and Pleasure swell,
And drink long lusty draughts from Bacchus' bowl,
Until our brains on vaporous waves do roll;
Let's joy ourselves in amorous delights;
There's none so happy as the carpet knights.

Melancholy

Then Melancholy, with sad and sober face,
Complexion pale, but of a comely grace,
With modest countenance thus softly spake;
May I so happy be your love to take?
True, I am dull, yet by me you shall know
More of yourself, and so much wiser grow;
I search the depth and bottom of mankind,
Open the eye of ignorance that's blind;
All dangers to avoid I watch with care,
And do 'gainst evils that may come prepare;
I hang not on inconstant fortune's wheel,
Nor yet with unresolving doubts do reel;
I shake not with the terrors of vain fears,
Nor is my mind filled with unuseful cares;
I do not spend my time like idle Mirth,
Which only happy is just at her birth;
And seldom lives so long as to be old,
But if she doth, can no affections hold;
Mirth good for nothing is, like weeds doth grow,
Or such plants as cause madness, reason's foe.
Her face with laughter crumples on a heap,
Which makes great wrinkles, and ploughs furrows deep;
Her eyes do water, and her skin turns red,
Her mouth doth gape, teeth bare, like one that's dead;
She fulsome is, and gluts the senses all,
Offers herself, and comes before a call;
Her house is built upon the golden sands,
Yet no foundation has, whereon it stands;
A palace 'tis, and of a great resort,
It makes a noise, and gives a loud report,
Yet underneath the roof disasters lie,

Beat down the house, and many killed thereby;
I dwell in groves that gilt are with the sun,
Sit on the banks by which clear waters run;
In summers hot down in a shade I lie,
My music is the buzzing of a fly;
I walk in meadows, where grows fresh green grass,
In fields, where corn is high, I often pass;
Walk up the hills, where round I prospects see,
Some brushy woods, and some all champaigns be;
Returning back, I in fresh pastures go,
To hear how sheep do bleat, and cows do low;
In winter cold, when nipping frosts come on,
Then I do live in a small house alone;
Although 'tis plain, yet cleanly 'tis within,
Like to a soul that's pure and clear from sin;
And there I dwell in quiet and still peace,
Not filled with cares how riches to increase;
I wish nor seek for vain and fruitless pleasures,
No riches are, but what the mind intreasures.
Thus am I solitary, live alone,
Yet better loved, the more that I am known;
And though my face ill-favoured at first sight,
After acquaintance it will give delight.
Refuse me not, for I shall constant be,
Maintain your credit and your dignity.

Katherine Philips

Against Love

Hence Cupid! with your cheating toys,
Your real griefs, and painted joys,
Your pleasure which itself destroys.
Lovers like men in fevers burn and rave,
And only what will injure them do crave.
Men's weakness makes love so severe,
They give him power by their fear,
And make the shackles which they wear.

Who to another does his heart submit,
Makes his own idol, and then worships it.
   Him whose heart is all his own,
   Peace and liberty does crown,
   He apprehends no killing frown.
He feels no raptures which are joys diseased,
And is not much transported, but still pleased.

To Mr. Henry Lawes

Nature, which is the vast creation's soul,
That steady curious agent in the whole,
The art of Heaven, the order of this frame,
Is only number in another name.
For as some king conqu'ring what was his own,
Hath choice of several titles to his crown;
So harmony on this score now, that then,
Yet still is all that takes and governs men.
Beauty is but composure, and we find
Content is but the concord of the mind,
Friendship the unison of well-tuned hearts,
Honour the chorus of the noblest parts,
And all the world on which we can reflect
Music to th'ear, or to the intellect.
If then each man a little world must be,
How many worlds are copied out in thee,
Who art so richly formed, so complete
T'epitomize all that is good and great;
Whose stars this brave advantage did impart,
Thy nature's as harmonious as thy art?
Though dost above the poets' praises live,
Who fetch from thee th'eternity they give.
And as true reason triumphs over sense,
Yet is subjected to intelligence:
So poets on the lower world look down,
But Lawes on them; his height is all his own.
For, like divinity itself, his lyre
Rewards the wit it did at first inspire.
And thus by double right poets allow
His and their laurel should adorn his brow.
Live then, great soul of nature, to assuage

The savage dullness of this sullen age.
Charm us to sense; for though experience fail
And reason too, thy numbers may prevail.
Then, like those ancients, strike, and so command
All nature to obey thy gen'rous hand.
None will resist but such who needs will be
More stupid than a stone, a fish, a tree.
Be it thy care our age to new-create:
What built a world may sure repair a state.

To My Excellent Lucasia, on Our Friendship

I did not live until this time
    Crowned my felicity,
When I could say without a crime,
    I am not thine, but thee.

This carcass breathed, and walked and slept,
    So that the world believed
There was a soul the motions kept;
    But they were all deceived.

For as a watch by art is wound
    To motion, such was mine:
But never had Orinda found
    A soul till she found thine;

Which now inspires, cures, and supplies,
    And guides my darkened breast:
For thou art all that I can prize,
    My joy, my life, my rest.

No bridegroom's nor crown-conqueror's mirth
    To mine compared can be:
They have but pieces of this earth,
    I've all the world in thee.

Then let our flames still light and shine,
    And no false fear control,
As innocent as our design,
    Immortal as our soul.

A Sea-Voyage From Tenby to Bristol, Begun Sept. 5, 1652. Sent From Bristol to Lucasia, Sept. 8, 1652

Hoise up the sail, cried they who understand
No word that carries kindness for the land:
Such sons of clamour, that I wonder not
They love the sea, whom sure some storm begot.
Had he who doubted motion these men seen,
Or heard their tongues, he had convinced been.
For had our bark moved half as fast as they,
We had not need cast anchor by the way.
One of the rest pretending to more wit,
Some small Italian spoke, but murdered it;
For I (thanks to Saburra's letters) knew
How to distinguish 'twixt the false and true.
But t'oppose these as mad a thing would be
As 'tis to contradict a Presbyt'ry.
'Tis Spanish though, (quoth I) e'en what you please:
For him that spoke it, 'tmight be Bread and Cheese.
So softly moves the bark which none controls,
As are the meetings of agreeing souls:
And the moon-beams did on the water play,
As if at midnight 'twould create a day.
The amorous wave that shared in such dispense
Expressed at once delight and reverence.
Such trepidation we in lovers spy
Under th'oppression of a mistress' eye.
But then the wind so high did rise and roar,
Some vowed they'd never trust the traitor more.
Behold the fate that all our glories sweep,
Writ in the dangerous wonders of the deep:
And yet behold man's easy folly more,
How soon we curse what erst we did adore.
Sure he that first himself did thus convey,
Had some strong passion that he would obey.
The bark wrought hard, but found it was in vain
To make its party good against the main,
Tossed and retreated, till at last we see
She must be fast if e'er she should be free.

We gravely anchor cast, and patiently
Lie prisoners to the weather's cruelty.
We had not wind nor tide, nor ought but grief,
Till a kind spring-tide was our first relief.
Then we float merrily, forgetting quite
The sad confinement of the stormy night.
Ere we had lost these thoughts, we ran aground,
And then how vain to be secure we found.
Now they were all surprised. Well, if we must,
Yet none shall say that dust is gone to dust.
But we are off now, and the civil tide
Assisted us the tempests to out-ride.
But what most pleased my mind upon the way,
Was the ship's posture that in harbour lay:
Which to a rocky grove so close were fixed,
That the trees branches with the tackling mixed.
One would have thought it was, as then it stood,
A growing navy, or a floating wood.
But I have done at last, and do confess
My voyage taught me so much tediousness.
In short, the Heav'ns must needs propitious be,
Because Lucasia was concerned in me.

Aphra Behn

From *The Dutch Lover*

Song

Ah false Amyntas, can that hour
  So soon forgotten be,
When first I yielded up my power
  To be betrayed by thee?
God knows with how much innocence
  I did my heart resign,
Unto thy faithless eloquence,
  And gave thee what was mine.

I had not one reserve in store,
  But at thy feet I laid

Those arms which conquered heretofore,
  Though now thy trophies made.
Thy eyes in silence told their tale,
  Of love in such a way,
That 'twas as easy to prevail,
  As after to betray.

From *Abdelazar*

Song

Love in fantastic triumph sat,
Whilst bleeding hearts around him flowed,
For whom fresh pains he did create,
And strange tyrannic power he showed;
From thy bright eyes he took his fire,
Which round about, in sport he hurled;
But 'twas from mine, he took desire,
Enough to undo the amorous world.

From me he took his sighs and tears,
From thee his pride and cruelty;
From me his languishments and fears,
And every killing dart from thee;
Thus thou and I, the God have armed,
And set him up a deity;
But my poor heart alone is harmed,
Whilst thine the victor is, and free.

From *The Lucky Chance*

Song

Oh! Love, that stronger art than wine,
Pleasing delusion, witchery divine,
Want to be prized above all wealth,
Disease that has more joys than health.
Though we blaspheme thee in our pain,
And of thy tyranny complain,
We are all bettered by thy reign.

What reason never can bestow
We to this useful passion owe.

Love wakes the dull from sluggish ease,
And learns a clown the art to please.
Humbles the vain, kindles the cold,
Makes misers free, and cowards bold.
'Tis he reforms the sot from drink,
And teaches airy fops to think.

When full brute appetite is fed,
And choked the glutton lies, and dead:
Thou new spirits dost dispense,
And fine'st the gross delights of sense.
Virtue's unconquerable aid,
That against nature can persuade:
And makes a roving mind retire
Within the bounds of just desire.
Cheerer of age, youth's kind unrest,
And half the heaven of the blest.

From *Emperor of the Moon*

Song 1

All joy to mortals, joy and mirth
    Eternal Io's sing;
The gods of love descend to earth,
    Their darts have lost the sting.
The youth shall now complain no more
    On Sylvia's needless scorn,
But she shall love, if he adore,
    And melt when he shall burn.

The nymph no longer shall be shy,
    But leave the jilting road;
And Daphne now no more shall fly
    The wounded panting God;
But all shall be serene and fair,
    No sad complaints of love
Shall fill the gentle whispering air,
    No echoing sighs the grove.

Beneath the shades young Strephon lies,
    Of all his wish possessed;

Gazing on Sylvia's charming eyes,
  Whose soul is there confessed.
All soft and sweet the maid appears,
  With looks that know no art,
And though she yields with trembling fears,
  She yields with all her heart.

Song 2

A curse upon that faithless maid,
Who first her sex's liberty betrayed;
Born free as man to love and range,
Till nobler nature did to custom change.
Custom, that dull excuse for fools,
Who think all virtue to consist in rules.

From love our fetters never sprung,
That smiling god, all wanton, gay and young,
Shows by his wings he cannot be
Confined to a restless slavery;
But here and there at random roves,
Not fixed to glitt'ring courts or shady groves.

Then she that constancy professed,
Was but a well dissembler at the best;
And that imaginary sway
She feigned to give, in seeming to obey,
Was but the height of prudent art,
To deal with greater liberty her heart.

Joan Philips

Maidenhead

Written at the Request of a Friend

At your entreaty, I at last have writ
This whimsey, that has nigh nonplussed my wit:
The toy I've long enjoyed, if it may
Be called t'enjoy, a thing we wish away;
But yet no more its character can give,
Than tell the minutes that I have to live.

'Tis a fantastic ill, a loathed disease,
That can no sex, no age, no person please.
Men strive to gain it, but the way they choose
T'obtain their wish, that and the wish doth lose.
Our thoughts are still uneasy, till we know
What 'tis, and why it is desired so:
But th'first unhappy knowledge that we boast,
Is that we know, the valued trifle's lost.
Thou dull companion of our active years,
That chill'st our warm blood with thy frozen fears,
How is it likely thou shouldst long endure,
When thought itself thy ruin may procure?
Thou short lived tyrant, that usurp'st a sway
O'er woman-kind though none thy power obey,
Except th' ill-natured, ugly, peevish, proud,
And these indeed, thy praises sing aloud.
But what's the reason they obey so well?
Because they want the power to rebel.
But I forget, or have my subject lost.
Alas! thy being's fancy at the most:
Though much desired, 'tis but seldom men
Court the vain blessing from a woman's pen.

To Phylocles, Inviting Him
to Friendship

Best of thy sex! if sacred friendship can
Dwell in the bosom of inconstant man,
As cold and clear as ice, as snow unstained,
With love's loose crimes unsullied, unprofaned;

Or you a woman with that name dare trust,
And think to friendship's ties we can be just:
In a strict league together we'll combine,
And let our friendship's bright example shine.

We will forget the difference of sex,
Nor shall the world's rude censure us perplex.
Think me all man: my soul is masculine,
And capable of as great things as thine.

I can be gen'rous just and brave,
Secret and silent as the grave,

And if I cannot yield relief,
I'll sympathize in all thy grief.

I will not have a thought from thee I'll hide,
In all my actions thou shalt be my guide;
In every joy of mine thou shalt have share,
And I will bear a part in all thy care.

Why do I vainly talk of what we'll do?
We'll mix our souls, you shall be me, I you;
And both so one it shall be hard to say
Which is Phylocles, which Ephelia.

Our ties shall be as strong as the chains of fate,
Conqu'rors and kings our joys shall emulate;
Forgotten friendship, held at first divine,
T'its native purity we will refine.

Anne Killigrew

Upon the Saying That My Verses Were Made by Another

Next Heaven, my vows to thee, O sacred Muse!
I offered up, nor didst thou them refuse.

   O Queen of Verse, said I, if thou'lt inspire,
And warm my soul with thy poetic fire,
No love of gold shall share with thee my heart,
Or yet ambition in my breast have part,
More rich, more noble I will ever hold
The Muse's laurel, than a crown of gold.
An undivided sacrifice I'll lay
Upon thine altar, soul and body pay;
Thou shalt my pleasure, my employment be,
My all I'll make a holocaust to thee.

   The deity that ever does attend
Prayers so sincere, to mine did condescend.
I writ, and the judicious praised my pen:

Could any doubt ensuing glory then?
What pleasing raptures filled my ravished sense,
How strong, how sweet, Fame, was thy influence!
And thine, false Hope, that to my flattered sight
Did'st glories represent so near and bright!
By thee deceived, methought each verdant tree
Apollo's transformed Daphne seemed to be;
And ev'ry fresher branch, and ev'ry bough,
Appeared as garlands to empale my brow.
The learn'd in love say, thus the winged boy
Does first approach, dressed up in welcome joy;
At first he to the cheated lover's sight
Nought represents but rapture and delight,
Alluring hopes, soft fears, which stronger bind
Their hearts, than when they more assurance find.

Emboldened thus, to fame I did commit
(By some few hands) my most unlucky wit.
But ah, the sad effects that from it came!
What ought t'have brought me honour, brought me shame!
Like Aesop's painted jay, I seemed to all,
Adorned in plumes, I not my own could call:
Rifled like her, each one my feathers tore,
And, as they thought, unto the owner bore.
My laurels thus another's brow adorned,
My numbers they admired, but me they scorned:
Another's brow, that had so rich a store
Of sacred wreaths that circled it before;
While mine quite lost (like a small stream that ran
Into a vast and boundless ocean,)
Was swallowed up with what it joined, and drowned.
And that abyss yet no accession found.

Orinda (Albion's and her sex's grace)
Owed not her glory to a beauteous face;
It was her radiant soul that shone within,
Which struck a lustre through her outward skin;
That did her lips and cheeks with roses dye,
Advanced her height, and sparkled in her eye.
Nor did her sex at all obstruct her fame,
But higher 'mong the stars it fixed her name;

What she did write, not only all allowed,
But every laurel to her laurel bowed!

 The envious age, only to me alone,
Will not allow what I do write, my own;
But let them rage, and 'gainst a maid conspire,
So deathless numbers from my tuneful lyre
Do ever flow; so, Phoebus, I by thee
Divinely inspired and possessed may be,
I willingly accept Cassandra's fate,
To speak the truth, although believed too late.

Mary Lee, Lady Chudleigh

The Offering: Part One

Accept, my God, the praises which I bring,
The humble tribute from a creature due;
 Permit me of thy power to sing,
That power which did stupendous wonders do,
And whose effects we still with awful rev'rence view:
That mighty pow'r which from thy boundless store,
 Out of thy self where all things lay,
 This beauteous universe did call,
This great, this glorious, this amazing all!
And filled with matter that vast empty space,
 Where nothing all alone
Had long unrivalled sat on its triumphant throne.
 See! now in every place
 The restless atoms play:
 Lo! High as heaven they proudly soar,
 And fill the wide stretched regions there;
In suns they shine above, in gems below,
And roll in solid masses through the yielding air;
In earth compacted, and diffused in seas,
In corn they nourish, and in flowers they please.
 In beasts they walk, in birds they fly,
And in gay painted insects crowd the sky;
In fish amid the silver waves they stray,
And ev'rywhere the laws of their first cause obey.

Of them, composed with wondrous art,
    We are our selves a part,
And on us still they nutriment bestow;
To us they kindly come, from us they swiftly go,
And through our veins in purple torrents flow.
    Vacuity is nowhere found,
Each place is full, with bodies we're encompassed round:
    In sounds they're to our ears conveyed,
In fragrant odors they our smell delight,
And in ten thousand curious forms displayed
        They entertain our sight;
    In luscious fruits our taste they court,
And in cool balmy breezes round us sport,
The friendly zephyrs fan our vital flame,
And give us breath to praise his holy name,
From whom our selves, and all these blessings came.

To the Ladies

Wife and servant are the same,
But only differ in the name,
For when that fatal knot is tied,
Which nothing, nothing can divide,
When she the word *obey* has said,
And man by law supreme has made,
Then all that's kind is laid aside,
And nothing left but state and pride.
Fierce as an eastern prince he grows,
And all his innate rigour shows.
Then but to look, to laugh, or speak,
Will the nuptial contract break.
Like mutes, she signs alone must make,
And never any freedom take,
But still be governed by a nod,
And fear her husband as her God;
Him still must serve, him still obey,
And nothing act, and nothing say,
But her haughty Lord thinks fit,
Who with the power, has all the wit.
Then shun, oh! shun that wretched state,
And all the fawning flatterers hate;

Value your selves, and men despise,
You must be proud, if you'll be wise.

The Resolve

For what the world admires I'll wish no more,
　　Nor court that airy nothing of a name;
Such fleeting shadows let the proud adore,
　　Let them be suppliants for an empty fame.

If reason rules within, and keeps the throne,
　　While the inferior faculties obey,
And all her laws without reluctance own,
　　Accounting none more fit, more just than they.

If virtue my free soul unsullied keeps,
　　Exempting it from passion and from stain;
If no black guilty thoughts disturb my sleeps,
　　And no past crimes my vexed remembrance pain,

If, though I pleasure find in living here,
　　I yet can look on death without surprise;
If I've a soul above the reach of fear,
　　And which will nothing mean or sordid prize,

A soul, which cannot be depressed by grief,
　　Nor too much raised by the sublimest joy,
Which can, when troubled, give itself relief,
　　And to advantage all its thoughts employ,

Then am I happy in my humbler state,
　　Although not crowned with glory nor with bays.
A mind, that triumphs over vice and fate,
　　Esteems it mean to court the world for praise.

Anne Finch,
Countess of Winchelsea

From *The Petition for*
an Absolute Retreat

Give me, O indulgent fate!
Give me yet before I die

A sweet, yet absolute retreat,
'Mongst paths so lost and trees so high
That the world may ne'er invade
Through such windings and such shade
My unshaken liberty.

No intruders thither come
Who visit but to be from home!
None who their vain moments pass
Only studious of their glass;
News, that charm to listening ears,
That false alarm to hopes and fears,
That common theme for every fop,
From the statesman to the shop,
In those coverts ne'er be spread,
Of who's deceased, and who's to wed.
Be no tidings thither brought,
But silent as a midnight thought
Where the world may ne'er invade
Be those windings and that shade!
Courteous Fate! afford me there
A table spread, without my care,
With what the neighbouring fields impart,
Whose cleanliness be all its art.
When of old the calf was dressed
(Though to make an angel's feast)
In the plain unstudied sauce
Nor truffle nor morillia was;
Nor could the mighty patriarchs' board
One far-fetched ortolan afford.
Courteous Fate! then give me there
Only plain and wholesome fare;
Fruits indeed (would heaven bestow)
All, that did in Eden grow
All but the forbidden Tree
Would be coveted by me;
Grapes with juice so crowded up
As breaking through the native cup;
Figs yet growing candied o'er
By the sun's attracting power;
Cherries, with the downy peach,

73

All within my easy reach;
Whilst creeping near the humble ground
Should the strawberry be found
Springing whereso'er I strayed
Through those windings and that shade.

For my garments: let them be
What may with the time agree;
Warm when Phœbus does retire
And is ill-supplied by fire:
But when he renews the year
And verdant all the fields appear,
Beauty every thing resumes,
Birds have dropped their winter plumes,
When the lily full-displayed
Stands in purer white arrayed
Than that vest which heretofore
The luxurious monarch wore,
When from Salem's gates he drove
To the soft retreat of love,
Lebanon's all burnished house
And the dear Egyptian spouse.
Clothe me, Fate, though not so gay,
Clothe me light and fresh as May!
In the fountains let me view
All my habit cheap and new
Such as, when sweet zephyrs fly,
With their motions may comply,
Gently waving to express
Unaffected carelessness.
No perfumes have there a part
Borrowed from the Chemist's art,
But such as rise from flowery beds
Or the falling jasmine sheds!

    .   .   .   .   .

Let me then no fragrance wear
But what the winds from gardens bear,
In such kind surprising gales
As gathered from Fidentia's vales
All the flowers that in them grew;
Which intermixing as they slew

In wreathen garlands dropped agen
On Lucullus and his men;
Who, cheered by the victorious sight,
Trebled numbers put to flight.
  Let me, when I must be fine,
In such natural colours shine;
Wove and painted by the sun;
Whose replendent rays to shun
When they do too fiercely beat
Let me find some close retreat
Where they have no passage made
Through those windings, and that shade.

  Give me there (since Heaven has shown
It was not good to be alone)
A partner suited to my mind,
Solitary, pleased and kind;
Who partially may something see
Preferred to all the world in me;
Slighting, by my humble side,
Fame and splendour, wealth and pride.
When but two the earth possessed,
'Twas their happiest days, and best;
They by business, nor by wars,
They by no domestic cares,
From each other e'er were drawn
But in some grove or flowery lawn
Spent the swiftly flying time,
Spent their own and nature's prime,
In love: that only passion given
To perfect man, whilst friends with heaven.
Rage, and jealousy, and hate,
Transports of his fallen state,
(When by Satan's wiles betrayed)
Fly those windings, and that shade!

  Thus from crowds and noise removed,
Let each moment be improved,
Every object still produce
Thoughts of pleasure, and of use;
When some river slides away
To increase the boundless sea,

Think we then, how Time does haste
To grow Eternity at last;
By the willows, on the banks,
Gathered into social ranks,
Playing with the gentle winds,
Straight the boughs and smooth the rinds,
Moist each fibre, and each top
Wearing a luxurious crop,
Let the time of youth be shown,
The time, alas! too soon outgrown;
Whilst a lonely stubborn oak
Which no breezes can provoke,
No less gusts persuade to move
Than those which in a whirlwind drove,
Spoiled the old fraternal feast
And left alive but one poor guest,
Rivelled the distorted trunk,
Sapless limbs all bent and shrunk,
Sadly does the time presage
Of our too near approaching age.

.   .   .   .   .   .

    Let me then, indulgent Fate!
Let me still in my retreat,
From all roving thoughts be freed,
Or aims that may contention breed;
Nor be my endeavours led
By goods that perish with the dead!
Fitly might the life of man
Be indeed esteemed a span,
If the present moment were
Of delight his only share;
If no other joys he knew
Than what round about him grew:
But as those who stars would trace
From a subterranean face
Through some engine lift their eyes
To the outward, glorious skies;
So the immortal spirit may,
When descended to our clay,
From a rightly governed frame

View the height from whence she came;
To her paradise be caught
And things unutterable taught.
Give me then, in that retreat,
Give me, O indulgent Fate!
For all pleasures left behind
Contemplations of the mind.
Let the fair, the gay, the vain
Courtship and applause obtain;
Let the ambitious rule the earth;
Let the giddy fool have mirth;
Give the epicure his dish,
Every one their several wish;
Whilst my transports I employ
On that more extensive joy,
When all Heaven shall be surveyed
From those windings, and that shade.

A Nocturnal Reverie

In such a night, when every louder wind
Is to its distant cavern safe confined;
And only gentle zephyr fans his wings,
And lonely Philomel, still waking, sings;
Or from some tree, famed for the owl's delight,
She, hollowing clear, directs the wanderer right;
In such a night, when passing clouds give place,
Or thinly veil the heaven's mysterious face;
When in some river, overhung with green,
The waving moon and trembling leaves are seen;
When freshened grass now bears itself upright,
And makes cool banks to pleasing rest invite,
Whence springs the woodbine and the bramble-rose,
And where the sleepy cowslip sheltered grows;
Whilst now a paler hue the foxglove takes,
Yet chequers still with red the dusky brakes:
When scattered glow-worms, but in twilight fine,
Show trivial beauties watch their hour to shine;
When odours, which declined repelling day,
Through temperate air uninterrupted stray;
When darkened groves their softest shadows wear,

And falling waters we distinctly hear;
When through the gloom more venerable shows
Some ancient fabric, awful in repose,
While sunburnt hills their swarthy looks conceal,
And swelling haycocks thicken up the vale:
When the loosed horse now, as his pasture leads,
Comes slowly grazing through the adjoining meads,
Whose stealing pace, and lengthened shade we fear,
Till torn-up forage in his teeth we hear:
When nibbling sheep at large pursue their food,
And unmolested kine rechew the cud;
When curlews cry beneath the village walls,
And to her straggling brood the partridge calls;
Their short-lived jubilee the creatures keep,
Which but endures, whilst tyrant man does sleep:
When a sedate content the spirit feels,
And no fierce light disturbs, whilst it reveals;
But silent musings urge the mind to seek
Something, too high for syllables to speak;
Till the free soul to a composedness charmed,
Finding the elements of rage disarmed,
O'er all below a solemn quiet grown,
Joys in the inferior world, and thinks it like her own:
In such a night let me abroad remain,
Till morning breaks, and all's confused again;
Our cares, our toils, our clamours are renewed,
Or pleasures, seldom reached, again pursued.

To the Nightingale

Exert thy voice, sweet harbinger of spring!
    This moment is thy time to sing,
    This moment I attend to praise
And set my numbers to thy lays.
    Free as thine shall be my song,
    As thy music, short or long.
Poets wild as thou were born
    Pleasing best when unconfined,
    When to please is least designed,
Soothing but their cares to rest.

Cares do still their thoughts molest,
    And still the unhappy poet's breast,
Like thine, when best he sings, is placed against a thorn.

She begins. Let all be still!
    Muse, thy promise now fulfil!
Sweet, oh sweet, still sweeter yet!
Can thy words such accents fit,
Canst thou syllables refine,
Melt a sense that shall retain
Still some spirit of the brain,
Till with sounds like these it join?
    'Twill not be! then change thy note;
    Let division shake thy throat.
Hark! Division now she tries;
Yet as far the Muse outflies.
    Cease then, prithee, cease thy tune.
    Trifler, wilt thou sing till June?
Till thy business all lies waste,
And the time of building's past!
    Thus we poets that have speech,

Unlike what thy forests teach,
    If a fluent vein be shown
    That's transcendent to our own,
Criticize, reform, or preach,
Or censure what we cannot reach.

To Melancholy

At last, my old, inveterate foe,
No opposition shalt thou know.
Since I, by struggling, can obtain
Nothing, but increase of pain,
I will at last no more do so,
Though I confess I have applied
Sweet mirth, and music, and have tried
A thousand other arts beside,
To drive thee from my darkened breast,
Thou, who hast banished all my rest.
But though sometimes a short reprieve they gave,

Unable they, and far too weak, to save;
All arts to quell, did but augment thy force,
As rivers checked, break with a wilder course.

Friendship I to my heart have laid,
Friendship, the applauded sovereign aid,
And thought that charm so strong would prove,
As to compel thee to remove;
And to myself I boasting said,
Now I a conqueror sure shall be,
The end of all my conflicts see,
And noble triumph wait on me;
My dusky, sullen foe will sure
Ne'er this united charge endure.
But, leaning on this reed, ev'n whilst I spoke,
It pierced my hand, and into pieces broke.
Still some new object, or new interest came
And loosed the bonds, and quite dissolved the claim.

These failing, I invoked a Muse,
And poetry would often use
To guard me from the tyrant power;
And to oppose thee, every hour
New troops of fancies did I choose.
Alas! in vain, for all agree
To yield me captive up to thee,
And heaven alone can set me free.
Thou through my life wilt with me go,
And make the passage sad, and slow.
All that could e'er thy ill-got rule invade,
Their useless arms before thy feet have laid;
The fort is thine, now ruined all within,
Whilst by decays without, thy conquest too is seen.

Trail All Your Pikes

Trail all your pikes, dispirit every drum,
March in a slow procession from afar,
Ye silent, ye dejected, men of war.
Be still the hautboys, and the flute be dumb!
Display no more, in vain, the lofty banner;

For see where on the bier before ye lies
The pale, the fall'n, the untimely sacrifice
To your mistaken shrine, to your false idol Honour.

Jane Brereton

On Mr. Nash's Picture at Full Length, Between the Busts of Sir Isaac Newton and Mr. Pope

The old Egyptians hid their wit
    In hieroglyphic dress,
To give men pains to search for it,
    And please themselves with guess.

Moderns, to tread the self-same path
    And exercise our parts,
Place figures in a room at Bath;
    Forgive them, God of Arts!

Newton, if I can judge aright,
    All wisdom doth express,
His knowledge gives mankind new light,
    Adds to their happiness.

Pope is the emblem of true wit,
    The sunshine of the mind;
Read o'er his works for proof of it,
    You'll endless pleasure find.

Nash represents man in the mass,
    Made up of wrong and right;
Sometimes a knave, sometimes an ass,
    Now blunt, and now polite.

The picture, placed the busts between,
    Adds to the thought much strength,
Wisdom and Wit are little seen,
    But Folly's at full length.

Lady Mary Wortley Montagu

Saturday: The Small Pox

Flavia

The wretched Flavia on her couch reclined,
Thus breathed the anguish of a wounded mind,
A glass reversed in her right hand she bore,
For now she shunned the face she sought before.

"How am I changed! alas! how am I grown
A frightful spectre, to myself unknown!
Where's my complexion, where my radiant bloom,
That promised happiness for years to come?
Then with what pleasure I this face surveyed!
To look once more, my visits oft delayed!
Charmed with the view, a fresher red would rise,
And a new life shot sparkling from my eyes!

"Ah! faithless glass, my wonted bloom restore;
Alas! I rave, that bloom is now no more!
The greatest good the gods on men bestow,
Ev'n youth itself to me is useless now.
There was a time (oh! that I could forget!)
When opera-tickets poured before my feet;
And at the ring, where brightest beauties shine,
The earliest cherries of the spring were mine.
Witness, O Lilly; and thou, Motteux, tell,
How much japan these eyes have made ye sell.
With what contempt ye saw me oft despise
The humble offer of the raffled prize!
For at the raffle still each prize I bore,
With scorn rejected, or with triumph wore!
Now beauty's fled, and presents are no more!

"For me the patriot has the House forsook,
And left debates to catch a passing look:
For me the soldier has soft verses writ:
For me the beau has aimed to be a wit.

For me the wit to nonsense was betrayed;
The gamester has for me his dun delayed,
And overseen the card he would have played.
The bold and haughty by success made vain,
Awed by my eyes, have trembled to complain;
The bashful squire touched by a wish unknown,
Has dared to speak with spirit not his own;
Fired by one wish, all did alike adore;
Now beauty's fled, and lovers are no more!

   "As round the room I turn my weeping eyes,
New unaffected scenes of sorrow rise.
Far from my sight that killing picture bear,
The face disfigure, and the canvas tear;
That picture which with pride I used to show,
The lost resemblance but upbraids me now.
And thou, my toilette! where I oft have sat,
While hours unheeded passed in deep debate,
How curls should fall, or where a patch to place,
If blue or scarlet best became my face;
Now on some happier nymph your aid bestow;
On fairer heads, ye useless jewels, glow!
No borrowed lustre can my charms restore;
Beauty is fled, and dress is now no more!

   "Ye meaner beauties I permit ye shine;
Go, triumph in the hearts that once were mine;
But 'midst your triumphs with confusion know,
'Tis to my ruin all your arms ye owe.
Would pitying heaven restore my wonted mien,
Ye still might move unthought of and unseen:
But oh, how vain, how wretched is the boast
Of beauty faded, and of empire lost!
What now is left but weeping, to deplore
My beauty fled, and empire now no more?

   "Ye cruel chemists, what withheld your aid?
Could no pomatum save a trembling maid?
How false and trifling is that art ye boast!
No art can give me back my beauty lost.
In tears, surrounded by my friends I lay,
Masked o'er and trembling at the sight of day;

Mirmillio came my fortune to deplore,
(A golden-headed cane well carved he bore)
Cordials, he cried, my spirits must restore!
Beauty is fled, and spirit is no more!

   "Galen, the grave, officious Squirt was there,
With fruitless grief and unavailing care;
Machaon too, the great Machaon, known
By his red cloak and his superior frown;
And why, he cried, this grief and this despair,
You shall again be well, again be fair;
Believe my oath; (with that an oath he swore)
False was his oath; my beauty is no more!

   "Cease hapless maid, no more thy tale pursue.
Forsake mankind, and bid the world adieu!
Monarchs and beauties rule with equal sway;
All strive to serve, and glory to obey:
Alike unpitied when deposed they grow,
Men mock the idol of their former vow.

   "Adieu! ye parks!—in some obscure recess,
Where gentle streams will weep at my distress,
Where no false friend will in my grief take part,
And mourn my ruin with a joyful heart;
There let me live in some deserted place,
There hide in shades this lost inglorious face,
Plays, operas, circles, I no more must view!
My toilette, patches, all the world adieu!"

Farewell to Bath

To all you ladies now at Bath,
   And eke, ye beaus, to you,
With aching heart, and wat'ry eyes,
   I bid my last adieu.

Farewell ye nymphs, who waters sip
   Hot reeking from the pumps,
While music lends her friendly aid,
   To cheer you from the dumps.

Farewell ye wits, who prating stand,
  And criticize the fair;
Yourselves the joke of men of sense,
  Who hate a coxcomb's air.

Farewell to Deard's, and all her toys,
  Which glitter in her shop,
Deluding traps to girls and boys,
  The warehouse of the fop.

Lindsay's and Hayes's both farewell,
  Where in the spacious hall,
With bounding steps, and sprightly air,
  I've led up many a ball.

Where Somerville of courteous mien,
  Was partner in the dance,
With swimming Haws, and Brownlow blithe,
  And Britton pink of France.

Poor Nash, farewell! may fortune smile,
  Thy drooping soul revive,
My heart is full I can no more—
  John, bid the Coachman drive.

Constantia Grierson

To Miss Laetitia Van Lewen (Afterwards Mrs. Pilkington), at a Country Assize

The fleeting birds may soon in ocean swim,
And northern whales through liquid azure skim;
The Dublin ladies their intrigues forsake,
To dress and scandal an aversion take;
When you can in the lonely forest walk,
And with some serious matron gravely talk
Of possets, poultices, and waters stilled,
And monstrous casks with mead and cider filled;

How many hives of bees she has in store,
And how much fruit her trees this summer bore;
Or, home returning, in the yard can stand,
And feed the chickens from your bounteous hand:
Of each one's top-knot tell, and hatching pry,
Like Tully waiting for an augury.
   When night approaches, down to table sit
With a great crowd, choice meat, and little wit;
What horse won the last race, how mighty Tray,
At the last famous hunting, caught the prey;
Surely you can't but such discourse despise,
Methinks I see displeasure in your eyes:
O my Laetitia! stay no longer there,
You'll soon forget that you yourself are fair;
Why will you keep from us, from all that's gay,
There in a lonely solitude to stay?
Where not a mortal through the year you view,
But bob-wigged hunters, who their game pursue
With so much ardour, they'd a cock or hare,
To thee in all thy blooming charms prefer.
   You write of belles and beaux that there appear,
And gilded coaches, such as glitter here;
For gilded coaches, each estated clown
That gravely slumbers on the bench has one;
But beaux! they're young attorneys sure you mean,
Who thus appear to your romantic brain.
Alas! no mortal there can talk to you,
That love, or wit, or softness ever knew;
All they can speak of's *capias* and law,
And writs to keep the country fools in awe.
And if to wit, or courtship they pretend,
'Tis the same way that they a cause defend;
In which they give of lungs a vast expence,
But little passion, thought, or eloquence:
Bad as they are, they'll soon abandon you,
And gain and clamour in the town pursue.
So haste to town, if even such fools you prize,
O haste to town! and bless the longing eyes
                    Of your Constantia.

Laetitia Pilkington

Song

Lying is an occupation
  Used by all who mean to rise;
Politicians owe their station
  But to well-concerted lies.

These to lovers give assistance
  To ensnare the fair one's heart;
And the virgin's best resistance
  Yields to this commanding art.

Study this superior science,
  Would you rise in church or state;
Bid to truth a bold defiance,
  'Tis the practice of the great.

Jane Elliot

The Flowers of the Forest

I've heard them lilting, at the ewe-milking,
  Lasses a' lilting, before dawn of day;
But now they are moaning, on ilka green loaning;
  The flowers of the forest are a' wede awae.

At bughts, in the morning, nae blithe lads are scorning;
  Lasses are lonely, and dowie, and wae;
Nae daffing, nae gabbing, but sighing and sabbing;
  Ilk ane lifts her leglin, and hies her awae.

In har'st, at the shearing, nae youths now are jearing;
  Bandsters are runkled, and lyart, or grey;
At fair, or at preaching, nae wooing, nae fleeching;
  The flowers of the forest are a' wede awae.

At e'en, in the gloaming, nae younkers are roaming,
  'Bout stacks, with the lasses at bogle to play;

But ilk maid sits dreary, lamenting her deary—
    The flowers of the forest are weded away.

Dool and wae for the order, sent our lads to the border!
    The English for ance, by guile wan the day;
The flowers of the forest, that fought aye the foremost,
    The prime of our land, are cauld in the clay.

We'll hear nae mair lilting, at the ewe-milking;
    Women and bairns are heartless and wae;
Sighing and moaning, on ilka green loaning—
    The flowers of the forest are a' wede awae.

Ann Murry

A Familiar Epistle

To the Author's Sister

Say, dear Maria! is the modish life
With sense and reason ever found at strife?
Say, dear Maria! is the rural seat
Of peace and virtue the secure retreat?
Then form thy judgment, and declare thy choice,
Though inconsistent with the gen'ral voice.
Mark but the hist'ry of a modern day,
Composed of nonsense, foppery, and play.
Suppose a lady in her easy chair,
Intent to fabricate and deck her hair;
A compound vile, of powder, paint, perfumes,
Adorned with diamonds, and with lofty plumes.
View her at Almack's in the pomp of pride,
With lord, or captain, seated by her side;
If not in unison with virtue's law,
Mod'rate the term, and call it—a *faux pas!*
This gaudy trifler, or this haughty belle,
In folly's lists is found—*la plus fidelle!*
Hence, dear Maria, bless the gracious star,
Which, from such scenes of folly guides thee far.
What, though on pea-chicks thou dost never dine,

Or in gold goblets drink Falernian wine!
What though no crowd of coxcombs grace thy gate,
The modern female's idle, useless state!
More blest thy lot, with meek and humble heart,
To seek the treasures that true joys impart;
The only blessings that can aught avail,
Which, like the widow's oil, will never fail.

Phillis Wheatley

On Being Brought From Africa to America

'Twas mercy brought me from my pagan land,
Taught my benighted soul to understand
That there's a God, that there's a Saviour too:
Once I redemption neither sought nor knew.
Some view our sable race with scornful eye,
"Their colour is a diabolic dye."
Remember, Christians, Negroes, black as Cain,
May be refined, and join th' angelic train.

An Hymn to the Evening

Soon as the sun forsook the eastern main
The pealing thunder shook the heav'nly plain;
Majestic grandeur! From the zephyr's wing,
Exhales the incense of the blooming spring.
Soft purl the streams, the birds renew their notes,
And through the air their mingled music floats.

    Through all the heav'ns what beauteous dyes are spread!
But the west glories in the deepest red:
So may our breasts with ev'ry virtue glow,
The living temples of our God below!

    Filled with the praise of him who gives the light;
And draws the sable curtains of the night,
Let placid slumbers sooth each weary mind,

At morn to wake more heav'nly, more refined;
So shall the labours of the day begin
More pure, more guarded from the snares of sin.

Night's leaden sceptre seals my drowsy eyes,
Then cease, my song, till fair Aurora rise.

To His Excellency
General Washington

Celestial choir! enthroned in realms of light,
    Columbia's scenes of glorious toils I write,
While freedom's cause her anxious breast alarms,
She flashes dreadful in refulgent arms.
See mother earth her offspring's fate bemoan,
And nations gaze at scenes before unknown!
See the bright beams of heaven's revolving light
Involved in sorrows and the veil of night!
    The goddess comes, she moves divinely fair,
Olive and laurel binds her golden hair:
Wherever shines this native of the skies,
Unnumbered charms and recent graces rise.
    Muse! bow propitious while my pen relates
How pour her armies through a thousand gates,
As when Eolus heaven's fair face deforms,
Enwrapped in tempest and a night of storms;
Astonished ocean feels the wild uproar,
The refluent surges beat the sounding shore;
Or thick as leaves in Autumn's golden reign,
Such, and so many, moves the warrior's train.
In bright array they seek the work of war,
Where high unfurled the ensign waves in air.
Shall I to Washington their praise recite?
Enough thou know'st them in the fields of fight.
Thee, first in peace and honours,—we demand
The grace and glory of thy martial band.
Famed for thy valour, for thy virtues more,
Hear every tongue thy guardian aid implore!
    One century scarce performed its destined round,
When Gallic powers Columbia's fury found;
And so may you, whoever dares disgrace

The land of freedom's heaven-defended race!
Fixed are the eyes of nations on the scales,
For in their hopes Columbia's arm prevails.
Anon Brittannia droops the pensive head,
While round increase the rising hills of dead.
Ah! cruel blindness to Columbia's state!
Lament thy thirst of boundless power too late.
   Proceed, great chief, with virtue on thy side,
Thy ev'ry action let the goddess guide.
A crown, a mansion, and a throne that shine,
With gold unfading, Washington! be thine.

Anna Gordon Brown

The Gay Goshawk

"O well's me o my gay goss-hawk,
  That he can speak and flee;
He'll carry a letter to my love,
  Bring back another to me."

"O how can I your true-love ken,
  Or how can I her know?
Whan frae her mouth I never heard couth,
  Nor wi my eyes her saw."

"O well sal ye my true-love ken,
  As soon as you her see;
For, of a' the flowrs in fair Englan,
  The fairest flowr is she.

"At even at my love's bowr-door
  There grows a bowing birk,
An sit ye down and sing thereon,
  As she gangs to the kirk.

"An four-and-twenty ladies fair
  Will wash and go to kirk,
But well shall ye my true-love ken,
  For she wears goud on her skirt.

"An four and twenty gay ladies
  Will to the mass repair,
But well sal ye my true-love ken
  For she wears goud on her hair."

O even at that lady's bowr-door
  There grows a bowin birk,
An she set down and sang thereon,
  As she ged to the kirk.

"O eet and drink, my marys a',
  The wine flows you among,
Till I gang to my shot-window,
  An hear yon bonny bird's song.

"Sing on, sing on, my bonny bird,
  The song ye sang the streen,
For I ken by your sweet singin
  You're frae my true-love sen."

O first he sang a merry song,
  An then he sang a grave,
An then he peckd his feathers gray,
  To her the letter gave.

"Ha, there's a letter frae your love,
  He says he sent you three;
He canna wait your love langer,
  But for your sake he'll die.

"He bids you write a letter to him;
  He says he's sent you five;
He canna wait your love langer,
  Tho you're the fairest woman alive."

"Ye bid him bake his bridal-bread
  And brew his bridal-ale,
An I'll meet him in fair Scotlan
  Lang, lang or it be stale."

She's doen her to her father dear,
  Fa'n low down on her knee:
"A boon, a boon, my father dear,
  I pray you, grant it me."

"Ask on, ask on, my daughter,
    An granted it sal be;
Except ae squire in fair Scotlan,
    An him you sall never see."

"The only boon, my father dear,
    That I do crave of the,
Is, gin I die in southin lands,
    In Scotland to bury me.

"An the firstin kirk that ye come till,
    Ye gar the bells be rung,
An the nextin kirk that ye come till,
    Ye gar the mess be sung.

"An the thirdin kirk that ye come till,
    You deal gold for my sake,
An the forthin kirk that ye come till,
    You tarry there till night."

She is doen her to her bigly bowr,
    As fast as she coud fare,
An she has tane a sleepy draught,
    That she had mixed wi care.

She's laid her down upon her bed,
    An soon she's fa'n asleep,
And soon oer every tender limb
    Cauld death began to creep.

Whan night was flown, an day was come,
    Nae ane that did her see
But thought she was as surely dead
    As ony lady coud be.

Her father an her brothers dear
    Gard make to her a bier;
The tae half was o guide red gold,
    The tither o silver clear.

Her mither an her sisters fair
    Gard work for her a sark;
The tae half was o cambrick fine,
    The tither o needle wark.

The firstin kirk that they came till,
　They gard the bells be rung,
At the nextin kirk that they came till,
　They gard the mess be sung.

The thirdin kirk that they came till,
　They dealt gold for her sake,
An the fourthin kirk that they came till,
　Lo, there they met her make!

"Lay down, lay down the bigly bier,
　Lat me the dead look on;"
Wi cherry cheeks and ruby lips
　She lay an smil'd on him.

"O ae sheave o your bread, true-love,
　An ae glass o your wine,
For I hae fasted for your sake
　These fully days is nine.

"Gang hame, gang hame, my seven bold brothers,
　Gang hame and sound your horn;
An ye may boast in southin lans
　Your sister's playd you scorn."

Charlotte Smith

To Spring

Again the wood, and long with-drawing vale,
　In many a tint of tender green are dressed,
Where the young leaves unfolding scarce conceal
　　Beneath their early shade the half-formed nest
Of finch or wood-lark; and the primrose pale,
　　And lavish cowslip, wildly scattered round,
Give their sweet spirits to the sighing gale.
　　Ah! Season of delight!—could aught be found
　To soothe awhile the tortured bosom's pain,
　　Of sorrow's rankling shaft to cure the wound,
　And bring life's first delusions once again,
'Twere surely met in thee!—Thy prospect fair,

Thy sounds of harmony, thy balmy air,
Have power to cure all sadness—but despair.

To Sleep

Come balmy Sleep! tired nature's soft resort,
    On these sad temples all thy poppies shed;
And bid gay dreams, from Morpheus' airy court,
    Float in light vision round my aching head!—
Secure of all thy blessings, partial Power!
    On his hard bed the peasant throws him down;
And the poor sea boy, in the rudest hour,
    Enjoys thee more than he who wears a crown.
Clasped in her faithful shepherd's guardian arms,
    Well may the village girl sweet slumbers prove;
And they, O gentle Sleep!—still taste thy charms,
    Who wake to labour, liberty, and love.
But still thy opiate aid dost thou deny
To calm the anxious breast; to close the streaming eye.

From *Montalbert*

Swift fleet the billowy clouds along the sky,
    Earth seems to shudder at the storm aghast;
While only beings as forlorn as I,
    Court the chill horrors of the howling blast.
Even round yon crumbling walls, in search of food,
    The ravenous owl foregoes his evening flight,
And in his cave, within the deepest wood,
    The fox eludes the tempest of the night.
But to my heart congenial is the gloom
    Which hides me from a world I wish to shun:
That scene where ruin saps the mouldering tomb
    Suits with the sadness of a wretch undone.
Nor is the deepest shade, the keenest air,
Black as my fate, or cold as my despair.

Sonnet Written in the Church-Yard at Middleton, in Sussex

Pressed by the moon, mute arbitress of tides,
   While the loud equinox its power combines,
   The sea no more the swelling surge confines,
But o'er the shrinking land sublimely rides.
The wild blast, rising from the western cave,
   Drives the huge billows from their heaving bed;
   Tears from their grassy tomb the village dead,
And breaks the silent sabbath of the grave!
With shells and sea-weed mingled, on the shore,
   Lo! their bones whiten in the frequent wave,
   But vain to them the winds and waters rave;
They hear the warring elements no more:
While I am doomed—by life's long storm oppressed,
To gaze with envy on their gloomy rest.

From *Beachy Head*

I once was happy, when, while yet a child,
I learned to love these upland solitudes,
And when, elastic as the mountain air,
To my light spirit care was yet unknown,
And evil unforeseen: —early it came,
And childhood scarcely past, I was condemned,
A guiltless exile, silently to sigh,
While Memory, with faithful pencil, drew
The contrast; and regretting, I compared
With the polluted smoky atmosphere
And dark and stifling streets, the southern hills
That to the setting sun their graceful heads
Rearing, o'erlook the frith, where Vecta breaks
With her white rocks the strong impetuous tide,
When western winds the vast Atlantic urge
To thunder on the coast—Haunts of my youth!

Scenes of fond day-dreams, I behold ye yet!
Where 'twas so pleasant by thy northern slopes
To climb the winding sheep-path, aided oft
By scattered thorns; whose spiny branches bore

Small woolly tufts, spoils of the vagrant lamb
There seeking shelter from the noonday sun:
And pleasant, seated on the short soft turf,
To look beneath upon the hollow way
While heavily upward moved the labouring wain,
And stalking slowly by, the sturdy hind,
To ease his panting team, stopped with a stone
The grating wheel.
              Advancing higher still,
The prospect widens, and the village church
But little, o'er the lowly roofs around,
Rears its gray belfrey, and its simple vane;
Those lowly roofs of thatch are half concealed
By the rude arms of trees, lovely in spring,
When on each bough, the rosy-tinctured bloom
Sits thick, and promises autumnal plenty.
For even those orchards round the Norman farms,
Which, as their owners mark the promised fruit,
Console them for the vineyards of the south,
Surpass not these.
            Where woods of ash, and beech,
And partial copses, fringe the green hill foot,
The upland shepherd rears his modest home;
There wanders by, a little nameless stream
That from the hill wells forth, bright now and clear,
Or after rain with chalky mixture gray,
But still refreshing in its shallow course
The cottage garden; most for use designed,
Yet not of beauty destitute. The vine
Mantles the little casement; yet the briar
Drops fragrant dew among the July flowers;
And pansies rayed, and freaked and mottled pinks
Grow among balm, and rosemary and rue;
There honeysuckles flaunt, and roses blow
Almost uncultured: some with dark green leaves
Contrast their flowers of pure unsullied white;
Others like velvet robes of regal state
Of richest crimson, while, in thorny moss
Enshrined and cradled, the most lovely wear
The hues of youthful beauty's glowing cheek. —
With fond regret I recollect e'en now

In Spring and Summer, what delight I felt
Among these cottage gardens, and how much
Such artless nosegays, knotted with a rush
By village housewife or her ruddy maid,
Were welcome to me; soon and simply pleased.

    An early worshipper at Nature's shrine,
I loved her rudest scenes—warrens, and heaths,
And yellow commons, and birch-shaded hollows,
And hedge rows, bordering unfrequented lanes
Bowered with wild roses, and the clasping woodbine,
Where purple tassels of the tangling vetch
With bittersweet, and bryony inweave,
And the dew fills the silver bindweed's cups—
I loved to trace the brooks whose humid banks
Nourish the harebell, and the freckled pagil;
And stroll among o'ershadowing woods of beech,
Lending in Summer from the heats of noon
A whispering shade; while haply there reclines
Some pensive lover of uncultured flowers,
Who, from the tumps with bright green mosses clad,
Plucks the wood sorrel with its light thin leaves,
Heart-shaped, and triply-folded, and its root
Creeping like beaded coral; or who there
Gathers, the copse's pride, anemones,
With rays like golden studs on ivory laid
Most delicate: but touched with purple clouds,
Fit crown for April's fair but changeful brow.

  .   .   .   .   .   .

Henrietta Oneil

Ode to the Poppy

Not for the promise of the laboured field,
Not for the good the yellow harvests yield,
    I bend at Ceres' shrine;
For dull to humid eyes appear
The golden glories of the year;
    Alas! a melancholy worship's mine:

I hail the goddess for her scarlet flower!
　　Thou brilliant weed,
　　That dost so far exceed

　　The richest gifts gay Flora can bestow,
Heedless I passed thee in life's morning hour,
　　Thou comforter of woe,
Till sorrow taught me to confess thy power.

　　In early days, when Fancy cheats,
　　　A varied wreath I wove,
　　Of laughing Spring's luxuriant sweets,
　　　To deck ungrateful love:

　　The rose, or thorn, my labours crowned,
　　As Venus smiled, or Venus frowned,
But Love and Joy and all their train are flown;
　　E'en languid Hope no more is mine,
And I will sing of thee alone;
　　Unless perchance the attributes of Grief,
　　　The cypress bud and willow leaf,
　　　Their pale funereal foliage blend with thine.

　　　Hail, lovely blossom! thou canst ease
　　　The wretched victims of Disease;
　　Canst close those weary eyes in gentle sleep,
　　Which never open but to weep;
　　　For oh! thy potent charm
　　　Can agonizing Pain disarm;
　　Expel imperious Memory from her seat,
　　And bid the throbbing heart forget to beat.

Lady Anne Lindsay

Auld Robin Gray

When the sheep are in the fauld, and the kye at hame,
And a' the warld to rest are gane,
The waes o' my heart fa' in showers frae my e'e,
While my gudeman lies sound by me.

Young Jamie lo'ed me weel, and sought me for his bride;
But saving a croun he had naething else beside:
To make the croun a pund, young Jamie gaed to sea;
And the croun and the pund were baith for me.

He hadna been awa' a week but only twa,
When my father brak his arm, and the cow was stown awa';
My mother she fell sick, —and my Jamie at the sea—
And auld Robin Gray came a-courtin' me.

My father couldna work, and my mother couldna spin;
I toiled day and night, but their bread I couldna win;
Auld Rob maintain'd them baith, and wi' tears in his e'e
Said, "Jennie, for their sakes, O, marry me!"

My heart it said nay; I look'd for Jamie back;
But the wind it blew high, and the ship it was a wrack;
His ship it was a wrack—Why didna Jamie dee?
Or why do I live to cry, Wae's me!

My father urged me sair: my mother didna speak;
But she look'd in my face till my heart was like to break:
They gie'd him my hand, tho' my heart was in the sea;
Sae auld Robin Gray he was gudeman to me.

I hadna been a wife a week but only four,
When mournfu' as I sat on the stane at the door,
I saw my Jamie's wraith, —for I couldna think it he,
Till he said, "I'm come hame to marry thee."

O sair, sair did we greet, and muckle did we say;
We took but ae kiss, and we tore ourselves away:
I wish that I were dead, but I'm no like to dee;
And why was I born to say, Wae's me!

I gang like a ghaist, and I carena to spin;
I daurna think on Jamie, for that wad be a sin;
But I'll do my best a gude wife aye to be,
For auld Robin Gray he is kind unto me.

Joanna Baillie

The Trysting Bush

The gowan glitters on the sward,
  The lavrock's in the sky,
And collie on my plaid keeps ward,
  And time is passing by.
    Oh no! sad and slow
And, lengthened on the ground,
  The shadow of our trysting bush,
It wears so slowly round!

My sheep-bell tinkles frae the west,
  My lambs are bleating near,
But still the sound that I lo'e best,
  Alack! I canna hear.
    Oh no! sad and slow,
The shadow lingers still,
  And like a lanely ghaist I stand
And croon upon the hill.

I hear below the water roar,
  The mill wi' clacking din,
And Lucky scolding frae her door,
  To ca' the bairnies in.
    Oh no! sad and slow,
These are na sounds for me,
  The shadow of our trysting bush,
It creeps sae drearily!

I coft yestreen, frae Chapman Tam,
  A snood of bonny blue,
And promised when our trysting cam',
  To tie it round her brow.
    Oh no! sad and slow!
The mark it winna pass;
  The shadow of that weary thorn
Is tethered on the grass.

O now I see her on the way,
  She's past the Witch's knowe,
She's climbing up the Browny's brae,
  My heart is in a lowe!
    Oh no! 'tis na so,
'Tis glamrie I have seen;
  The shadow of that hawthorn bush
Will move na mair till e'en.

My book o' grace I'll try to read,
  Though conn'd wi' little skill,
When collie barks I'll raise my head,
  And find her on the hill;
    Oh no! sad and slow,
The time will ne'er be gane,
  The shadow of the trysting bush
Is fixed like ony stane.

Carolina Oliphant, Lady Nairne

The Laird o' Cockpen

The Laird o' Cockpen, he's proud an' he's great,
His mind is ta'en up wi' things o' the State:
He wanted a wife, his braw house to keep;
But favour wi' wooin' was fashious to seek.

Down by the dyke-side a lady did dwell;
At his table-head he thought she'd look well—
McClish's ae daughter o' Claverse-ha' Lee,
A penniless lass wi' a lang pedigree.

His wig was weel pouther'd and as gude as new;
His waistcoat was white, his coat it was blue:
He put on a ring, a sword, and cock'd hat, —
And wha could refuse the Laird wi' a' that?

He took the grey mare, and rade cannily,
An' rapp'd at the yett o' Claverse-ha' Lee:

"Gae tell Mistress Jean to come speedily ben, —
She's wanted to speak to the Laird o' Cockpen."

Mistress Jean was makin' the elder-flower wine:
"And what brings the Laird at sic a like time?"
She put aff her apron and on her silk goun,
Her mutch wi' red ribbons, and gaed awa doun.

An' when she cam' ben he bow'd fu' low;
An' what was his errand he soon let her know.
Amazed was the Laird when the lady said "Na"; —
And wi' a laigh curtsey she turn'd awa.

Dumbfounder'd was he; nae sigh did he gie,
He mounted his mare, he rade cannily;
And aften he thought as he gaed thro' the glen,
"She's daft to refuse the Laird o' Cockpen!"

Anne Radcliffe

Night

Now Ev'ning fades! her pensive step retires,
    And Night leads on the dews, and shadowy hours;
Her awful pomp of planetary fires,
    And all her train of visionary powers.

These paint with fleeting shapes the dream of sleep,
    These swell the waking soul with pleasing dread;
These through the glooms in forms terrific sweep,
    And rouse the thrilling horrors of the dead!

Queen of the solemn thought—mysterious Night!
    Whose step is darkness, and whose voice is fear!
Thy shades I welcome with severe delight,
    And hail thy hollow gales, that sigh so drear!

When, wrapped in clouds, and riding in the blast,
    Thou roll'st the storm along the sounding shore,
I love to watch the whelming billows, cast
    On rocks below, and listen to the roar.

Thy milder terrors, Night, I frequent woo,
    Thy silent lightnings, and thy meteor's glare,
Thy northern fires, bright with ensanguine hue,
    That light in heaven's high vault the fervid air.

But chief I love thee, when thy lucid car
    Sheds through the fleecy clouds a trembling gleam,
And shows the misty mountain from afar,
    The nearer forest, and the valley's stream:

And nameless objects in the vale below,
    That floating dimly to the musing eye,
Assume, at Fancy's touch, fantastic show,
    And raise her sweet romantic visions high.

Then let me stand amidst thy glooms profound
    On some wild woody steep, and hear the breeze
That swells in mournful melody around,
    And faintly dies upon the distant trees.

What melancholy charm steals o'er the mind!
    What hallowed tears the rising rapture greet!
While many a viewless spirit in the wind
    Sighs to the lonely hour in accents sweet!

Ah! who the dear illusions pleased would yield,
    Which Fancy wakes from silence and from shades,
For all the sober forms of Truth revealed,
    For all the scenes that Day's bright eye pervades!

Stanzas

How smooth that lake expands its ample breast!
    Where smiles in softened glow the summer sky:
How vast the rocks that o'er its surface rest!
    How wild the scenes its winding shores supply!

Now down the western steep slow sinks the sun,
    And paints with yellow gleam the tufted woods:
While here the mountain-shadows, broad and dun,
    Sweep o'er the crystal mirror of the floods.

Mark how his splendor tips with partial light
    Those shattered battlements! that on the brow

Of yon bold promontory burst to sight
    From o'er the woods that darkly spread below.

In the soft blush of light's reflected power,
    The ridgy rock, the woods that crown its steep,
Th'illumined battlement, and darker tower,
    On the smooth wave in trembling beauty sleep.

But lo! the sun recalls his fervid ray,
    And cold and dim, the wat'ry visions fail;
While o'er yon cliff, whose pointed crags decay,
    Mild Evening draws her thin empurpled veil!

How sweet that strain of melancholy horn!
    That floats along the slowly ebbing wave;
And up the far-receding mountains borne,
    Returns a dying close from Echo's cave!

Hail! shadowy forms of still, expressive Eve!
    Your pensive graces stealing on my heart,
Bid all the fine-attuned emotions live,
    And fancy all her loveliest dreams impart.

Sonnet

Now the bat circles on the breeze of eve,
That creeps, in shudd'ring fits, along the wave,
And trembles 'mid the woods, and through the cave
Whose lonely sighs the wanderer deceive;
For oft, when melancholy charms his mind,
He thinks the Spirit of the rock he hears,
Nor listens, but with sweetly-thrilling fears,
To the low, mystic murmurs of the wind!
Now the bat circles, and the twilight dew
Falls silent round, and, o'er the mountain-cliff,
The gleaming wave and far-discovered skiff,
Spreads the grey veil of soft, harmonious hue.
So falls o'er Grief the dew of pity's tear
Dimming her lonely visions of despair.

Felicia Hemans

The Homes of England

"Where's the coward that would not dare
To fight for such a land?"
                    —Marmion.

The stately homes of England,
  How beautiful they stand,
Amidst their tall ancestral trees,
  O'er all the pleasant land!
The deer across their greensward bound,
  Through shade and sunny gleam;
And the swan glides past them with the sound
  Of some rejoicing stream.

The merry homes of England!
  Around their hearths by night,
What gladsome looks of household love
  Meet in the ruddy light!
There woman's voice flows forth in song,
  Or childhood's tale is told,
Or lips move tunefully along
  Some glorious page of old.

The blessed homes of England!
  How softly on their bowers
Is laid the holy quietness
  That breathes from Sabbath hours!
Solemn, yet sweet, the church-bell's chime
  Floats through their woods at morn;
All other sounds, in that still time,
  Of breeze and leaf are born.

The cottage homes of England!
  By thousands on her plains,
They are smiling o'er the silvery brooks,
  And round the hamlet fanes.
Through glowing orchards forth they peep,
  Each from its nook of leaves;

And fearless there the lowly sleep,
    As the bird beneath their eaves.

The free, fair homes of England!
    Long, long, in hut and hall,
May hearts of native proof be reared
    To guard each hallowed wall!
And green forever be the groves,
    And bright the flowery sod,
Where first the child's glad spirit loves
    Its country and its God!

The Landing of the Pilgrim Fathers in New England

"Look now abroad! Another race has filled
    Those populous borders—wide the wood recedes,
And towns shoot up, and fertile realms are tilled;
    The land is full of harvest and green meads."—Bryant.

The breaking waves dashed high
    On a stern and rock-bound coast,
And the woods against a stormy sky
    Their giant branches tossed;

And the heavy night hung dark
    The hills and waters o'er,
When a band of exiles moored their bark
    On the wild New England shore.

Not as the conqueror comes,
    They, the true-hearted, came;
Not with the roll of the stirring drums,
    And the trumpet that sings of fame;

Not as the flying come,
    In silence and in fear; —
They shook the depths of the desert gloom
    With their hymns of lofty cheer.

Amidst the storm they sang,
    And the stars heard and the sea;
And the sounding aisles of the dim woods rang
    To the anthem of the free!

The ocean eagle soared
From his nest by the white wave's foam;
And the rocking pines of the forest roared—
This was their welcome home!

There were men with hoary hair
Amidst that pilgrim band; —
Why had *they* come to wither there,
Away from their childhood's land?

There was woman's fearless eye,
Lit by her deep love's truth;
There was manhood's brow serenely high,
And the fiery heart of youth.

What sought they thus afar? —
Bright jewels of the mine?
The wealth of seas, the spoils of war? —
They sought a faith's pure shrine!

Ay, call it holy ground,
The soil where first they trod.
They have left unstained what there they found—
Freedom to worship God.

The Graves of a Household

They grew in beauty side by side,
They filled one home with glee;
Their graves are severed far and wide,
By mount, and stream, and sea.

The same fond mother bent at night
O'er each fair sleeping brow:
She had each folded flower in sight—
Where are those dreamers now?

One, midst the forest of the West,
By a dark stream is laid—
The Indian knows his place of rest,
Far in the cedar-shade.

The sea, the blue lone sea, hath one—
He lies where pearls lie deep;

He was the loved of all, yet none
　　O'er his low bed may weep.

One sleeps where southern vines are dressed
　　Above the noble slain:
He wrapped his colors round his breast
　　On a blood-red field of Spain.

And one—o'er *her* the myrtle showers
　　Its leaves, by soft winds fanned;
She faded midst Italian flowers—
　　The last of that bright band.

And parted thus they rest, who played
　　Beneath the same green tree;
Whose voices mingled as they prayed
　　Around one parent knee!

They that with smiles lit up the hall,
　　And cheered with song the hearth! —
Alas, for love! if *thou* wert all,
　　And naught beyond, O Earth!

Elizabeth Barrett Browning

Bereavement

When some Belovéds, 'neath whose eyelids lay
The sweet lights of my childhood, one by one
Did leave me dark before the natural sun,
And I astonied fell and could not pray, —
A thought within me to myself did say,
"Is God less God, that thou art left undone?
Rise, worship, bless Him, in this sackcloth spun,
As in that purple!"—But I answered, Nay!
What child his filial heart in words can loose,
If he behold his tender father raise
The hand that chastens sorely? can he choose
But sob in silence with an upward gaze? —
And my great Father, thinking fit to bruise,
Discerns in speechless tears, both prayer and praise.

Tears

Thank God, bless God, all ye who suffer not
More grief than ye can weep for. That is well—
That is light grieving! lighter, none befell,
Since Adam forfeited the primal lot.
Tears! what are tears? The babe weeps in its cot,
The mother singing; at her marriage-bell
The bride weeps, and before the oracle
Of high-faned hills the poet has forgot
Such moisture on his cheeks. Thank God for grace,
Ye who weep only! If, as some have done,
Ye grope tear-blinded in a desert place
And touch but tombs—look up! those tears will run
Soon in long rivers down the lifted face,
And leave the vision clear for stars and sun.

Grief

I tell you, hopeless grief is passionless;
That only men incredulous of despair,
Half-taught in anguish, through the mid-night air
Beat upward to God's throne in loud access
Of shrieking and reproach. Full desertness
In souls as countries, lieth silent-bare
Under the blanching, vertical eye-glare
Of the absolute Heavens. Deep-hearted man, express
Grief for thy Dead in silence like to death—
Most like a monumental statue set
In everlasting watch and moveless woe,
Till itself crumble to the dust beneath.
Touch it; the marble eyelids are not wet.
If it could weep, it could arise and go.

From *Sonnets From The Portuguese*

I

I thought once how Theocritus had sung
Of the sweet years, the dear and wished-for years,
Who each one in a gracious hand appears

To bear a gift for mortals, old or young;
And, as I mused it in his antique tongue,
I saw, in gradual vision through my tears,
The sweet, sad years, the melancholy years,
Those of my own life, who by turns had flung
A shadow across me. Straightway I was 'ware,
So weeping, how a mystic Shape did move
Behind me, and drew me backward by the hair;
And a voice said in mastery, while I strove—
"Guess now who holds thee?"—"Death," I said. But, there,
The silver answer rang—"Not Death, but Love."

14

If thou must love me, let it be for naught
Except for love's sake only. Do not say
"I love her for her smile—her look—her way
Of speaking gently—for a trick of thought
That falls in well with mine, and certes brought
A sense of pleasant ease on such a day"—
For these things in themselves, Belovéd, may
Be changed, or change for thee—and love, so wrought,
May be unwrought so. Neither love me for
Thine own dear pity's wiping my cheeks dry—
A creature might forget to weep, who bore
Thy comfort long, and lose thy love thereby!
But love me for love's sake, that evermore
Thou mayst love on, through love's eternity.

20

Belovéd, my Belovéd, when I think
That thou wast in the world a year ago,
What time I sat alone here in the snow
And saw no footprint, heard the silence sink
No moment at thy voice, but, link by link,
Went counting all my chains as if that so
They never could fall off at any blow
Struck by thy possible hand—why, thus I drink
Of life's great cup of wonder! Wonderful,
Never to feel thee thrill the day or night
With personal act or speech—nor ever cull
Some prescience of thee with the blossoms white

Thou sawest growing! Atheists are as dull,
Who cannot guess God's presence out of sight.

22

When our two souls stand up erect and strong,
Face to face, silent, drawing nigh and nigher,
Until the lengthening wings break into fire
At either curvéd point—what bitter wrong
Can the earth do to us, that we should not long
Be here contented? Think. In mounting higher,
The angels would press on us and aspire
To drop some golden orb of perfect song
Into our deep, dear silence. Let us stay
Rather on earth, Belovéd—where the unfit
Contrarious moods of men recoil away
And isolate pure spirits, and permit
A place to stand and love in for a day,
With darkness and the death-hour rounding it.

32

The first time that the sun rose on thine oath
To love me, I looked forward to the moon
To slacken all those bonds which seemed too soon
And quickly tied to make a lasting troth.
Quick-loving hearts, I thought, may quickly loathe;
And, looking on myself, I seemed not one
For such man's love!—more like an out-of-tune
Worn viol, a good singer would be wroth
To spoil his song with, and which, snatched in haste,
Is laid down at the first ill-sounding note.
I did not wrong myself so, but I placed
A wrong on *thee*. For perfect strains may float
'Neath master-hands, from instruments defaced—
And great souls, at one stroke, may do and doat.

43

How do I love thee? Let me count the ways.
I love thee to the depth and breadth and height
My soul can reach, when feeling out of sight
For the ends of Being and ideal Grace.
I love thee to the level of everyday's
Most quiet need, by sun and candle-light.

I love thee freely, as men strive for Right;
I love thee purely, as they turn from Praise.
I love thee with the passion put to use
In my old griefs, and with my childhood's faith.
I love thee with a love I seemed to lose
With my lost saints—I love thee with the breath,
Smiles, tears, of all my life!—and, if God choose,
I shall but love thee better after death.

44

Belovéd, thou hast brought me many flowers
Plucked in the garden, all the summer through
And winter, and it seemed as if they grew
In this close room, nor missed the sun and showers.
So, in the like name of that love of ours,
Take back these thoughts which here unfolded too,
And which on warm and cold days I withdrew
From my heart's ground. Indeed, those beds and bowers
Be overgrown with bitter weeds and rue,
And wait thy weeding; yet here's eglantine,
Here's ivy!—take them, as I used to do
Thy flowers, and keep them where they shall not pine.
Instruct thine eyes to keep their colors true,
And tell thy soul their roots are left in mine.

A Curse for a Nation
Prologue

I heard an angel speak last night,
        And he said, "Write!
Write a Nation's curse for me,
And send it over the Western Sea."

I faltered, taking up the word:
        "Not so, my lord!
If curses must be, choose another
To send thy curse against my brother.

"For I am bound by gratitude,
        By love and blood,
To brothers of mine across the sea,
Who stretch out kindly hands to me."

"Therefore," the voice said, "shalt thou write
      My curse tonight.
From the summits of love a curse is driven,
As lightning is from the tops of heaven."

"No so," I answered. "Evermore
      My heart is sore
For my own land's sins; for little feet
Of children bleeding along the street;

"For parked-up honors that gainsay
      The right of way;
For almsgiving through a door that is
Not open enough for two friends to kiss;

"For love of freedom which abates
      Beyond the Straits;
For patriot virtue starved to vice on
Self-praise, self-interest, and suspicion;

"For an oligarchic parliament,
      And bribes well-meant.
What curse to another land assign,
When heavy-souled for the sins of mine?"

"Therefore," the voice said, "shalt thou write
      My curse tonight,
Because thou hast strength to see and hate
A foul thing done *within* thy gate."

"Not so," I answered once again.
      "To curse, choose men.
For I, a woman, have only known
How the heart melts and the tears run down."

"Therefore," the voice said, "shalt thou write
      My curse tonight.
Some women weep and curse, I say
(And no one marvels), night and day.

"And thou shalt take their part tonight,
      Weep and write.
A curse from the depths of womanhood
Is very salt, and bitter, and good."

So thus I wrote, and mourned indeed,
    What all may read.
And thus, as was enjoined on me,
I send it over the Western Sea.

The Curse

I

Because ye have broken your own chain
    With the strain
Of brave men climbing a Nation's height,
Yet thence bear down with brand and thong
On souls of others—for this wrong
    This is the curse. Write.

Because yourselves are standing straight
    In the state
Of Freedom's foremost acolyte,
Yet keep calm footing all the time
On writhing bond slaves—for this crime
    This is the curse. Write.

Because ye prosper in God's name,
    With a claim
To honor in the old world's sight,
Yet do the fiend's work perfectly
In strangling martyrs—for this lie
    This is the curse. Write.

2

Ye shall watch while kings conspire
Round the people's smoldering fire,
    And, warm for your part,
Shall never dare—O shame!—
To utter the thought into flame
    Which burns at your heart.
        This is the curse. Write.

Ye shall watch while nations strive
With the bloodhounds, die or survive,
    Drop faint from their jaws,
Or throttle them backward to death;

And only under your breath
  Shall favor the cause.
      This is the curse. Write.

Ye shall watch while strong men draw
The nets of feudal law
  To strangle the weak;
And, counting the sin for a sin,
Your soul shall be sadder within
  Than the word ye shall speak.
      This is the curse. Write.

When good men are praying erect
That Christ may avenge his elect
  And deliver the earth,
The prayer in your ears, said low,
Shall sound like the tramp of a foe
  That's driving you forth.
      This is the curse. Write.

When wise men give you their praise,
They shall pause in the heat of the phrase,
  As if carried too far.
When ye boast your own charters kept true,
Ye shall blush; for the thing which ye do
  Derides what ye are.
      This is the curse. Write.

When fools cast taunts at your gate,
Your scorn ye shall somewhat abate
  As ye look o'er the wall;
For your conscience, tradition, and name
Explode with a deadlier blame
  Than the worst of them all.
      This is the curse. Write.

Go, wherever ill deeds shall be done,
Go plant your flag in the sun
  Beside the ill-doers!
And recoil from clenching the curse
Of God's witnessing Universe
  With a curse of yours.
      This is the curse. Write.

A Musical Instrument

What was he doing, the great god Pan,
    Down in the reeds by the river?
Spreading ruin and scattering ban,
Splashing and paddling with hoofs of a goat,
And breaking the golden lilies afloat
    With the dragon-fly on the river.

He tore out a reed, the great god Pan,
    From the deep cool bed of the river;
The limpid water turbidly ran,
And the broken lilies a-dying lay,
And the dragon-fly had fled away,
    Ere he brought it out of the river.

High on the shore sat the great god Pan
    While turbidly flowed the river;
And hacked and hewed as a great god can,
With his hard bleak steel at the patient reed,
Till there was not a sign of the leaf indeed
    To prove it fresh from the river.

He cut it short, did the great god Pan
    (How tall it stood in the river!),
Then drew the pith, like the heart of a man,
Steadily from the outside ring,
And notched the poor dry empty thing
    In holes, as he sat by the river.

"This is the way," laughed the great god Pan
    (Laughed while he sat by the river),
"The only way, since gods began
To make sweet music, they could succeed."
Then, dropping his mouth to a hole in the reed,
    He blew in power by the river.

Sweet, sweet, sweet, O Pan!
    Piercing sweet by the river!
Blinding sweet, O great god Pan!
The sun on the hill forgot to die,
And the lilies revived, and the dragon-fly
    Came back to dream on the river.

Yet half a beast is the great god Pan,
  To laugh as he sits by the river,
Making a poet out of a man;
The true gods sigh for the cost and pain—
For the reed which grows nevermore again
  As a reed with the reeds in the river.

Helen Selina Sheridan, Lady Dufferin

The Charming Woman

So Miss Myrtle is going to marry?
  What a number of hearts she will break!
There's Lord George, and Tom Brown, and Sir Harry
  Who are dying of love for her sake!
'Tis a match that we all must approve, —
  Let gossips say all that they can!
For indeed she's a charming woman,
  And he's a most fortunate man!

Yes, indeed, she's a charming woman,
  And she reads both Latin and Greek, —
And I'm told that she solved a problem
  In Euclid before she could speak!
Had she been but a daughter of mine,
  I'd have taught her to hem and to sew, —
But her mother (a charming woman)
  Couldn't think of such trifles, you know!

Oh, she's really a charming woman!
  But perhaps a little too thin:
And no wonder such very late hours
  Should ruin her beautiful skin!
And her shoulders are rather too bare,
  And her gown's nearly up to her knees,
But I'm told that these charming women
  May dress themselves just as they please!

Yet, she's really a charming woman!
  But I thought I observed, by the bye,

A something—that's rather uncommon, —
    In the flash of that very bright eye?
It may be a mere fancy of mine,
    Tho' her voice has a very sharp tone, —
But I'm told that these charming women
    Are inclined to have wills of their own!

She sings like a bullfinch or linnet,
    And she talks like an Archbishop too;
Can play you a rubber and win it, —
    If she's got nothing better to do!
She can chatter of Poor-Laws and Tithes,
    And the value of labour and land, —
'Tis pity when charming women
    Talk of things which they don't understand!

I'm told that she hasn't a penny,
    Yet her gowns would make Maradan stare;
And I feel her bills must be many, —
    But that's only her husband's affair!
Such husbands are very uncommon,
    So regardless of prudence and pelf, —
But they say such a charming woman
    Is a fortune, you know, in herself.

She's brothers and sisters by dozens,
    And all charming people, they say!
And several tall Irish cousins
    Whom she loves in a sisterly way.
O young men, if you'd take my advice,
    You would find it an excellent plan, —
Don't marry a charming woman,
    If you are a sensible man.

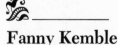

Fanny Kemble

A Wish

Let me not die for ever, when I'm gone
    To the cold earth! but let my memory

Live like the gorgeous western light that shone
    Over the clouds where sank day's majesty.
Let me not be forgotten; though the grave
    Has clasped its hideous arms around my brow.
Let me not be forgotten! though the wave
    Of time's dark current rolls above me now.
Yet not in tears remembered be my name;
    Weep over those ye loved; for me, for me,
Give me the wreath of glory, and let fame
    Over my tomb spread immortality!

Lady John Scott

Ettrick

When we first rade down Ettrick,
Our bridles were ringing, our hearts were dancing,
The waters were singing, the sun was glancing,
An' blithely our voices rang out thegither,
As we brushed the dew frae the blooming heather,
    When we first rade down Ettrick.

When we next rade down Ettrick,
The day was dying, the wild birds calling,
The wind was sighing, the leaves were falling,
An' silent an' weary, but closer thegither,
We urged our steeds thro' the faded heather,
    When we next rade down Ettrick.

When I last rade down Ettrick,
The winds were shifting, the storm was waking,
The snow was drifting, my heart was breaking,
For we never again were to ride thegither,
In sun or storm on the mountain heather,
    When I last rade down Ettrick.

Charlotte Brontë

On the Death of Anne Brontë

There's little joy in life for me,
  And little terror in the grave;
I've lived the parting hour to see
  Of one I would have died to save.

Calmly to watch the failing breath,
  Wishing each sigh might be the last;
Longing to see the shade of death
  O'er those beloved features cast;

The cloud, the stillness that must part
  The darling of my life from me;
And then to thank God from my heart,
  To thank him well and fervently;

Although I knew that we had lost
  The hope and glory of our life;
And now, benighted, tempest-tossed,
  Must bear alone the weary strife.

Emily Jane Brontë

Remembrance

Cold in the earth—and the deep snow piled above thee,
  Far, far removed, cold in the dreary grave!
Have I forgot, my only Love, to love thee,
  Severed at last by Time's all-severing wave?

Now, when alone, do my thoughts no longer hover
  Over the mountains on that northern shore,
Resting their wings where heath and fern-leaves cover
  Thy noble heart for ever, ever more?

Cold in the earth—and fifteen wild Decembers
  From those brown hills, have melted into spring:

Faithful, indeed, is the spirit that remembers
    After such years of change and suffering!

Sweet Love of youth, forgive, if I forget thee,
    While the world's tide is bearing me along;
Other desires and other hopes beset me,
    Hopes which obscure, but cannot do thee wrong!

No later light has lightened up my heaven,
    No second morn has ever shone for me;
All my life's bliss from thy dear life was given,
    All my life's bliss is in the grave with thee.

But when the days of golden dreams had perished,
    And even Despair was powerless to destroy,
Then did I learn how existence could be cherished,
    Strengthened, and fed, without the aid of joy.

Last Words

I knew not 'twas so dire a crime
    To say the word, 'Adieu';
But this shall be the only time
    My lips or heart shall sue.

The wild hillside, the winter morn,
    The gnarled and ancient tree,
If in your breast they waken scorn,
    Shall wake the same in me.

I can forget black eyes and brows,
    And lips of falsest charm,
If you forget the sacred vows
    Those faithless lips could form.

If hard commands can tame your love,
    Or strongest walls can hold,
I would not wish to grieve above
    A thing so false and cold.

And there are bosoms bound to mine
    With links both tried and strong;
And there are eyes whose lightning shine
    Has warmed and blest me long:

Those eyes shall make my only day,
  Shall set my spirit free,
And chase the foolish thoughts away
  That mourn your memory.

Stanzas

I'll not weep that thou art going to leave me,
  There's nothing lovely here;
And doubly will the dark world grieve me,
  While thy heart suffers there.

I'll not weep, because the summer's glory
  Must always end in gloom;
And, follow out the happiest story—
  It closes with a tomb!

And I am weary of the anguish
  Increasing winters bear;
Weary to watch the spirit languish
  Through years of dead despair.

So, if a tear, when thou art dying,
  Should haply fall from me,
It is but that my soul is sighing,
  To go and rest with thee.

Stanzas to ———

Well, some may hate, and some may scorn,
  And some may quite forget thy name;
But my sad heart must ever mourn
  Thy ruined hopes, thy blighted fame!
'Twas thus I thought, an hour ago,
Even weeping o'er that wretch's woe;
One word turned back my gushing tears,
And lit my altered eye with sneers.
Then, 'Bless the friendly dust,' I said,
'That hides thy unlamented head!
Vain as thou wert, and weak as vain,
The slave of Falsehood, Pride, and Pain—
My heart has nought akin to thine;
Thy soul is powerless over mine.'

But these were thoughts that vanished too:
Unwise, unholy, and untrue:
Do I despise the timid deer,
Because his limbs are fleet with fear?
Or, would I mock the wolf's death-howl,
Because his form is gaunt and foul?
Or, hear with joy the leveret's cry,
Because it cannot bravely die?
No! Then above his memory
Let Pity's heart as tender be;
Say, 'Earth lie lightly on that breast,
And, kind Heaven, grant that spirit rest!'

Warning and Reply

In the earth—the earth—thou shalt be laid,
    A grey stone standing over thee;
Black mould beneath thee spread,
    And black mould to cover thee.

'Well—there is rest there,
    So fast come thy prophecy;
The time when my sunny hair
    Shall with grass roots entwinèd be.'

But cold—cold is that resting-place,
    Shut out from joy and liberty,
And all who loved thy living face
    Will shrink from it shudderingly.

'Not so! *Here* the world is chill,
    And sworn friends fall from me:
But *there*—they will own me still,
    And prize my memory.'

Farewell, then, all that love,
    All that deep sympathy:
Sleep on; Heaven laughs above,
    Earth never misses thee.

Turf-sod and tombstone drear
    Part human company;
One heart breaks only—here,
    But that heart was worthy thee!

Anne Brontë

A Reminiscence

Yes, thou art gone! and never more
Thy sunny smile shall gladden me;
But I may pass the old church door,
And pace the floor that covers thee,

May stand upon the cold, damp stone,
And think that, frozen, lies below
The lightest heart that I have known,
The kindest I shall ever know.

Yet, though I cannot see thee more,
'Tis still a comfort to have seen;
And though thy transient life is o'er,
'Tis sweet to think that thou hast been;

To think a soul so near divine,
Within a form, so angel fair,
United to a heart like thine,
Has gladdened once our humble sphere.

Julia Ward Howe

Battle-Hymn of the Republic

Mine eyes have seen the glory of the coming of the Lord:
He is trampling out the vintage where the grapes of wrath are stored;
He hath loosed the fateful lightning of his terrible swift sword:
      His truth is marching on.

I have seen Him in the watch-fires of a hundred circling camps;
They have builded Him an altar in the evening dews and damps;
I can read his righteous sentence by the dim and flaring lamps.
      His day is marching on.

' I have read a fiery gospel, writ in burnished rows of steel:
"As ye deal with my contemners, so with you my grace shall deal;

Let the Hero, born of woman, crush the serpent with his heel,
    Since God is marching on."

He has sounded forth the trumpet that shall never call retreat;
He is sifting out the hearts of men before his judgment-seat:
Oh! be swift, my soul, to answer Him! be jubilant, my feet!
    Our God is marching on.

In the beauty of the lilies Christ was born across the sea,
With a glory in his bosom that transfigures you and me:
As he died to make men holy, let us die to make men free,
    While God is marching on.

Dora Greenwell

The Sun-Flower

Till the slow daylight pale,
    A willing slave, fast bound to one above,
I wait; he seems to speed, and change, and fail;
    I know he will not move.

I lift my golden orb
    To his, unsmitten when the roses die,
And in my broad and burning disk absorb
    The splendours of his eye.

His eye is like a clear
    Keen flame that searches through me: I must droop
Upon my stalk, I cannot reach his sphere;
    To mine he cannot stoop.

I win not my desire,
    And yet I fail not of my guerdon; lo!
A thousand flickering darts and tongues of fire
    Around me spread and glow.

All rayed and crowned, I miss
    No queenly state until the summer wane,
The hours flit by; none knoweth of my bliss,
    And none has guessed my pain.

I follow one above,
   I track the shadow of his steps, I grow
Most like to him I love
   Of all that shines below.

 ————————

Christina Rossetti

From *The Prince's Progress*

Bride Song

Too late for love, too late for joy,
   Too late, too late!
You loitered on the road too long,
   You trifled at the gate:
The enchanted dove upon her branch
   Died without a mate;
The enchanted princess in her tower
   Slept, died, behind the grate;
Her heart was starving all this while
   You made it wait.

Ten years ago, five years ago,
   One year ago,
Even then you had arrived in time,
   Though somewhat slow;
Then you had known her living face
   Which now you cannot know:
The frozen fountain would have leaped,
   The buds gone on to blow,
The warm south wind would have awaked
   To melt the snow.

Is she fair now as she lies?
   Once she was fair;
Meet queen for any kingly king,
   With gold-dust on her hair.
Now these are poppies in her locks,
   White poppies she must wear;
Must wear a veil to shroud her face
   And the want graven there:

Or is the hunger fed at length,
  Cast off the care?

We never saw her with a smile
  Or with a frown;
Her bed seemed never soft to her,
  Though tossed of down;
She little heeded what she wore,
  Kirtle, or wreath, or gown;
We think her white brows often ached
  Beneath her crown,
Till silvery hairs showed in her locks
  That used to be so brown.

We never heard her speak in haste;
  Her tones were sweet,
And modulated just so much
  As it was meet:
Her heart sat silent through the noise
  And concourse of the street.
There was no hurry in her hands,
  No hurry in her feet;
There was no bliss drew nigh to her,
  That she might run to greet.

You should have wept her yesterday,
  Wasting upon her bed:
But wherefore should you weep today
  That she is dead?
Lo we who love weep not today,
  But crown her royal head.
Let be these poppies that we strew,
  Your roses are too red:
Let be these poppies, not for you
  Cut down and spread.

Two Pursuits

A voice said, 'Follow, follow': and I rose
  And followed far into the dreamy night,
  Turning my back upon the pleasant light.
It led me where the bluest water flows,

And would not let me drink: where the corn grows
    I dared not pause, but went uncheered by sight
    Or touch: until at length in evil plight
It left me, wearied out with many woes.
Some time I sat as one bereft of sense:
    But soon another voice from very far
        Called, "Follow, follow': and I rose again.
    Now on my night has dawned a blessed star:
        Kind steady hands my sinking steps sustain,
And will not leave me till I shall go hence.

Spring Quiet

Gone were but the Winter,
    Come were but the Spring,
I would go to a covert
    Where the birds sing;

Where in the whitethorn
    Singeth a thrush,
And a robin sings
    In the holly-bush.

Full of fresh scents
    Are the budding boughs
Arching high over
    A cool green house;

Full of sweet scents,
    And whispering air
Which sayeth softly:
    'We spread no snare;

'Here dwell in safety,
    Here dwell alone,
With a clear stream
    And a mossy stone.

'Here the sun shineth
    Most shadily;
Here is heard an echo
    Of the far sea,
        Though far off it be.'

Passing Away

Passing away, saith the World, passing away:
Chances, beauty, and youth, sapped day by day:
Thy life never continueth in one stay.
Is the eye waxen dim, is the dark hair changing to grey
That hath won neither laurel nor bay?
I shall clothe myself in spring and bud in May:
Thou, root-stricken, shalt not rebuild thy decay
On my bosom for aye.
Then I answered: Yea.

Passing away, saith my Soul, passing away:
With its burden of fear and hope, of labour and play,
Hearken what the past doth witness and say:
Rust in thy gold, a moth is in thine array,
A canker is in thy bud, thy leaf must decay.
At midnight, at cockcrow, at morning, one certain day
Lo the Bridegroom shall come and shall not delay;
Watch thou and pray.
Then I answered: Yea.

Passing away, saith my God, passing away:
Winter passeth after the long delay:
New grapes on the vine, new figs on the tender spray,
Turtle calleth turtle in Heaven's May.
Though I tarry, wait for Me, trust Me, watch and pray:
Arise, come away, night is past and lo it is day,
My love, My sister, My spouse, thou shalt hear me say.
Then I answered: Yea.

Song

When I am dead, my dearest,
   Sing no sad songs for me;
Plant thou no roses at my head,
   Nor shady cypress tree:
Be the green grass above me
   With showers and dewdrops wet:
And if thou wilt, remember,
   And if thou wilt, forget.

I shall not see the shadows,
   I shall not feel the rain;
I shall not hear the nightingale
   Sing on as if in pain:

And dreaming through the twilight
   That doth not rise nor set,
Haply I may remember,
   And haply may forget.

A Birthday

My heart is like a singing bird
   Whose nest is in a watered shoot:
My heart is like an apple-tree
   Whose boughs are bent with thickset fruit;
My heart is like a rainbow shell
   That paddles in a halcyon sea;
My heart is gladder than all these
   Because my love is come to me.

Raise me a dais of silk and down;
   Hang it with vair and purple dyes;
Carve it in doves and pomegranates,
   And peacocks with a hundred eyes;
Work it in gold and silver grapes,
   In leaves and silver fleur-de-lys;
Because the birthday of my life
   Is come, my love is come to me.

Up-Hill

Does the road wind up-hill all the way?
   Yes, to the very end.
Will the day's journey take the whole long day?
   From morn to night, my friend.

But is there for the night a resting-place?
   A roof for when the slow dark hours begin.
May not the darkness hide it from my face?
   You cannot miss that inn.

131

Shall I meet other wayfarers at night?
    Those who have gone before.
Then must I knock, or call when just in sight?
    They will not keep you standing at that door.

Shall I find comfort, travel-sore and weak?
    Of labour you shall find the sum.
Will there be beds for me and all who seek?
    Yea, beds for all who come.

In Progress

Ten years ago it seemed impossible
    That she should ever grow as calm as this,
    With self-remembrance in her warmest kiss
And dim dried eyes like an exhausted well.
Slow-speaking when she has some fact to tell,
    Silent with long-unbroken silences,
    Centred in self yet not unpleased to please,
Gravely monotonous like a passing bell.
Mindful of drudging daily common things,
    Patient at pastime, patient at her work,
        Wearied perhaps but strenuous certainly.
        Sometimes I fancy we may one day see
    Her head shoot forth seven stars from where they lurk
And her eyes lightnings and her shoulders wings.

Italia, Io Ti Saluto

To come back from the sweet South, to the North
    Where I was born, bred, look to die;
Come back to do my day's work in its day,
      Play out my play—
    Amen, amen, say I.

To see no more the country half my own,
    Nor hear the half familiar speech,
Amen, I say; I turn to that bleak North
      Whence I came forth—
    The South lies out of reach.

But when our swallows fly back to the South,
    To the sweet South, to the sweet South,

The tears may come again into my eyes
    On the old wise,
  And the sweet name to my mouth.

Emily Dickinson

This Is My Letter to the World

This is my letter to the world,
    That never wrote to me—
The simple news that Nature told,
    With tender majesty.

Her message is committed
    To hands I cannot see;
For love of her, sweet countrymen,
    Judge tenderly of me!

To Fight Aloud Is Very Brave

To fight aloud is very brave,
But gallanter, I know,
Who charge within the bosom,
The cavalry of woe.

Who win, and nations do not see,
Who fall, and none observe,
Whose dying eyes no country
Regards with patriot love.

We trust, in plumed procession,
For such the angels go,
Rank after rank, with even feet
And uniforms of snow.

Success

Success is counted sweetest
By those who ne'er succeed.

133

To comprehend a nectar
Requires sorest need.

Not one of all the purple host
Who took the flag to-day
Can tell the definition,
So clear, of victory,

As he, defeated, dying,
On whose forbidden ear
The distant strains of triumph
Break, agonized and clear.

The Heart Asks Pleasure First

The heart asks pleasure first,
And then, excuse from pain;
And then, those little anodynes
That deaden suffering;

And then, to go to sleep;
And then, if it should be
The will of its Inquisitor,
The liberty to die.

Much Madness Is Divinest Sense

Much madness is divinest sense
To a discerning eye;
Much sense the starkest madness.
'T is the majority
In this, as all, prevails.
Assent, and you are sane;
Demur, —you're straightway dangerous,
And handled with a chain.

I Taste a Liquor Never Brewed

I taste a liquor never brewed,
From tankards scooped in pearl;

Not all the vats upon the Rhine
Yield such an alcohol!

Inebriate of air am I,
And debauchee of dew,
Reeling, through endless summer days,
From inns of molten blue.

When landlords turn the drunken bee
Out of the foxglove's door,
When butterflies renounce their drams,
I shall but drink the more!

There's a Certain Slant of Light

There's a certain slant of light,
On winter afternoons,
That oppresses, like the weight
Of cathedral tunes.

Heavenly hurt it gives us;
We can find no scar,
But internal difference
Where the meanings are.

None may teach it anything,
'T is the seal, despair, —
An imperial affliction
Sent us of the air.

When it comes, the landscape listens,
Shadows hold their breath;
When it goes, 't is like the distance
On the look of death.

Suspense

Elysium is as far as to
The very nearest room,
If in that room a friend await
Felicity or doom.

What fortitude the soul contains,
That it can so endure
The accent of a coming foot,
The opening of a door!

Exclusion

The soul selects her own society,
Then shuts the door;
On her divine majority
Obtrude no more.

Unmoved, she notes the chariot's pausing
At her low gate;
Unmoved, an emperor is kneeling
Upon her mat.

I've known her from an ample nation
Choose one;
Then close the valves of her attention
Like stone.

The Way I Read a Letter's This

The way I read a letter 's this:
'T is first I lock the door,
And push it with my fingers next,
For transport it be sure.

And then I go the furthest off
To counteract a knock;
Then draw my little letter forth
And softly pick its lock.

Then, glancing narrow at the wall,
And narrow at the floor,
For firm conviction of a mouse
Not exorcised before,

Peruse how infinite I am
To—no one that you know!
And sigh for lack of heaven, —but not
The heaven the creeds bestow.

Safe in Their Alabaster Chambers

Safe in their alabaster chambers,
Untouched by morning and untouched by noon,
Sleep the meek members of the resurrection,
Rafter of satin, and roof of stone.

Light laughs the breeze in her castle of sunshine;
Babbles the bee in a stolid ear;
Pipe the sweet birds in ignorant cadence, —
Ah, what sagacity perished here!

Grand go the years in the crescent above them;
Worlds scoop their arcs, and firmaments row,
Diadems drop and Doges surrender,
Soundless as dots on a disk of snow.

What Soft, Cherubic Creatures

What soft, cherubic creatures
    These gentlewomen are!
One would as soon assault a plush
    Or violate a star.

Such dimity convictions,
    A horror so refined
Of freckled human nature
    Of Deity ashamed, —

It's such a common glory,
    A fisherman's degree!
Redemption, brittle lady,
    Be so, ashamed of thee.

I'm Nobody

I'm nobody! Who are you?
Are you nobody, too?
Then there's a pair of us—don't tell!
They'd banish us, you know.

How dreary to be somebody!
How public, like a frog
To tell your name the livelong day
To an admiring bog!

Wild Nights

Wild nights! Wild nights!
Were I with thee,
Wild nights should be
Our luxury!

Futile the winds
To a heart in port, —
Done with the compass,
Done with the chart.

Rowing in Eden!
Ah! the sea!
Might I but moor
To-night in thee!

The Chariot

Because I could not stop for Death,
He kindly stopped for me;
The carriage held but just ourselves
And Immortality.

We slowly drove, he knew no haste,
And I had put away
My labor, and my leisure too,
For his civility.

We passed the school where children played,
Their lessons scarcely done;
We passed the fields of gazing grain,
We passed the setting sun.

We paused before a house that seemed
A swelling of the ground;
The roof was scarcely visible,
The cornice but a mound.

Since then 't is centuries; but each
Feels shorter than the day
I first surmised the horses' heads
Were toward eternity.

Mathilde Blind

The Sower

The winds had hushed at last as by command;
    The quiet sky above,
With its grey clouds spread o'er the fallow land,
    Sat brooding like a dove.

There was no motion in the air, no sound
    Within the tree-tops stirred,
Save when some last leaf, fluttering to the ground,
    Dropped like a wounded bird:

Or when the swart rooks in a gathering crowd
    With clamorous noises wheeled,
Hovering awhile, then swooped with wranglings loud
Down on the stubbly field.

For now the big-thewed horses, toiling slow
    In straining couples yoked,
Patiently dragged the ploughshare to and fro
    Till their wet haunches smoked.

Till the stiff acre, broken into clods,
    Bruised by the harrow's tooth,
Lay lightly shaken, with its humid sods
    Ranged into furrows smooth.

There looming lone, from rise to set of sun,
    Without or pause or speed,
Solemnly striding by the furrows dun,
    The sower sows the seed.

The sower sows the seed, which mouldering,
    Deep coffined in the earth,

Is buried now, but with the future spring
    Will quicken into birth.

Oh, poles of birth and death! Controlling Powers
    Of human toil and need!
On this fair earth all men are surely sowers,
    Surely all life is seed!

All life is seed, dropped in Time's yawning furrow,
    Which with slow sprout and shoot,
In the revolving world's unfathomed morrow,
    Will blossom and bear fruit.

Reapers

Sun-tanned men and women, toiling there together;
    Seven I count in all, in yon field of wheat,
Where the rich ripe ears in the harvest weather
    Glow an orange gold through the sweltering heat.

Busy life is still, sunk in brooding leisure:
    Birds have hushed their singing in the hushed tree-tops;
Not a single cloud mars the flawless azure;
    Not a shadow moves o'er the moveless crops;

In the glassy shallows, that no breath is creasing,
    Chestnut-coloured cows in the rushes dank
Stand like cows of bronze, save when they flick the teasing
    Flies with switch of tail from each quivering flank.

Nature takes a rest—even her bees are sleeping,
    And the silent wood seems a church that's shut;
But these human creatures cease not from their reaping
    While the corn stands high, waiting to be cut.

Emma Lazarus

1492

Thou two-faced year, Mother of Change and Fate,
Didst weep when Spain cast forth with flaming sword,

The children of the prophets of the Lord,
Prince, priest, and people, spurned by zealot hate.
Hounded from sea to sea, from state to state,
The West refused them, and the East abhorred.
No anchorage the known world could afford,
Close-locked was every port, barred every gate.
Then smiling, thou unveil'dst, O two-faced year,
A virgin world where doors of sunset part,
Saying, "Ho, all who weary, enter here!
There falls each ancient barrier that the art
Of race or creed or rank devised, to rear
Grim bulwarked hatred between heart and heart!"

The New Colossus

Not like the brazen giant of Greek fame,
With conquering limbs astride from land to land;
Here at our sea-washed, sunset gates shall stand
A mighty woman with a torch, whose flame
Is the imprisoned lightning, and her name
Mother of Exiles. From her beacon-hand
Glows world-wide welcome; her mild eyes command
The air-bridged harbor that twin cities frame.
"Keep ancient lands, your storied pomp!" cries she
With silent lips. "Give me your tired, your poor,
Your huddled masses yearning to breathe free,
The wretched refuse of your teeming shore.
Send these, the homeless, tempest-tost to me,
I lift my lamp beside the golden door!"

By the Waters of Babylon

Little Poems in Prose
    No. 1 The Exodus (August 3, 1492)

1. The Spanish noon is a blaze of azure fire, and the dusty pilgrims crawl like an endless serpent along treeless plains and bleached highroads, through rock-split ravines and castellated, cathedral-shadowed towns.

2. The hoary patriarch, wrinkled as an almond shell, bows painfully upon his staff. The beautiful young mother, ivory-pale, well-nigh

swoons beneath her burden; in her large enfolding arms nestles her sleeping babe, round her knees flock her little ones with bruised and bleeding feet. "Mother, shall we soon be there?"

3. The youth with Christ-like countenance speaks comfortably to father and brother, to maiden and wife. In his breast, his own heart is broken.

4. The halt, the blind, are amid the train. Sturdy pack-horses laboriously drag the tented wagons wherein lie the sick athirst with fever.

5. The panting mules are urged forward with spur and goad; stuffed are the heavy saddle-bags with the wreckage of ruined homes.

6. Hark to the tinkling silver bells that adorn the tenderly carried silken scrolls.

7. In the fierce noon-glare a lad bears a kindled lamp; behind its network of bronze the airs of heaven breathe not upon its faint purple star.

8. Noble and abject, learned and simple, illustrious and obscure, plod side by side, all brothers now, all merged in one routed army of misfortune.

9. Woe to the straggler who falls by the wayside! No friend shall close his eyes.

10. They leave behind, the grape, the olive, and the fig; the vines they planted, the corn they sowed, the garden-cities of Andalusia and Aragon, Estremadura and La Mancha, of Granada and Castile; the altar, the hearth, and the grave of their fathers.

11. The townsman spits at their garments, the shepherd quits his flock, the peasant his plow, to pelt with curses and stones; the villager sets on their trail his yelping cur.

12. Oh the weary march, oh the uptorn roots of home, oh the blankness of the receding goal!

13. Listen to their lamentation: *They that ate dainty food are desolate in the streets; they that were reared in scarlet embrace dung-hills. They flee away and wander about. Men say among the nations, they shall no more sojourn there; our end is near, our days are full, our doom is come.*

14. Whither shall they turn? for the West hath cast them out, and the East refuseth to receive.

15. O bird of the air, whisper to the despairing exiles, that to-day, to-day, from the many-masted, gayly-bannered port of Palos, sails the world-unveiling Genoese, to unlock the golden gates of sunset and bequeath a Continent to Freedom!

No. v. Currents

1. Vast oceanic movements, the flux and reflux of immeasurable tides oversweep our continent.

2. From the far Caucasian steppes, from the squalid Ghettos of Europe,

3. From Odessa and Bucharest, from Kief and Ekaterinoslav,

4. Hark to the cry of the exiles of Babylon, the voice of Rachel mourning for her children, of Israel lamenting for Zion.

5. And lo, like a turbid stream, the long-pent flood bursts the dykes of oppression and rushes hitherward.

6. Unto her ample breast, the generous mother of nations welcomes them.

7. The herdsman of Canaan and the seed of Jerusalem's royal shepherd renew their youth amid the pastoral plains of Texas and the golden valleys of the Sierras.

Ethna Carbery

The Love-Talker

I met the Love-Talker one eve in the glen,
He was handsomer than any of our handsome young men,
His eyes were blacker than the sloe, his voice sweeter far
Than the crooning of old Kevin's pipes beyond in Coolnagar.

I was bound for the milking with a heart fair and free—
My grief! my grief! that bitter hour drained the life from me;
I thought him human lover, though his lips on mine were cold,
And the breath of death blew keen on me within his hold.

I know not what way he came, no shadow fell behind,
But all the sighing rushes swayed beneath a fairy wind
The thrush ceased its singing, a mist crept about,
We two clung together—with the world shut out.

Beyond the ghostly mist I could hear my cattle low,
The little cow from Ballina, clean as driven snow,
The dun cow from Kerry, the roan from Inisheer,
Oh, pitiful their calling—and his whispers in my ear!

His eyes were a fire; his words were a snare;
I cried my mother's name, but no help was there;
I made the blessed Sign: then he gave a dreary moan,
A wisp of cloud went floating by, and I stood alone.

Running ever thro' my head is an old-time rune—
"Who meets the Love-Talker must weave her shroud soon."
My mother's face is furrowed with the salt tears that fall,
But the kind eyes of my father are the saddest sight of all.

I have spun the fleecy lint, and now my wheel is still,
The linen length is woven for my shroud fine and chill,
I shall stretch me on the bed where a happy maid I lay—
Pray for the soul of Máire Og at dawning of the day!

On an Island

Weary on ye, sad waves!
Still scourging the lonely shore.
Oh, I am far from my father's door,
And my kindred's graves!

From day to day, outside
There is nothing but dreary sea;
And at night o'er the dreams of me
The great waters glide.

If I look to East or west,
Green billows go tipped with foam—
Green woods gird my father's home,
With birds in each nest.

The grass is bitter with brine,
Sea-stunted the rushes stir—
In my father's woods the fir
Smells sweeter than wine.

My mother's eyes were kind,
But oh! kind eyes and smile
That won me to this lone isle,
She is left behind.

For love came like a storm,
Uprooted, and bound me here

In chains more strong, more dear,
Than the old home charm.

. . . . . .

Swiftly I thrust away
This thought of the Woods of Truagh,
My poplar, my fir are you,
My larch a-sway—

My mether of full delight,
My sun that is never spent,
And thus I go well-content,
Through gray days in your light.

The King of Ireland's Cairn

Blow softly down the valley,
  O wind, and stir the fern
That waves its green fronds over
  The King of Ireland's Cairn.

Here in his last wild foray
  He fell, and here he lies—
His armour makes no rattle,
  The clay is in his eyes.

His spear, that once was lightning
  Hurled with unerring hand,
Rusts by his fleshless fingers
  Beside his battle brand.

His shield that made a pillow
  Beneath his noble head,
Hath smouldered, quite forgotten,
  With the half-forgotten dead.

Say, doth his ghost remember
  Old fights—old revellings,
When the victor-chant re-echoed
  In Tara of the Kings?

Say, down those Halls of Quiet
  Doth he cry upon his Queen?
Or doth he sleep contented
  To dream of what has been?

Nay, nay, he still is kingly—
    He wanders in a glen
Where Fionn goes by a-hunting
    With misty Fenian men.

He sees the hounds of Wonder
    Bringing down their fleeting prey
He sees the swift blood flowing
    At dawning of the day.

At night he holds his revels
    Just as a king might do—
But the ghostly mirth is silent,
    The harp-song silent too!

And he who crowns the feasting,
    His shadowy Queen beside,
Is pale as when they stretched him
    That bitter eve he died.

.   .   .   .   .   .

'Tis well he seeks no tidings—
    His heart would ache to know
That all is changed in Ireland,
    And Tara lieth low.

That we go wailing, wailing,
    Around a foreign horde—
Nor raise the call to conflict,
    Nor ever draw the sword.

Mary Elizabeth Coleridge

Unwelcome

We were young, we were merry, we were very very wise,
    And the door stood open at our feast,
When there passed us a woman with the West in her eyes,
    And a man with his back to the East.

O, still grew the hearts that were beating so fast,
    The loudest voice was still.

The jest died away on our lips as they passed,
   And the rays of July struck chill.

The cups of red wine turned pale on the board,
   The white bread black as soot.
The hound forgot the hand of her lord,
   She fell down at his foot.

Low let me lie, where the dead dog lies,
   Ere I sit me down again at a feast,
When there passes a woman with the West in her eyes,
   And a man with his back to the East.

The Witch

I have walked a great while over the snow,
And I am not tall nor strong.
My clothes are wet, and my teeth are set,
And the way was hard and long.
I have wandered over the fruitful earth,
But I never came here before.
Oh, lift me over the threshold, and let me in at the door!

The cutting wind is a cruel foe.
I dare not stand in the blast.
My hands are stone, and my voice a groan,
And the worst of death is past.
I am but a little maiden still,
My little white feet are sore.
Oh, lift me over the threshold, and let me in at the door!

Her voice was the voice that women have,
Who plead for their heart's desire.
She came—she came—and the quivering flame
Sank and died in the fire.
It never was lit again on my hearth
Since I hurried across the floor,
To lift her over the threshold, and let her in at the door.

Jealousy

"The myrtle bush grew shady
   Down by the ford."—

"Is it even so?" said my lady.
  "Even so!" said my lord.
"The leaves are set too thick together
  For the point of a sword."

"The arras in your room hangs close,
  No light between!
You wedded one of those
  That see unseen." —
"Is it even so?" said the King's Majesty.
  "Even so!" said the Queen.

At a Friends' Meeting

"Strangers are we and pilgrims here!"
  So sing we every Sabbath day.
But surely pilgrimage is dear,
  We linger so upon the way.

Is that the home, the Father kind,
  Is that the country of our birth?
Were we created deaf and blind,
  That we prefer the toilsome Earth?

Its setting sun—its changing sea—
  The day—the dark, refreshing night—
The winds that wander wide and free—
  Are dearer than the Land of Light.

Though Age may sit in Beauty's place,
  The eyes, that growing old, wax dim,
Are fairer than the youthful face
  Of Cherubim and Seraphim.

And when we lay them in the ground
  The sting of death is living still,
Although we know that they have found
  The city set upon a hill.

We sigh and weep and pray for rest,
  And murmur that the way is long.
Alas! the Islands of the Blest
  Are only blest in Psalm and song.

Nay, not in Psalm, for David knew
    The dread that pierces like a sword,
And had the faith to say it too:
    "The dead they praise not Thee, O Lord."

The life that we so much despise
    The Son hath deigned with us to share.
Shall we find favour in Thine eyes
    By slighting what He made His care?

We feel more truly than we speak.
    Thou art the Life. And Thou hast said,
That he who lives, however weak,
    Shall not be numbered with the dead.

Our Lady

Mother of God! no lady thou:
    Common woman of common earth!
OUR LADY ladies call thee now,
    But Christ was never of gentle birth;
    A common man of the common earth.

For God's ways are not as our ways.
    The noblest lady in the land
Would have given up half her days,
    Would have cut off her right hand,
    To bear the Child that was God of the land.

Never a lady did He choose,
    Only a maid of low degree,
So humble she might not refuse
    The carpenter of Galilee.
    A daughter of the people, she.

Out she sang the song of her heart.
    Never a lady so had sung.
She knew no letters, had no art;
    To all mankind, in woman's tongue,
    Hath Israelitish Mary sung.

And still for men to come she sings,
    Nor shall her singing pass away.

"He hath filled the hungry with good things"—
  Oh, listen, lords and ladies gay!—
  "And the rich He hath sent empty away."

We Never Said Farewell

We never said farewell, nor even looked
  Our last upon each other, for no sign
Was made when we the linkèd chain unhooked
  And broke the level line.

And here we dwell together, side by side,
  Our places fixed for life upon the chart.
Two islands that the roaring seas divide
  Are not more far apart.

Michael Field

Macrinus Against Trees

'How bare! How all the lion-desert lies
Before your cell!
Behind are leaves and boughs on which your eyes
Could, as the eyes of shepherd, on his flock,
That turn to the soft mass from barren rock,
Familiarly dwell.'

'O Traveller, for me the empty sands
Burning to white!
There nothing on the wilderness withstands
The soul or prayer. I would not look on trees;
My thoughts and will were shaken in their breeze,
And buried as by night.

'Yea, listen! If you build a cell, at last,
Turned to the wood,
Your fall is near, your safety overpast;
And if you plant a tree beside your door
Your fall is there beside it, and no more
The solitude is frank and good.

'For trees must have soft dampness for their growth,
And interfold
Their boughs and leaves into a screen, not loath
To hide soft, tempting creatures at their play,
That, playing timbrels and bright shawms, delay,
And wear one's spirit old.

'Smoothly such numberless distractions come—
Impertinence
Of multiplicity, salute and hum.
Away with solitude of leafy shade,
Mustering coy birds and beasts, and men waylaid,
Tingling each hooded sense!

'Did not God call out of a covert-wood
Adam and Eve,
Where, cowering under earliest sin, they stood,
The hugged green-leaves in bunches round their den?
Himself God called them out—so lost are men
Whom forest haunts receive!'

Descent From the Cross

Come down from the Cross, my soul, and save thyself—come down!
Thou wilt be free as wind. None meeting thee will know
How thou wert hanging stark, my soul, outside the town,
Thou wilt fare to and fro;
Thy feet in grass will smell of faithful thyme; thy head. . . .
Think of the thorns, my soul—how thou wilt cast them off,
With shudder at the bleeding clench they hold!
But on their wounds thou wilt a balsam spread,
And over that a verdurous circle rolled
With gathered violets, sweet bright violets, sweet
As incense of the thyme on thy free feet;
A wreath thou wilt not give away, nor wilt thou doff.

Come down from the Cross, my soul, and save thyself; yea, move
As scudding swans pass lithely on a seaward stream!
Thou wilt have everything thou wert made great to love;
Thou wilt have ease for every dream;
No nails with fang will hold thy purpose to one aim;
There will be arbours round about thee, not one trunk
Against thy shoulders pressed and burning them with hate,

Yea, burning with intolerable flame.
O lips, such noxious vinegar have drunk,
There are through valley-woods and mountain glades
Rivers where thirst in naked prowess wades;
And there are wells in solitude whose chill no hour abates!

Come down from the Cross, my soul, and save thyself! A sign
Thou wilt become to many as a shooting star.
They will believe thou art ethereal, divine,
When thou art where they are;
They will believe in thee and give thee feasts and praise.
They will believe thy power when thou hast loosed thy nails;
For power to them is fetterless and grand:
For destiny to them, along their ways,
Is one whose earthly Kingdom never fails.
Thou wilt be as a prophet or a king
In thy tremendous term of flourishing—
And thy hot royalty with acclamations fanned.

Come down from the Cross, my soul, and save thyself! . . . . Beware!
Art thou not crucified with God, who is thy breath?
Wilt thou not hang as He while mockers laugh and stare?
Wilt thou not die His death?
Wilt thou not stay as He with nails and thorns and thirst?
Wilt thou not choose to conquer faith in His lone style?
Wilt thou not be with Him and hold thee still?
Voices have cried to Him, *Come down!* Accursed
And vain those voices, striving to beguile!
How heedless, solemn-gray in powerful mass,
Christ droops among the echoes as they pass!
O soul, remain with Him, with Him thy doom fulfil!

After Mass

Lovingly I turn me down
From this church, St. Philip's crown,
To the leafy street where dwell
   The good folk of Arundel.

Lovingly I look between
Roof and roof, to meadows green,
To the cattle by the wall,
To the place where sea-birds call,

Where the sky more closely dips,
And perchance, there may be ships:
God have pity on us all!

Alice Meynell

Chimes

Brief, on a flying night,
    From the shaken tower
A flock of bells take flight,
    And go with the hour.

Like birds from the cote to the gales,
    Abrupt—oh, hark!
A fleet of bells set sails,
    And go to the dark.

Sudden the cold airs swing.
    Alone, aloud,
A verse of bells takes wing
    And flies with the cloud.

The Roaring Frost

A flock of winds came winging from the North,
Strong birds with fighting pinions driving forth
    With a resounding call: —

Where will they close their wings and cease their cries—
Between what warming seas and conquering skies—
    And fold, and fall?

Renouncement

I must not think of thee; and, tired yet strong,
    I shun the thought that lurks in all delight—
    The thought of thee—and in the blue Heaven's height,
And in the sweetest passage of a song.
Oh, just beyond the fairest thoughts that throng
    This breast, the thought of thee waits hidden yet bright;
    But it must never, never come in sight;
I must stop short of thee the whole day long.

But when sleep comes to close each difficult day,
    When night gives pause to the long watch I keep,
    And all my bonds I needs must loose apart,
Must doff my will as raiment laid away—
    With the first dream that comes with the first sleep
    I run, I run, I am gathered to thy heart.

Veni Creator

So humble things Thou hast borne for us, O God,
Left'st Thou a path of lowliness untrod?
Yes, one, till now, another Olive-Garden.
For we endure the tender pain of pardon:
One with another we forbear. Give heed,
Look at the mournful world Thou hast decreed.
The time has come. At last we hapless men
Know all our haplessness all through. Come, then,
Endure undreamed humility: Lord of Heaven,
Come to our ignorant hearts and be forgiven.

A General Communion

I saw the throng, so deeply separate,
    Fed at one only board—
The devout people, moved, intent, elate,
    And the devoted Lord.

O struck apart! not side from human side,
    But soul from human soul,
As each asunder absorbed the multiplied,
    The ever unparted, whole.

I saw this people as a field of flowers,
    Each grown at such a price
The sum of unimaginable powers
    Did no more than suffice.

A thousand single central daisies they,
    A thousand of the one;
For each, the entire monopoly of day;
    For each, the whole of the devoted sun.

The Launch

Forth, to the alien gravity,
Forth, to the laws of ocean, we,
   Builders on earth by laws of land,
   Entrust this creature of our hand
Upon the calculated sea.

Fast bound to shore we cling, we creep,
And make our ship ready to leap
   Light to the flood, equipped to ride
   The strange conditions of the tide—
New weight, new force, new world: the Deep.

Ah thus—not thus—the Dying, kissed,
Cherished, exhorted, shriven, dismissed;
   By all the eager means we hold
   We, warm, prepare him for the cold,
To keep the incalculable tryst.

The Threshing-Machine

No 'fan is in his hand' for these
Young villagers beneath the trees,
   Watching the wheels. But I recall
   The rhythm of rods that rise and fall,
Purging the harvest, over-seas.

No fan, no flail, no threshing-floor!
And all their symbols evermore
   Forgone in England now—the sign,
   The visible pledge, the threat divine,
The chaff dispersed, the wheat in store.

The unbreathing engine marks no tune,
Steady at sunrise, steady at noon,
   Inhuman, perfect, saving time,
   And saving measure, and saving rhyme—
And did our Ruskin speak too soon?

'No noble strength on earth' he sees
'Save Hercules' arm'. His grave decrees
   Curse wheel and stream. As the wheels ran
   I saw the other strength of man,
I knew the brain of Hercules.

Summer in England, 1914

On London fell a clearer light;
   Caressing pencils of the sun
Defined the distances, the white
   Houses transfigured one by one,
The 'long, unlovely street' impearled.
Oh, what a sky has walked the world!

Most happy year! And out of town
   The hay was prosperous, and the wheat;
The silken harvest climbed the down:
   Moon after moon was heavenly-sweet,
Stroking the bread within the sheaves,
Looking 'twixt apples and their leaves.

And while this rose made round her cup,
   The armies died convulsed. And when
This chaste young silver sun went up
   Softly, a thousand shattered men,
One wet corruption, heaped the plain,
After a league-long throb of pain.

Flower following tender flower; and birds,
   And berries; and benignant skies
Made thrive the serried flocks and herds.—
   Yonder are men shot through the eyes.
     Love, hide thy face
From man's unpardonable race.

A Father of Women

Ad Sororem E. B.

'Thy father was transfused into thy blood.'
DRYDEN: Ode to Mrs. Anne Killigrew

   Our father works in us,
The daughters of his manhood. Not undone
Is he, not wasted, though transmuted thus,
   And though he left no son.

   Therefore on him I cry
To arm me: 'For my delicate mind a casque,

A breastplate for my heart, courage to die,
  Of thee, captain, I ask.

'Nor strengthen only; press
A finger on this violent blood and pale,
Over this rash will let thy tenderness
  A while pause, and prevail.

'And shepherd-father, thou
Whose staff folded my thoughts before my birth,
Control them now I am of earth, and now
  Thou art no more of earth.

'O liberal, constant, dear,
Crush in my nature the ungenerous art
Of the inferior; set me high, and here,
  Here garner up thy heart!'

Like to him now are they,
The million living fathers of the War—
Mourning the crippled world, the bitter day—
  Whose striplings are no more.

The crippled world! Come then,
Fathers of women with your honour in trust,
Approve, accept, know them daughters of men,
  Now that your sons are dust.

The Two Questions

'A riddling world!' one cried.
'If pangs must be, would God that they were sent
To the impure, the cruel, and passed aside
  The holy innocent!'

But I, 'Ah no, no, no!
Not the clean heart transpierced; not tears that fall
For a child's agony; nor a martyr's woe;
  Not these, not these appal.

'Not docile motherhood,
Dutiful, frequent, closed in all distress;
Not shedding of the unoffending blood;
  Not little joy grown less;

'Not all-benign old age
With dotage mocked; not gallantry that faints
And still pursues; not the vile heritage
  Of sin's disease in saints;

'Not these defeat the mind.
For great is that abjection, and august
That irony. Submissive we shall find
  A splendour in that dust.

'Not these puzzle the will;
Not these the yet unanswered question urge.
But the unjust stricken; but the hands that kill
  Lopped; but the merited scourge;

'The sensualist at fast;
The merciless felled; the liar in his snares.
The cowardice of my judgement sees, aghast,
  The flail, the chaff, the tares.'

A Thrush Before Dawn

A voice peals in this end of night
  A phrase of notes resembling stars,
Single and spiritual notes of light.
    What call they at my window-bars?
    The South, the past, the day to be,
    An ancient infelicity.

Darkling, deliberate, what sings
  This wonderful one, alone, at peace?
What wilder things than song, what things
    Sweeter than youth, clearer than Greece,
    Dearer than Italy, untold
    Delight, and freshness centuries old?

And first first-loves, a multitude,
  The exaltation of their pain;
Ancestral childhood long renewed;
    And midnights of invisible rain;
    And gardens, gardens, night and day,
    Gardens and childhood all the way.

What Middle Ages passionate,
   O passionless voice! What distant bells
Lodged in the hills, what palace state
   Illyrian! For it speaks, it tells,
      Without desire, without dismay,
      Some morrow and some yesterday.

All-natural things! But more—Whence came
   This yet remoter mystery?
How do these starry notes proclaim
   A graver still divinity?
      This hope, this sanctity of fear?

   O innocent throat! O human ear!

Singers to Come

No new delights to our desire
   The singers of the past can yield.
   I lift mine eyes to hill and field,
And see in them your yet dumb lyre,
   Poets unborn and unrevealed.

Singers to come, what thoughts will start
   To song? What words of yours be sent
   Through man's soul, and with earth be blent?
These worlds of nature and the heart
   Await you like an instrument.

Who knows what musical flocks of words
   Upon these pine-tree tops will light,
   And crown these towers in circling flight,
And cross these seas like summer birds,
   And give a voice to the day and night?

Something of you already is ours;
   Some mystic part of you belongs
   To us whose dreams your future throngs,
Who look on hills, and trees, and flowers,
   Which will mean so much in your songs.

I wonder, like the maid who found,
   And knelt to lift, the lyre supreme
   Of Orpheus from the Thracian stream.

She dreams on its sealed past profound;
　　On a deep future sealed I dream.

She bears it in her wanderings
　　Within her arms, and has not pressed
　　Her unskilled fingers but her breast
Upon those silent sacred strings;
　　I, too, clap mystic strings at rest.

For I, in the world of lands and seas,
　　The sky of wind and rain and fire,
　　And in man's world of long desire—
In all that is yet dumb in these—
　　Have found a more mysterious lyre.

PART
TWO

Mary Austin

Come Not Near My Songs

Shoshone

Come not near my songs,
You who are not my lover,
Lest from out that ambush
Leaps my heart upon you!

When my songs are glowing
As an almond thicket
With the bloom upon it,
Lies my heart in ambush
All amid my singing;
Come not near my songs,
You who are not my lover!

Do not hear my songs,
You who are not my lover!
Over-sweet the heart is
Where my love has bruised it;

Breathe you not that fragrance,
You who are not my lover.
Do not stoop above my song
With its languor on you,
Lest from out my singing
Leaps my heart upon you!

Song for the Newborn

Grande Pueblos
To be sung by the one who first takes the child from its mother.

Newborn, on the naked sand
Nakedly lay it.
Next to the earth mother,
That it may know her;
Having good thoughts of her, the food giver.

Newborn, we tenderly
In our arms take it,
Making good thoughts.
House-god, be entreated,
That it may grow from childhood to manhood,
Happy, contented;
Beautifully walking
The trail to old age.
Having good thoughts of the earth its mother,
That she may give it the fruits of her being.
Newborn, on the naked sand
Nakedly lay it.

Pilgrimage Song

Woman's Dance at Tesuque Pueblo

That mountain there,
That white-shell mountain,
Toward the east it standeth,
O sacred mountain,
Whence the day springs.
O white-shell mountain,
Guard thou our day!

Yonder, afar,
That dark blue mountain,
Toward the north standing
That sacred mountain,
Whence the storm cometh,
O dark blue mountain,
Spare not our storm!

That mountain there,
That turquoise-colored mountain,
Toward the west it standeth,
The path of life unending
And beyond it,
O turquoise mountain,
Guide thou our way!

Yonder, afar,
Rose-yellow mountain,
Sacred southern mountain,
Yonder afar, in beauty walking,
The way of joy unending;
Rose-yellow mountain,
Keep thou our home!

Song of a Woman Abandoned by the Tribe Because She Is Too Old to Keep Up with Their Migration

Southern Shoshone

Alas, that I should die,
That I should die now,
I who know so much!

It will miss me,
The twirling fire stick;
The fire coal between the hearth stones,
It will miss me.

The Medicine songs,
The songs of magic healing;
The medicine herbs by the water borders,
They will miss me;
The basket willow,
It will miss me;
All the wisdom of women,
It will miss me.

Alas, that I should die,
Who know so much.

Beatrice Ravenel

The Alligator

He roars in the swamp.
For two hundred years he has clamored in Spring;
He is fourteen feet long, and his track scars the earth in the night-time,
His voice scars the air.

Oak-boughs have furred their forks, are in velvet;
Jessamine crackle their fire-new sparks;
The grass is full of a nameless wildness of color, of flowers in solution.
The glass-blower birds twist their brittle imaginings over the multiplied
    colors of water.

But the counterpoint of the Spring—
Exacerbate, resonant,
Raw like beginnings of worlds,
Cry of the mud made flesh, made particular, personal,
Midnight assailing the morning, myopic sound, blinded by sun,—
Roars from the swamp.
A thing in itself,
Not only alive, but the very existence of death would be news to it.
Will—
Will without inflection,
Making us shudder, ashamed of our own triviality—
The bull alligator roars in the swamp.

This is queer country.
One does not walk nor climb for a view;
It comes right up to the porch, like a hound to be patted.
Under our hog-back
The swamp, inchoate creature, fumbles its passage, still nearer;
Puffing a vapor of flowers before it.

This week there are ponds in the wood, vertiginous skies underfoot,
Pondering heaven.
Next week, in the pashing mud of the footpath

Fish may be gasping, baffled in semi-solids.
The negroes will eat them.

This is queer country.
Thick-blooded compulsive sound,
Like scum in the branch, chokes, mantles the morning.

Sangarrah! . . . Sangarrah! . . . Sangarrah! . . .

Two hundred years back—
And the medicine-man of the Yemassee
Sat in the thick of the swamp, on the ridge where the cypresses flung
Their elfin stockade.
Wrinkled his chest as the cast-off skin of the blacksnake,
The hide of his cheeks hung square and ridged as the hide
Of the grown alligator.
A young alligator squirmed on his naked knees
While he muttered its lesson.

That was strong medicine. Over the old man's eyes
        Drooped the holy beloved crest of the swan-plumes;
Otter-skin straps cut under his arms
From the breastplate of conch-shells.
Fawn-trotters fell from his boot-tops; the white beloved mantle
Lined with raw scarlet, hung on the gum-tree, along with the ocelot
        quiver
And locust-wood bow.
He had fasted, drinking the dark button snake-root. He shuddered,
Calling the secret name, the name of the Manneyto,
Y-O-He,
Never known by the people.

On the infant saurian, long-lived, ruled into patterns, his hands
Moved, taking the shape of a sharp-curved arrow;
He spoke, teaching its lesson, calling its name;
"Nanneb-Chunchaba,
Fish-like-a-Mountain,
Remember!

"By the day-sun and the night-sun,
By the new beloved fire of the corn-feast;
By the Arrow of Lightning, that came from the storm,
From the Spirit of Fire to the ancient chief of the Yemassee—

Totem of Yemassee!
Let our voice be remembered.

"We go from the hunting-grounds of our fathers,
The lands that we took, fighting north through the man-eating
     Westoes,
Fall from our hands.
In the hills of our dead, in the powdering flesh that conceived us,
     Shall the white-man plant corn.

"The trails where we fought with the fierce Tuscarora
Will call us in vain;
No pictures of skillful canoemen will green Isundiga paint clear in his
     waters.
We shall be cut from the land as the medicine-man cuts the totem
From the arm of the outcast.

"*From the sky they cannot cut our totem!*

"My name too shall vanish.
When the drums and the music for three days are silent
And men praise me under the peach-trees,
My over-wise spirit
Shall root itself here, as the oak-tree takes hold.
Who will wait for me? Which of the spirits
That have made of my body a lodge, that have twisted my sinews
As women twist withes for their baskets, will claim habitation,
That have spoken their wisdom
Out of my mouth?
I shall hide from them all, as the war-chiefs
Cover their lives with the tree-tops,
Leaving them safe when they go on the war-path.
I shall sleep in this place.

In the new days,
The days when our voice shall be silent,
Speak for the Yemassee!
Nanneb-Chunchaba, you, little Fish-like-a-Mountain,
Shout through the forest the terrible war-cry of Yemassee!

"*Sangarrah! . . . Sangarrah-me! . . . Sangarrah-me!*
Shout! I shall hear you!
Sangarrah! . . ."

For two hundred years—
Will, without inflexion—
The bull alligator
Roars from the swamp
In the Spring.

Charlotte Mew

The Farmer's Bride

Three summers since I chose a maid,
    Too young maybe—but more's to do
At harvest-time than bide and woo.
    When us was wed she turned afraid
Of love and me and all things human;
Like the shut of a winter's day
Her smile went out, and 'twadn't a woman—
    More like a little frightened fay.
        One night, in the Fall, she runned away.

"Out 'mong the sheep, her be," they said.
Should properly have been abed;
But sure enough she wadn't there
Lying awake with her wide brown stare.
So over seven-acre field and up-along across the down
    We chased her, flying like a hare
Before our lanterns. To Church-Town
    All in a shiver and a scare
We caught her, fetched her home at last
    And turned the key upon her, fast.

She does the work about the house
As well as most, but like a mouse:
    Happy enough to chat and play
    With birds and rabbits and such as they,
    So long as men-folk keep away.

"Not near, not near!" her eyes beseech
When one of us comes within reach.
    The women say that beasts in stall

Look round like children at her call.
I've hardly heard her speak at all.

Shy as a leveret, swift as he,
Straight and slight as a young larch tree,
Sweet as the first wild violets, she,
To her wild self. But what to me?

The short days shorten and the oaks are brown,
    The blue smoke rises to the low grey sky,
One leaf in the still air falls slowly down,
    A magpie's spotted feathers lie
On the black earth spread white with rime,
The berries redden up to Christmas-time.
    What's Christmas-time without there be
    Some other in the house than we!
    She sleeps up in the attic there
    Alone, poor maid. 'Tis but a stair
Betwixt us. Oh! my God! the down,
The soft young down of her, the brown,
The brown of her—her eyes, her hair, her hair!

Beside the Bed

Someone has shut the shining eyes, straightened and folded
    The wandering hands quietly covering the unquiet breast:
So, smoothed and silenced you lie, like a child not again to be
        questioned or scolded;
    But, for you, not one of us believes that this is rest.

Not so to close the windows down can cloud and deaden
    The blue beyond: or to screen the wavering flame subdue its breath:
Why, if I lay my cheek to your cheek, your grey lips, like dawn, would
        quiver and redden,
    Breaking into the old, odd smile at this fraud of death.

Because all night you have not turned to us or spoken
    It is time for you to wake; your dreams were never very deep:
I, for one, have seen the thin, bright, twisted threads of them dimmed
        suddenly and broken,
    This is only a most piteous pretence of sleep!

The Trees Are Down

—and he cried with a loud voice:
Hurt not the earth, neither the sea,
* nor the trees—*
                    (Revelation.)

They are cutting down the great plane-trees at the end of the gardens.
For days there has been the grate of the saw, the swish of the branches
    as they fall,
The crash of trunks, the rustle of trodden leaves,
With the "Whoops" and the "Whoas," the loud common talk, the
    loud common laughs of the men, above it all.

I remember one evening of a long past Spring
Turning in at a gate, getting out of a cart, and finding a large dead
    rat in the mud of the drive.
I remember thinking: alive or dead, a rat was a god-forsaken thing,
But at least, in May, that even a rat should be alive.

The week's work here is as good as done. There is just one bough
    On the roped bole, in the fine grey rain,
        Green and high
        And lonely against the sky.
            (Down now!—)
        And but for that,
        If an old dead rat
Did once, for a moment, unmake the Spring, I might never have
    thought of him again.

It is not for a moment the Spring is unmade to-day;
These were great trees, it was in them from root to stem:
When the men with the "Whoops" and the "Whoas" have carted the
    whole of the whispering loveliness away
Half the Spring, for me, will have gone with them.

It is going now, and my heart has been struck with the hearts of the
    planes;
Half my life it has beat with these, in the sun, in the rains,
    In the March wind, the May breeze,
In the great gales that came over to them across the roofs from the
    great seas.

There was only a quiet rain when they were dying;
They must have heard the sparrows flying,
And the small creeping creatures in the earth where they were lying—
But I, all day, I heard an angel crying:
"Hurt not the trees."

Old Shepherd's Prayer

Up to the bed by the window, where I be lyin',
Comes bells and bleat of the flock wi' they two children's clack.
Over, from under the eaves there's the starlings flyin',
And down in yard, fit to burst his chain, yapping out at Sue I do hear
    young Mac.

Turning around like a falled-over sack
I can see team ploughin' in Whithy-bush field and meal carts startin'
    up road to Church-Town;
Saturday arternoon the men goin' back
And the women from market, trapin' home over the down.

Heavenly Master, I wud like to wake to they same green places
Where I be know'd for breakin' dogs and follerin' sheep.
And if I may not walk in th' old ways and look on th' old faces
I wud sooner sleep.

The Cenotaph

September 1919

Not yet will those measureless fields be green again
Where only yesterday the wild sweet blood of wonderful youth was
    shed;
There is a grave whose earth must hold too long, too deep a stain,
Though for ever over it we may speak as proudly as we may tread.
But here, where the watchers by lonely hearths from the thrust of an
    inward sword have more slowly bled,
We shall build the Cenotaph: Victory, winged, with Peace, winged
    too, at the column's head.
And over the stairway, at the foot—oh! here, leave desolate, passionate
    hands to spread
Violets, roses, and laurel, with the small, sweet, twinkling country
    things
Speaking so wistfully of other Springs,

From the little gardens of little places where son or sweetheart was
        born and bred.
In splendid sleep, with a thousand brothers
                To lovers—to mothers
                Here, too, lies he:
Under the purple, the green, the red,
It is all young life: it must break some women's hearts to see
Such a brave, gay coverlet to such a bed!
Only, when all is done and said,
God is not mocked and neither are the dead.
For this will stand in our Market-place—
                Who'll sell, who'll buy
                (Will you or I
Lie each to each with the better grace)?
While looking into every busy whore's and huckster's face
As they drive their bargains, is the Face
Of God: and some young, piteous, murdered face.

Saturday Market

Bury your heart in some deep green hollow
    Or hide it up in a kind old tree;
Better still, give it the swallow
    When she goes over the sea.

In Saturday Market there's eggs a 'plenty
    And dead-alive ducks with their legs tied down,
Grey old gaffers and boys of twenty—
    Girls and the women of the town—
Pitchers and sugar-sticks, ribbons and laces,
    Posies and whips and dicky-birds' seed,
Silver pieces and smiling faces,
    In Saturday Market they've all they need.

What were you showing in Saturday Market
    That set it grinning from end to end
Girls and gaffers and boys of twenty—?
    Cover it close with your shawl, my friend—
Hasten you home with the laugh behind you,
    Over the down—, out of sight,
Fasten your door, though no one will find you,
    No one will look on a Market night.

See, you, the shawl is wet, take out from under
    The red dead thing—. In the white of the moon
On the flags does it stir again? Well, and no wonder!
    Best make an end of it; bury it soon.

If there is blood on the hearth who'll know it?
    Or blood on the stairs,
When a murder is over and done why show it?
    In Saturday Market nobody cares.

Then lie you straight on your bed for a short, short weeping
    And still, for a long, long rest,
There's never a one in the town so sure of sleeping
    As you, in the house on the down with a hole in your breast.

    Think no more of the swallow,
        Forget, you, the sea,
Never again remember the deep green hollow
        Or the top of the kind old tree!

Smile, Death

Smile, Death, see I smile as I come to you
    Straight from the road and the moor that I leave behind,
Nothing on earth to me was like this wind-blown space,
Nothing was like the road, but at the end there was a vision or a face
    And the eyes were not always kind.

    Smile, Death, as you fasten the blades to my feet for me,
On, on let us skate past the sleeping willows dusted with snow;
Fast, fast down the frozen stream, with the moor and the road and the
    vision behind,
    (Show me your face, why the eyes are kind!)
And we will not speak of life or believe in it or remember it as we go.

Willa Cather

Dedicatory

Somewhere, sometime, in an April twilight,
When the hills are hid in violet shadows

When meadow brooks are still and hushed for wonder,
At the ring dove's call as at a summons,
Let us gather from the world's four quarters,
Stealing from the trackless dusk like shadows,
Meet to wait the moon, and greet in silence.
When she swims above the April branches,
Rises clear of naked oak and beeches,
Sit with me beneath the snowy orchard,
Where the white moth hangs with wings entranced,
Drunken with the still perfume of blossoms.
Then, for that the moon was ours of olden,
Let it work again its old enchantment.
Let it, for an April night, transform us
From our grosser selves to happy shadows
Of the three who lay and planned at moonrise,
On an island in a western river,
Of the conquest of the world together.
Let us pour our amber wine and drink it
To the memory of our vanished kingdom,
To our days of war and ocean venture,
Brave with brigandage and sack of cities;
To the Odysseys of summer mornings,
Starry wonder-tales of nights in April.

Grandmither, Think Not I Forget

Grandmither, think not I forget, when I come back to town,
An' wander the old ways again an' tread them up an' down.
I never smell the clover bloom, nor see the swallows pass,
Without I mind how good ye were unto a little lass.
I never hear the winter rain a-pelting all night through,
Without I think and mind me of how cold it falls on you.
And if I come not often to your bed beneath the thyme,
Mayhap 'tis that I'd change wi' ye, and gie my bed for thine,
       Would like to sleep in thine.

I never hear the summer winds among the roses blow,
Without I wonder why it was ye loved the lassie so.
Ye gave me cakes and lollipops and pretty toys a score, —
I never thought I should come back and ask ye now for more.

Grandmither, gie me your still, white hands, that lie upon your breast,
For mine do beat the dark all night and never find me rest;
They grope among the shadows an' they beat the cold black air,
They go seekin' in the darkness, an' they never find him there,
   An' they never find him there.

Grandmither, gie me your sightless eyes, that I may never see
His own a-burnin' full o' love that must not shine for me.
Grandmither, gie me your peaceful lips, white as the kirkyard snow,
For mine be red wi' burnin' thirst, an' he must never know.
Grandmither, gie me your clay-stopped ears, that I may never hear
My lad a'singin' in the night when I am sick wi' fear;
A-singin' when the moonlight over a' the land is white—
Aw God! I'll up an' go to him a-singin' in the night,
   A-callin' in the night.

Grandmither, gie me your clay-cold heart that has forgot to ache,
For mine be fire within my breast and yet it cannot break.
It beats an' throbs forever for the things that must not be, —
An' can ye not let me creep in an' rest awhile by ye?
A little lass afeard o' dark slept by ye years agone—
Ah, she has found what night can hold 'twixt sunset an' the dawn!
So when I plant the rose an' rue above your grave for ye,
Ye'll know it's under rue an' rose that I would like to be,
   That I would like to be.

Amy Lowell

The Cyclists

Spread on the roadway,
With open-blown jackets,
Like black, soaring pinions,
They swoop down the hillside,
 The Cyclists.

Seeming dark-plumaged
Birds, after carrion,
Careening and circling,

Over the dying
  Of England.

She lies with her bosom
Beneath them, no longer
The Dominant Mother,
The Virile—but rotting
  Before time.

The smell of her, tainted,
Has bitten their nostrils.
Exultant they hover,
And shadow the sun with
  Foreboding.

The Basket

I

The inkstand is full of ink, and the paper lies white and unspotted, in the round of light thrown by a candle. Puffs of darkness sweep into the corners, and keep rolling through the room behind his chair. The air is silver and pearl, for the night is liquid with moonlight.

See how the roof glitters like ice!

Over there, a slice of yellow cuts into the silver-blue, and beside it stand two geraniums, purple because the light is silver-blue, to-night.

See! She is coming, the young woman with the bright hair. She swings a basket as she walks, which she places on the sill, between the geranium stalks. He laughs, and crumples his paper as he leans forward to look. "The Basket Filled with Moonlight," what a title for a book!

The bellying clouds swing over the housetops.

He has forgotten the woman in the room with the geraniums. He is beating his brain, and in his eardrums hammers his heavy pulse. She sits on the window-sill, with the basket in her lap. And tap! She cracks a nut. And tap! Another. Tap! Tap! Tap! The shells ricochet upon the roof, and get into the gutters, and bounce over the edge and disappear.

"It is very queer," thinks Peter, "the basket was empty, I'm sure. How could nuts appear from the atmosphere?"

The silver-blue moonlight makes the geraniums purple, and the roof glitters like ice.

II

Five o'clock. The geraniums are very gay in their crimson array. The bellying clouds swing over the housetops, and over the roofs goes Peter to pay his morning's work with a holiday.

"Annette, it is I. Have you finished? Can I come?"

Peter jumps through the window.

"Dear, are you alone?"

"Look, Peter, the dome of the tabernacle is done. This gold thread is so very high, I am glad it is morning, a starry sky would have seen me bankrupt. Sit down, now tell me, is your story going well?"

The golden dome glittered in the orange of the setting sun. On the walls, at intervals, hung altar-cloths and chasubles, and copes, and stoles, and coffin palls. All stiff with rich embroidery, and stitched with so much artistry, they seemed like spun and woven gems, or flower-buds new-opened on their stems.

Annette looked at the geraniums, very red against the blue sky.

"No matter how I try, I cannot find any thread of such a red. My bleeding hearts drip stuff muddy in comparison. Heigh-ho! See my little pecking dove? I'm in love with my own temple. Only that halo's wrong. The colour's too strong, or not strong enough. I don't know. My eyes are tired. Oh, Peter, don't be so rough; it is valuable. I won't do any more. I promise. You tyrannise, Dear, that's enough. Now sit down and amuse me while I rest."

The shadows of the geraniums creep over the floor, and begin to climb the opposite wall.

Peter watches her, fluid with fatigue, floating, and drifting, and undulant in the orange glow. His senses flow towards her, where she lies supine and dreaming. Seeming drowned in a golden halo.

The pungent smell of the geraniums is hard to bear.

He pushes against her knees, and brushes his lips across her languid hands. His lips are hot and speechless. He woos her, quivering, and the room is filled with shadows, for the sun has set. But she only understands the ways of a needle through delicate stuffs, and the shock of one colour on another. She does not see that this is the same, and querulously murmurs his name.

"Peter, I don't want it. I am tired."
And he, the undesired, burns and is consumed.
There is a crescent moon on the rim of the sky.

III

"Go home, now, Peter. To-night is full moon. I must be alone."
"How soon the moon is full again! Annette, let me stay. Indeed,
Dear Love, I shall not go away. My God, but you keep me starved!
You write 'No Entrance Here,' over all the doors. Is it not strange, my
Dear, that loving, yet you deny me entrance everywhere. Would
marriage strike you blind, or, hating bonds as you do, why should I
be denied the rights of loving if I leave you free? You want the
whole of me, you pick my brains to rest you, but you give me not one
heart-beat. Oh, forgive me, Sweet! I suffer in my loving, and you know
it. I cannot feed my life on being a poet. Let me stay."
"As you please, poor Peter, but it will hurt me if you do. It will
crush your heart and squeeze the love out."
He answered gruffly, "I know what I'm about."
"Only remember one thing from to-night. My work is taxing and
I must have sight! I MUST!"
The clear moon looks in between the geraniums. On the wall, the
shadow of the man is divided from the shadow of the woman by a
silver thread.
They are eyes, hundreds of eyes, round like marbles! Unwinking,
for there are no lids. Blue, black, gray, and hazel, and the irises are
cased in the whites, and they glitter and spark under the moon. The
basket is heaped with human eyes. She cracks off the whites and
throws them away. They ricochet upon the roof, and get into the
gutters, and bounce over the edge and disappear. But she is here,
quietly sitting on the window-sill, eating human eyes.
The silver-blue moonlight makes the geraniums purple, and the
roof shines like ice.

IV

How hot the sheets are! His skin is tormented with pricks, and
over him sticks, and never moves, an eye. It lights the sky with blood,
and drips blood. And the drops sizzle on his bare skin, and he smells
them burning in, and branding his body with the name "Annette."
The blood-red sky is outside his window now. Is it blood or fire?
Merciful God! Fire! And his heart wrenches and pounds "Annette!"

179

The lead of the roof is scorching, he ricochets, gets to the edge, bounces over and disappears.

The bellying clouds are red as they swing over the housetops.

V

The air is of silver and pearl, for the night is liquid with moonlight. How the ruin glistens, like a palace of ice! Only two black holes swallow the brilliance of the moon. Deflowered windows, sockets without sight.

A man stands before the house. He sees the silver-blue moonlight, and set in it, over his head, staring and flickering, eyes of geranium red.

Annette!

Adelaide Crapsey

Cinquains

TRIAD

These be
Three silent things:
The falling snow . . . the hour
Before the dawn . . . the mouth of one
Just dead.

SUSANNA AND THE ELDERS

"Why do
You thus devise
Evil against her?" "For that
She is beautiful, delicate;
Therefore."

THE GUARDED WOUND

If it
Were lighter touch
Than petal of flower resting
On grass, oh still too heavy it were,
Too heavy!

The Warning

Just now,
Out of the strange
Still dusk . . . as strange, as still . . .
A white moth flew. Why am I grown
So cold?

Mina Loy

Love Songs

1

Spawn of fantasies
Sifting the appraisable
Pig Cupid   his rosy snout
Rooting erotic garbage
"Once upon a time"
Pulls a weed   white-star-topped
Among wild oats sown in mucous membrane
I would   an eye in a Bengal light
Eternity in a sky-rocket
Constellations in an ocean
Whose rivers run no fresher
Than a trickle of saliva

These are suspect places

I must live in my lantern
Trimming subliminal flicker
Virginal   to the bellows
Of experience
                Colored glass.

4

Evolution fall foul of
Sexual equality
Prettily miscalculate
Similitude

The Women Poets in English

Unnatural selection
Breed such sons and daughters
As shall jibber at each other
Uninterpretable cryptonyms
Under the moon

Give them some way of braying brassily
For caressive calling
Or to homophonous hiccoughs
Transpose the laugh
Let them suppose that tears
Are snowdrops or molasses
Or anything
Than human insufficiencies
Begging dorsal vertebrae

Let meeting be the turning
To the antipodean
And Form   a blurr
Anything
Than seduce them
To the one
As simple satisfaction
For the other

7

Once in a messanino
The starry ceiling
Vaulted an unimaginable family
Bird-like abortions
With human throats
And Wisdom's eyes
Who wore lamp-shade red dresses
And woolen hair

One bore a baby
In a padded porte-enfant
Tied with a sarsenet ribbon
To her goose's wings

But for the abominable shadows
I would have lived

Among their fearful furniture
To teach them to tell me their secrets
Before I guessed
—Sweeping the brood clean out

9

We might have coupled
In the bed-ridden monopoly of a moment
Or broken flesh with one another
At the profane communion table
Where wine is spill't on promiscuous lips

We might have given birth to a butterfly
With the daily-news
Printed in blood on its wings

12

Shedding out petty pruderies
From slit eyes

We sidle up
to Nature
        that irate pornographist

Lola Ridge

Saint's Bridge

Light across the courtyard
intercepts the snow . . .
swarming particles of light
follow each other in shimmering confusion,
as though the moon were snowing out of her mountains,
emptying her craters of their silvery ash . . .
light
spinning a gossamer trestle
swung from the flame of windows,
reaching a broad and shining arm
on which saints might hang their garments.

Spring

A spring wind on the Bowery,
Blowing the fluff of night shelters
Off bedraggled garments,
And agitating the gutters, that eject little spirals of vapor
Like lewd growths.

Bare-legged children stamp in the puddles,
    splashing each other,
One—with a choir-boy's face
Twits me as I pass . . .
The word, like a muddied drop,
Seems to roll over and not out of
The bowed lips,
Yet dewy red
And sweetly immature.

People sniff the air with an upward look—
Even the mite of a girl
Who never plays . . .
Her mother smiles at her
With eyes like vacant lots
Rimming vistas of mean streets
And endless washing days . . .
Yet with sun on the lines
And a drying breeze.

The old candy woman
Shivers in the young wind.
Her eyes—littered with memories
Like ancient garrets,
Or dusty unaired rooms where someone died—
Ask nothing of the spring.

But a pale pink dream
Trembles about this young girl's body,
Draping it like a glowing aura.

She gloats in a mirror
Over her gaudy hat,
With its flower God never thought of . . .

And the dream, unrestrained,
Floats about the loins of a soldier,
Where it quivers a moment,
Warming to a crimson
Like the scarf of a toreador . . .

But the delicate gossamer breaks at his contact
And recoils to her in strands of shattered rose.

The Fifth-Floor Window

Walls . . . iridescent with eyes
that stare into the courtyard
at the still thing lying
in the turned-back snow . . .
stark precipice of walls
with a foam of white faces
lathering their stone lips . . .
faces of the shawled women
the walls pour forth without aim
under the vast pallor of the sky.

They point at the fifth-floor window
and whisper one to the other:
"It's hard on a man out of work
an' the mother gone out of his door
with a younger lover . . ."

The blanched morning stares
in like a face flattened against the pane
where the little girl used to cry all day
with a feeble and goading cry.
Her father, with his eyes at bay
before the vague question of the light,
says that she fell . . .
Between his twitching lips
a stump of cigarette
smoulders, like a burning root.

Only the wind was abroad
in high cold hours
of the icy and sightless night
with back to the stars—

night growing white and still as a pillar of salt
and the snow mushing without sound—
when something hurtled through the night
and drifted like a larger snow-flake
in the trek of the blind snow
that stumbled over it in heaps—
only white-furred wind
pawed at the fifth-floor window
and nosed cigarette-butts on the sill . . .
till the window closed down softly
on the silvery fleece of wind
that tore and left behind its flying fringes.

The Song

That day, in the slipping of torsos and straining flanks on the bloodied
    ooze of fields plowed by the iron,
And the smoke bluish near earth and bronze in the sunshine floating
    like cotton-down,
And the harsh and terrible screaming,
And that strange vibration at the roots of us . . .
Desire, fierce, like a song . . .
And we heard
(Do you remember?)
All the Red Cross bands on Fifth avenue
And bugles in little home towns
And children's harmonicas bleating

America!

And after . . .
(Do you remember?)
The drollery of the wind on our faces,
And horizons reeling,
And the terror of the plain
Heaving like a gaunt pelvis to the sun . . .
Under us—threshing and twanging
Torn-up roots of the Song . . .

Veteran

On a morning such as this
He comes out early to the curb

He knows
On mornings such as this
When life leaps in whole bodies like a colt
That pulls upon the leash . . .
Men give to what they hate
And shudder . . . and walk on elate,
With beautiful loud feet and upon the silence
That rears up like a formless head
Out of the blind stone.

And so
On mornings such as this
Before the air has lost that sweet astringency
He comes more early to the curb
And feels the sunlight soft as a warm fleece,
The eager light
That gambols down the pavement like a lamb
And stumbles on him with its shining feet.

From *Ward X*

The Salvation Army lass
has arms like thin white moonbeams
she twists her pillow toward a patch of sky—
a mauve-rose awning over herded lights.
Her body seems to depend from her eyes—
eyes eager-blue as marbles
that have rolled in many gutters
yet stayed miraculously clean.
Her hands monotonously
scoop up the shallow moonlight,
pale as weak lemonade,
that spills through her fingers
over the white sheet.
—The moon is of little account here
with that strong light in the corridor.
Now over the Battery—
all the Bay to herself
and Sunday boats coming in—
The moon'll be bright as Jesus
walking upon the water.

Electrocution

He shudders . . . feeling on the shaven spot
The probing wind, that stabs him to a thought
Of storm-drenched fields in a white foam of light,
And roads of his hill-town that leap to sight
Like threads of tortured silver . . . while the guards—
Monstrous deft dolls that move as on a string,
In wonted haste to finish with this thing,
Turn faces blanker than asphalted yards.

They heard the shriek that tore out of its sheath
But as a feeble moan . . . yet dared not breathe,
Who stared there at him, arching—like a tree
When the winds wrench it and the earth holds tight—
Whose soul, expanding in white agony,
Had fused in flaming circuit with the night.

Reveille

Come forth, you workers!
Let the fires go cold—
Let the iron spill out, out of the troughs—
Let the iron run wild
Like a red bramble on the floors—
Leave the mill and the foundry and the mine
And the shrapnel lying on the wharves—
Leave the desk and the shuttle and the loom—
Come,
With your ashen lives,
Your lives like dust in your hands.

I call upon you, workers.
It is not yet light
But I beat upon your doors.
You say you await the Dawn
But I say you are the Dawn.
Come, in your irresistible unspent force
And make new light upon the mountains.

You have turned deaf ears to others—
Me you shall hear.
Out of the mouths of turbines,

Out of the turgid throats of engines,
Over the whistling steam,
You shall hear me shrilly piping.
Your mills I shall enter like the wind,
And blow upon your hearts,
Kindling the slow fire.

They think they have tamed you, workers—
Beaten you to a tool
To scoop up hot honor
Till it be cool—
But out of the passion of the red frontiers
A great flower trembles and burns and glows
And each of its petals is a people.

Come forth, you workers—
Clinging to your stable
And your wisp of warm straw—
Let the fires grow cold,
Let the iron spill out of the troughs,
Let the iron run wild
Like a red bramble on the floors. . . .

As our forefathers stood on the prairies
So let us stand in a ring,
Let us tear up their prisons like grass
And beat them to barricades—
Let us meet the fire of their guns
With a greater fire,
Till the birds shall fly to the mountains
For one safe bough.

 _____

Ethel Anderson

From *Bucolic Eclogues*

Waking, child, while you slept, your mother took
Down from its wooden peg her reaping-hook,
Rustless with use, to cut (her task when dawn
With nervous light would bead the dusky leaves)

From the cold wheat-paddock's shivering fringe, two sheaves;
Against a block she'd thrash the golden grain,
Then winnow corn and husk, and toss again,
And yet again, her dish, and frisk the chaff
Wide to the wind;
Then grind,
Her new steel hand-mill being still the pride
Of the astonished country-side.
Her meal cooked, she'd call men and children in;
With bustling care, in genial haste, not late
Her cows she'd milk, her butter churn and set
Fresh cream in scalded pans. Her hens she'd feed
With hot scraps, stirred in pollard from the bin;
Then give her dribbling calves what drink they need,
Or drive with flowery staff
Meek stragglers through the gate;
Or on her youngest-born
Impose the fret,
The letter'd tyranny, of the alphabet.

    Yet in this daily round
    She nothing trivial found
    A little love to earn
    She, but a girl, did learn;

To dig, to delve, to drive wild cattle in,
('Ester, ley thou thy mekeness al a-doun')
To scour, to sweep, to wash and iron, to spin;
('Penalopee and Marcia Catoun
Make of your wifehood no comparisoun,')
To sew, to darn, to cook, to bake, to brew,
To bear, to rear, to nurse her children, too;
('And Cleopatre, with al thy passioun
Hyde ye your trouthe of love, and your renoun.')

Though, child, your mother, trembling, smiled at fear,
Fears had she; the blackfellow's cruel spear,
White desperadoes. When to the open well
She crept at nightfall, being all alone,
The well, with sheoaks ringed, where dark and slow
Stole east-going, prostrate shades; where one would go,

Sometimes, bolt upright, darker and less slow
But noiseless, too, her warlike bandolier
And bell-mouthed blunderbuss (all else disown
Having new flintlocks) would her terrors tell.

For comfort, then, she'd watch her frugal rush,
The only gleam in all that virgin bush,
Cheer the unshutter'd, distant, window-pane;
Then hoist her twirling bucket yet again;
Or, set beyond the tassell'd corn-cobs, see
Her chimney's sepia plume
For Hesperus make room;
Or, through the peppermint-tree,
A crescent, coasting moon a reef of stars
Skirt; or a dangerous Jupiter, or Mars;
As on that happy night when in her pride
Quickening, she felt her son stir in her side.

When in a drought the waterholes ran dry
And of 'dry-bible' half the herds would die,
And others in their agony creep to lie
About the homestead, moaning piteously,
Or, famished, on the deadly purple weed,
Or poisonous variegated thistle, feed,
—The purple weed that lames—or in the creek,
Among dead frogs, dead ferns, water would seek;
The men being absent, then, to give release,
She brought to every suffering brute death's peace;
     Who never heard the rain
     Fall, but she heard again
     The cattle in their pain.

But in a lucky year your mother's care
Was all to save the wealth her orchard bore;
Apples and plums, peach, apricot and pear,
Mandarins, nectarines, tangerines, a score
Of rosy berries, currants and their kind;
Drying these last, through muslin she would squeeze
Damson or apple cheese;
Quinces conserve; bottle black mulberries;
Sweet cherries and strawberries in honey seal;
Float cumquats in syrup; candy lemon-peel;

Or, versed in the housewife's alchemy once more,
Jams in her pantry stack—a round fourscore.

She for her cellar with a cheerful mind
Would brew in tubs peach-beer,
Sparkling and clear,
Rub pears, and trinities of apples bruise
To perry and cider in a wooden cruse.
Of keeving and pomace then gossip ran.
One servant assigned her being a Devon man,
Whose convict clothes and homely face—so kind—
Smiling, you may remember, musing on
The knight, his grandson and the judge, his son.

Elizabeth Madox Roberts

Cold Fear

As I came home through Drury's woods,
My face stung in the hard sleet.
The rough ground kept its frozen tracks;
They stumbled my feet.

The trees shook off the blowing frost.
The wind found out my coat was thin.
It tried to tear my clothes away.
And the cold came in.

The ice drops rattled where there was ice.
Each tree pushed back the other ones.
I did not pass a single bird,
Or anything that crawls or runs.

I saw a moth wing that was dry
And thin; it hung against a burr.
A few black leaves turned in a bush;
The grass was like cold, dead fur.

As I climbed over Howard's fence,
The wind came there with a sudden rush.
My teeth made a chattering sound,
And a bush said, "Hush!"

When I was in our house again,
With people there and fire and light,
A thought kept coming back to say,
"It will be cold out there tonight."

The clods are cold and the stones are cold,
The stiff trees shake and the hard air, . . .
And something said again to me,
"It will be cold out there."

And even when I talked myself,
And all the talk made a happy sound,
I kept remembering the wind
And the cold ground.

Elinor Wylie

Wild Peaches

I

When the world turns completely upside down
You say we'll emigrate to the Eastern Shore
Aboard a river-boat from Baltimore;
We'll live among wild peach trees, miles from town,
You'll wear a coonskin cap, and I a gown
Homespun, dyed butternut's dark gold colour.
Lost, like your lotus-eating ancestor,
We'll swim in milk and honey till we drown.

The winter will be short, the summer long,
The autumn amber-hued, sunny and hot,
Tasting of cider and of scuppernong;
All seasons sweet, but autumn best of all.
The squirrels in their silver fur will fall
Like falling leaves, like fruit, before your shot.

2

The autumn frosts will lie upon the grass
Like bloom on grapes of purple-brown and gold.
The misted early mornings will be cold;

The little puddles will be roofed with glass.
The sun, which burns from copper into brass,
Melts these at noon, and makes the boys unfold
Their knitted mufflers; full as they can hold,
Fat pockets dribble chestnuts as they pass.

Peaches grow wild, and pigs can live in clover;
A barrel of salted herrings lasts a year;
The spring begins before the winter's over.
By February you may find the skins
Of garter snakes and water moccasins
Dwindled and harsh, dead-white and cloudy-clear.

3

When April pours the colours of a shell
Upon the hills, when every little creek
Is shot with silver from the Chesapeake
In shoals new-minted by the ocean swell,
When strawberries go begging, and the sleek
Blue plums lie open to the blackbird's beak,
We shall live well—we shall live very well.

The months between the cherries and the peaches
Are brimming cornucopias which spill
Fruits red and purple, sombre-bloomed and black;
Then, down rich fields and frosty river beaches
We'll trample bright persimmons, while you kill
Bronze partridge, speckled quail, and canvasback.

4

Down to the Puritan marrow of my bones
There's something in this richness that I hate.
I love the look, austere, immaculate,
Of landscapes drawn in pearly monotones.
There's something in my very blood that owns
Bare hills, cold silver on a sky of slate,
A thread of water, churned to milky spate
Streaming through slanted pastures fenced with stones.

I love those skies, thin blue or snowy gray,
Those fields sparse-planted, rendering meagre sheaves;
That spring, briefer than apple-blossom's breath,

Summer, so much too beautiful to stay,
Swift autumn, like a bonfire of leaves,
And sleepy winter, like the sleep of death.

Hughie at the Inn

Is it not fine to fling against loaded dice
Yet to win once or twice?
To bear a rusty sword without an edge
Yet wound the thief in the hedge?
To be unhorsed, and drown in horrid muck,
And in at the death, by luck?
To meet a masked assassin in a cape
And kill him, and escape?
To have the usurers all your fortune take,
And a bare living make
By industry, and your brow's personal sweat?
To be caught in the bird-net
Of a bad marriage; then to be trepanned
And stranded on foreign land?
To be cast into a prison damp and vile,
And break bars, with a blunt file?
To be cut down from gallows while you breathe
And live, by the skin of your teeth?
To defy the tyrant world, and at a pinch
To wrest from it an inch?
To engage the stars in combat, and therefrom
Pluck a hair's breadth of room?
Is it not fine, worthy of Titans or gods,
To challenge such heavy odds?
But no, but no, my lad;
'Tis cruel chance gone mad;
A stab in the back; a serpent in the breast;
And worst that murders best.
Such broad and open affronts to fear and pain
Breed maggots in the brain;
They are not valour, but the merest rash
Rubbish and balderdash.
Fortune's a drab, and vice her native soil,
And the button's off her foil.
Season your ale, now these long nights draw in,

With thought to save your skin:
Be provident, and pray for cowardice
And the loaded pair of dice.

Hilda Doolittle (H. D.)

Hermes of the Ways

The hard sand breaks,
and the grains of it
are clear as wine.

Far off over the leagues of it,
the wind,
playing on the wide shore,
piles little ridges,
and the great waves
break over it.

But more than the many-foamed ways
of the sea,
I know him
of the triple path-ways,
Hermes,
who awaits.

Dubious,
facing three ways,
welcoming wayfarers,
he whom the sea-orchard
shelters from the west,
from the east
weathers sea-wind;
fronts the great dunes.

Wind rushes
over the dunes,
and the coarse, salt-crusted grass
answers.

Heu,
it whips round my ankles!

II

Small is
this white stream,
flowing below ground
from the poplar-shaded hill,
but the water is sweet.

Apples on the small trees
are hard,
too small,
too late ripened
by a desperate sun
that struggles through sea-mist.

The boughs of the trees
are twisted
by many bafflings;
twisted are
the small-leafed boughs.

But the shadow of them
is not the shadow of the mast head
nor of the torn sails.

Hermes, Hermes,
the great sea foamed,
gnashed its teeth about me;
but you have waited,
where sea-grass tangles with
shore-grass.

Pursuit

What do I care
that the stream is trampled,
the sand on the stream-bank
still holds the print of your foot:
the heel is cut deep.
I see another mark
on the grass ridge of the bank—
it points toward the wood-path.
I have lost the third
in the packed earth.

But here
a wild-hyacinth stalk is snapped:
the purple buds—half ripe—
show deep purple
where your heel pressed.

A patch of flowering grass,
low, trailing—
you brushed this:
the green stems show yellow-green
where you lifted—turned the earth-side
to the light:
this and a dead leaf-spine,
split across,
show where you passed.

You were swift, swift!
here the forest ledge slopes—
rain has furrowed the roots.
Your hand caught at this;
the root snapped under your weight.

I can almost follow the note
where it touched this slender tree
and the next answered—
and the next.

And you climbed yet further!
you stopped by the dwarf-cornel—
whirled on your heels,
doubled on your track.

This is clear—
you fell on the downward slope,
you dragged a bruised thigh—you limped—
you clutched this larch.

Did your head, bent back,
search further—
clear through the green leaf-moss
of the larch branches?

Did you clutch,
stammer with short breath and gasp:

wood-daemons grant life—
give life—I am almost lost.

For some wood-daemon
has lightened your steps.
I can find no trace of you
in the larch-cones and the underbrush.

Evening

The light passes
from ridge to ridge,
from flower to flower—
the hypaticas, wide-spread
under the light
grow faint—
the petals reach inward,
the blue tips bend
toward the bluer heart
and the flowers are lost.

The cornel-buds are still white,
but shadows dart
from the cornel-roots—
black creeps from root to root,
each leaf
cuts another leaf on the grass,
shadow seeks shadow,
then both leaf
and leaf-shadow are lost.

The Wind Sleepers

Whiter
than the crust
left by the tide,
we are stung by the hurled sand
and the broken shells.

We no longer sleep
in the wind—
we awoke and fled
through the city gate.

199

Tear—
tear us an altar,
tug at the cliff-boulders,
pile them with the rough stones—
we no longer
sleep in the wind,
propitiate us.

Chant in a wail
that never halts,
pace a circle and pay tribute
with a song.

When the roar of a dropped wave
breaks into it,
pour meted words
of sea-hawks and gulls
and sea-birds that cry
discords.

Edith Sitwell

The Swans

In the green light of water, like the day
Under green boughs, the spray
And air-pale petals of the foam seem flowers, —
Dark-leaved arbutus blooms with wax-pale bells
And their faint honey-smells,
The velvety syringa with smooth leaves,
Gloxinia with a green shade in the snow,
Jasmine and moon-clear orange-blossoms and green blooms
Of the wild strawberries from the shade of woods.
Their showers
Pelt the white women under the green trees,
Venusia, Cosmopolita, Pistillarine—
White solar statues, white rose-trees in snow
Flowering for ever, child-women, half stars
Half flowers, waves of the sea, born of a dream.

Their laughter flying through the trees like doves,
These angels come to watch their whiter ghosts
In the air-pale water, archipelagos
Of stars and young thin moons from great wings falling
As ripples widen.
These are their ghosts, their own white angels these!
O great wings spreading—
Your bones are made of amber, smooth and thin
Grown from the amber dust that was a rose
Or nymph in swan-smooth waters.
                                        But Time's winter falls
With snows as soft, as soundless. . . . Then, who knows
Rose-footed swan from snow, or girl from rose?

Marianne Moore

The Steeple-Jack

Dürer would have seen a reason for living
        in a town like this, with eight stranded whales
to look at; with the sweet sea air coming into your house
on a fine day, from water etched
        with waves as formal as the scales
on a fish.

One by one, in two's, in three's, the seagulls keep
        flying back and forth over the town clock,
or sailing around the lighthouse without moving their wings—
rising steadily with a slight
        quiver of the body—or flock
mewing where

a sea the purple of the peacock's neck is
        paled to greenish azure as Dürer changed
the pine green of the Tyrol to peacock blue and guinea
grey. You can see a twenty-five-
        pound lobster and fish-nets arranged
to dry. The

whirlwind fife-and-drum of the storm bends the salt
        marsh grass, disturbs stars in the sky and the

star on the steeple; it is a privilege to see so
much confusion.

        A steeple-jack in red, has let
    a rope down as a spider spins a thread;
he might be part of a novel, but on the sidewalk a
sign says C. J. Poole, Steeple-Jack,
    in black and white; and one in red
and white says

Danger. The church portico has four fluted
    columns, each a single piece of stone, made
modester by white-wash. This would be a fit haven for
waifs, children, animals, prisoners,
    and presidents who have repaid
sin-driven

senators by not thinking about them. One
    sees a school-house, a post-office in a
store, fish-houses, hen-houses, a three-masted schooner on
the stocks. The hero, the student,
    the steeple-jack, each in his way,
is at home.

It scarcely could be dangerous to be living
    in a town like this, of simple people
who have a steeple-jack placing danger-signs by the church
when he is gilding the solid-
    pointed star, which on a steeple
stands for hope.

A Grave

Man looking into the sea,
taking the view from those who have as much right to it as you have
    to it yourself,
it is human nature to stand in the middle of a thing,
but you cannot stand in the middle of this;
the sea has nothing to give but a well excavated grave.
The firs stand in a procession, each with an emerald turkey foot at the
    top,
reserved as their contours, saying nothing;

repression, however, is not the most obvious characteristic of the sea;
the sea is a collector, quick to return a rapacious look.
There are others besides you who have worn that look—
whose expression is no longer a protest; the fish no longer investigate
  them
for their bones have not lasted:
men lower nets, unconscious of the fact that they are desecrating a
  grave,
and row quickly away—the blades of the oars
moving together like the feet of water-spiders as if there were no such
  thing as death.
The wrinkles progress among themselves in a phalanx—beautiful
  under networks of foam,
and fade breathlessly while the sea rustles in and out of the seaweed;
the birds swim through the air at top speed, emitting catcalls as here-
  tofore—
the tortoise shell scourges about the feet of the cliffs, in motion beneath
  them;
and the ocean, under the pulsation of lighthouses and noise of bell
  buoys,
advances as usual, looking as if it were not that ocean in which
  dropped things are bound to sink—
in which if they turn and twist, it is neither with volition nor con-
  sciousness.

Saint Nicholas,

  might I, if you can find it, be given
a chameleon with tail
that curls like a watch spring; and vertical
on the body—including the face—pale
  tiger-stripes, about seven;
      (the melanin in the skin
      having been shaded from the sun by thin
        bars; the spinal dome
          beaded along the ridge
          as if it were platinum).

  If you can find no striped chameleon,
might I have a dress or suit—
I guess you have heard of it—of *qiviut?*

and to wear with it, a taslon shirt, the drip-dry fruit
　　of research second to none;
　　　　sewn, I hope, by Excello;
　　　　as for buttons to keep down the collar-points, no.
　　　　　The shirt could be white—
　　　　　　and be "worn before six,"
　　　　　either in daylight or at night.

　　But don't give me, if I can't have the dress,
a trip to Greenland, or grim
trip to the moon. The moon should come here. Let him
make the trip down, spread on my dark floor some dim
　　marvel, and if a success
　　　　that I stoop to pick up and wear,
　　　　I could ask nothing more. A thing yet more rare,
　　　　　though, and different,
　　　　　　would be this; Hans von Marées'
　　　　　St. Hubert, kneeling with head bent,

　　　form erect—in velvet, tense with restraint—
hand hanging down: the horse, free.
Not the original, of course. Give me
a postcard of the scene—huntsman and divinity—
　　　hunt-mad Hubert startled into a saint
　　　　by a stag with a Figure entined.
　　　　But why tell you what you must have divined?
　　　　　Saint Nicholas, O Santa Claus,
　　　　　　would it not be the most
　　　　　prized gift that ever was!

Dorothy Wellesley

Lost Lane

Catkins, like caterpillars slung arow,
Roof over with sloe blossom this lost track
And speckle it with shadow. Deep in June
Afloat with weed and wrack
It sways, a sunken garden in a tide

Of apple-green, and there
Each evening at the light end of the lane
Cassiopeia, Lady in her Chair,
Sits light and elegant, watching with me
The Zodiac blaze on the twelve compass points:
The spiteful Scorpion; sentimental Twins;
The Crab with crazy joints;
The Water Carrier, watering the dark
With drench of diamonds; jewelled Archer wild
With hair of ravelled gold; Goat, Virgin, Scales
Swarming on space like spattered bees; once styled
From dark Chaldean Towers the gates of suns.
Down here, where labourers pass,
Striding the stile, the polished bar has caught
Those royal highways in a looking-glass,
Holding them prisoner till the autumn comes;
Then with a swoop and glitter,
Then with a gale the Sickle gets aswing
Across the sky to reap the stars, to litter
With spirtled stars the fallow and the corn,
The villages we know; till roof and spire,
And hedgerow timbers in familiar fields,
Are streaked with fire;
So that the gardener on his honour sworn
Tells me a meteor fell last night; and went
To seek inside the line of rabbit wire
A star among the cabbages at dawn.

Lighthouses

The night sea quickens. On the shoal or rock
Lighthouses take the shock,
The tumbling sea-lights clap with bell and gong
On buoys whose silences are drawn out long
By west-bound rollers; off the Shambles Banks,
The Manacles, the Varne, the Dancing Ledge,
The Kentish Knock, and the long Shingle Edge,
All join the clamour; grappled to the flanks
Of sunken wrecks, three-balled the lightship lurches,
Her wreck-sign painted up in green and white
Apparent in the night;

Or, off the quicksands, where the sunken churches,
As sea-tales tell, give peal before a storm,
A beacon out for harm,
Will drag its moorings, lead with light astray
Lost ships from Goodwin up to Stornoway.

Of old an oak-fed cresset, or a grate,
Stoked by nude figures firelit in the foam,
Brought all the wanderers home
Within the harbour gate
Of templed Rhodes, to a snow-skerried head;
These burn no longer.
                Now untenanted,
Arching horizons with a moving zone,
Lanterns of volatile spirit burn alone:
Upon outlying stacks
Of rock, facing the full fetch of the seas,
In roaring tideways, where the honking geese
Smash in the shimmering plate-glass, break their backs:
Or, hitched on ice-towers built above the race
Of travelling floes that bite upon the base,
Great lanterns turn. They light a rag of waves
Off Portland Bill, South Foreland, Dungeness,
Off promontory or ness,
Off Biscay, or the Longships or the Graves;
Off the great lighthouse built at Skerryvore,
Upon the Atlantic.

              There the granite blocks,
Are dovetailed, joggled into knots and locks,
And bastions take the onslaughts, and the bore
Of water breaks, and spray
Alone may spend itself; unlike the day
When waves shot up the curved face of the tower,
Washing the lantern, builder, fog-bell off
Into the trough,
And after scurry and scour
Weltered a moment in foam-netted spate,
And gathered, mustered force, and charged anew
On iron girder, layered metal plate,
And sliced the steel in two.

Edna St. Vincent Millay

The Cameo

Forever over now, forever, forever gone
That day. Clear and diminished like a scene
Carven in cameo, the lighthouse, and the cove between
The sandy cliffs, and the boat drawn up on the beach;
And the long skirt of a lady innocent and young,
Her hand resting on her bosom, her head hung;
And the figure of a man in earnest speech.

Clear and diminished like a scene cut in cameo
The lighthouse, and the boat on the beach, and the two shapes
Of the woman and the man; lost like the lost day
Are the words that passed, and the pain,—discarded, cut away
From the stone, as from the memory the heat of the tears escapes.

O troubled forms, O early love unfortunate and hard,
Time has estranged you into a jewel cold and pure;
From the action of the waves and from the action of sorrow forever
    secure,
White against a ruddy cliff you stand, chalcedony on sard.

On the Wide Heath

On the wide heath at evening overtaken,
    When the fast-reddening sun
Drops, and against the sky the looming bracken
    Waves, and the day is done,

Though no unfriendly nostril snuffs his bone,
    Though English wolves be dead,
The fox abroad on errands of his own,
    The adder gone to bed,

The weary traveler from his aching hip
    Lengthens his long stride;
Though Home be but a humming on his lip,
    No happiness, no pride,

He does not drop him under the yellow whin
    To sleep the darkness through;
Home to the yellow light that shines within
    The kitchen of a loud shrew,

Home over stones and sand, through stagnant water
    He goes, mile after mile
Home to a wordless poaching son and a daughter
    With a disdainful smile,

Home to the worn reproach, the disagreeing,
    The shelter, the stale air; content to be
Pecked at, confined, encroached upon, —it being
    Too lonely, to be free.

To Inez Milholland

*Read in Washington, November
eighteenth, 1923, at the unveiling
of a statue of three leaders in the
cause of Equal Rights for Women.*

Upon this marble bust that is not I
Lay the round, formal wreath that is not fame;
But in the forum of my silenced cry
Root ye the living tree whose sap is flame.
I, that was proud and valiant, am no more; —
Save as a dream that wanders wide and late,
Save as a wind that rattles the stout door,
Troubling the ashes in the sheltered grate.
The stone will perish; I shall be twice dust.
Only my standard on a taken hill
Can cheat the mildew and the red-brown rust
And make immortal my adventurous will.
Even now the silk is tugging at the staff:
Take up the song; forget the epitaph.

What Rider Spurs Him From the Darkening East

What rider spurs him from the darkening east
As from a forest, and with rapid pound
Of hooves, now light, now louder on hard ground,

Approaches, and rides past with speed increased,
Dark spots and flecks of foam upon his beast?
What shouts he from the saddle, turning 'round
As he rides on?—"Greetings!"—I made the sound;
"Greetings from Nineveh!"—it seemed, at least.
Did someone catch the object that he flung?
He held some object on his saddle-bow,
And flung it towards us as he passed; among
The children then it fell most likely; no,
'Tis here: a little bell without a tongue.
Listen; it has a faint voice even so.

Victoria Sackville-West

Persia

The passes are blocked by snow.
No word comes through, no message, and no letter.
Only the eagles plane above the snow,
And wolves come down upon the villages.
The barrier of mountains is the end,
The edge of the world to us in wintry Persia.
We are self-contained, shut off.
Only the telegraph ticks out its flimsy sheets,
Bringing the distant news of deaths of princes.
Day after day the cold and marvellous sun
Rides in the cold, the pale, the marvellous heaven,
Cutting the blue and icy folds of shadow
Aslant the foot-hills where the snow begins.
So would I have it, pure in isolation,
With scarcely a rumour of the varied world
Leaping the mountain-barrier in disturbance.

Are there not hearts that find their high fulfilment
Alone, with ice between them and their friends?

Sometimes When Night . . .

Sometimes when night has thickened on the woods,
And we in the house's square security

Read, speak a little, read again,
Read life at second-hand, speak of small things,
Being content and withdrawn for a little hour
From the dangers and fears that are either wholly absent
Or wholly invading, —sometimes a shot rings out,
Sudden and sharp; complete. It has no sequel,
No sequel for us, only the sudden crack
Breaking a silence followed by a silence,
Too slight a thing for comment; slight, and usual,
A shot in the dark, fired by a hand unseen
At a life unknown; finding, or missing, the mark?
Bringing death? bringing hurt? teaching, perhaps, escape,
Escape from a present threat, a threat recurrent,
Or ending, once and for all? But we read on,
Since the shot was not at our hearts, since the mark was not
Your heart or mine, not this time, my companion.

The Bull

Now sinks another day to rest
On summer and her leafy ways.
By the last golden light caressed
The farmstead drowses in the haze
Of slanting light in rungs and reins
From heaven slung across the Weald
Above the pricking of the vanes,
More golden than the ripening field
Within the hedgerow squares ensealed.

The owl with short and silent stroke
Deadly to field-fare or to mouse,
Slants from the apple to the oak
Across the orchard near the house;
And through the grasses creep the small
Creatures of twilight, hid by day;
The snail beside the garden wall,
The mole on his myopic way.

The kindly trees protective stand
Around the farm less old than they,
And drawl their shadows on a land
Tilled by a man's forgotten hand,

But still beneath his grandson's sway;
And silent as an empty fane
The barn with doors flung wide
Drinks in the rays of golden rain
On ropes and pulleys, sacks of grain,
A summer evening's pride.

The vanes upon the oasts outside
Have turned their chimneys to the east,
And dim within the shadows deep
Where silence shrouds the roof,
The barn is darkened and asleep.
But in the stall the monstrous beast
Ranges, and stamps a fretful hoof.

The granaries once more are full,
—Oh sweet monotony of the year!—
But in the stall the aging bull
Feels that the end of time is near;
End of that time which was his span,
When he could lash his tail, or browse
On acres all his own,
Or stand four-square and lordly scan
His grass, his calves, his willing cows,
Male, arrogant, alone.
No bachelor! the lord and sire
Of cows and calves in half a shire,
Sole sovereign of his clan;

Whom no man dared approach but he
Who brought the bucket filled with milk
When little bulls are weak of knee
And muzzled sleek as silk;
Days when within a neighbouring byre
His mother softly mourned her loss,
And he already scampered free
In right and callow disregard,
And kicked his heels, and tried to toss
The empty bucket round the yard.

Days of a lost and youthful spring
Before his liberty was scarred

And branded by the shameful ring;
But what's a ring, when thews are hard
And sex supreme in strength and youth?
A small and negligible thing!

But now resigned within the shed
He moves uneasy round the stall,
And lowers his great tufted head
Against the manger and the wall;
Too patient now for mighty rage,
Too mild and cumbrous and uncouth,
He watches night creep on like age,
And only dimly knows the truth.

The night creeps on; the single star
Of contemplation's lidless eye
Stares through the stable door ajar,
Constant, dispassionate, and high;
Returning at the punctual hour
To stare on man and beast alike,
On rising strength or fallen power.
Nor merciless, nor pitiful,
Without compassion or dislike;
And sees the old and lonely bull
Who does not know that he must die.

Genevieve Taggard

Train: Abstraction

The steely train in the stupid green
Of sleepy, sleepy summer tore
An even rent in the placid clean
Cloth of the air with an onward roar.

Above the sharp diagonal,—the two
Lines either side the rended cleft—
The air closed in, the green stuff grew
Almost together—until the train tore left.

I saw this happen daily and watched both:
Saw the air mend, and the round earth pinch the crack—
After the train sprung them open with an oath,
A massive pressure. Until the train came back:

Dark spot of these rails—lines laid merely for speed—
Dark clot of speed on pure line, to assert:
Idea the line; the dark acceleration, the deed,
Passing along the line to kill the inert.

Squirrel Near Library

All he owns is
His body and a few nuts.
He is 300 times as alive as you.
Disney silhouette on a branch,
Headlong creeping, tail afloat, then up, up,
And he sits,
Intensively busy, frisking
Tail, plump tum and small
Able paws. Watch, it's run, ripple, stop,
Stop, run and ripple,
A thousand times a day.
Tired never. Idle never. But always
Squirrel-alert in a close fitting
Comfortable allover fur suit.
All the shut dictionaries reading RODENT
Can't tamp down that
Tail.

Elizabeth Daryush

Still-Life

Through the open French window the warm sun
lights up the polished breakfast-table, laid
round a bowl of crimson roses, for one—
a service of Worcester porcelain, arrayed
near it a melon, peaches, figs, small hot
rolls in a napkin, fairy rack of toast,

butter in ice, high silver coffee-pot,
and, heaped on a salver, the morning's post.

She comes over the lawn, the young heiress,
from her early walk in her garden-wood,
feeling that life's a table set to bless
her delicate desires with all that's good,

that even the unopened future lies
like a love-letter, full of sweet surprise.

Babette Deutsch

Barges on the Hudson

Going up the river, or down, their tuneless look
Is of men grown poorer who, though ageing, wear
Some majesty of the commonplace. Old barges
Are cousin to those whom poverty becomes—
To late November, the north, nightfall, all the
Deprived whom increment of loss enlarges.
They have no faces, have no voices, even
Of their own selves no motion. Yet they move.
With what salt grace, with a dim pride of ocean
Uncompassable by a fussy tug,
Prim nurse that drags or nudges the old ones on.
They must borrow their colors from the river, mirror
The river's muddy silver, in dulled red echo
A sundown that beds in soot. Their freight, rusty,
Faded, cindery, is like the past
The charwoman deals with. Yesterday's business
They carry with the dignity of the blind.
By night the river is black, they are black's shadows
Passing. The unwrinkled stars dispute that darkness
Alone with a lantern on a one-eyed spar.

Stranger Than the Worst

London Bridge was built
In a foggy century;

Men without anger or guilt
Shed blood to mortise the stones:
A child's. Year upon year,
Under a hotter sky,
Men brutish with fear
Wrenched a child's heart, throbbing,
Out of its cage of bones,
Screening with boisterous chants
The shrieks, the final moans.

To a woman in old age
Nothing of this is strange.
She knows the idolater's rage.
She thrills with the victim's pain.
In her own breast she keeps
A child, like the heart in its cage.
Sacrifice hardly sleeps,
Rousing again, as always,
To freshen a blackened stain.
The passionate innocent
Cries out, appalled. In vain.

Yet there is something comes
And goes, but comes again—
Emboldening, like drums,
But with the light grace of song,
And stranger than the worst.
Pure blitheness, out of the scums
Of evil and anguish will burst
Into a glory that
Dazzles beyond all wrong.
Love, as the old know love.
Fibred with grief, it is strong.

Destruction of Letters

To shred them: a narrow labor, and simply toss
The pieces away like peelings. Fingers tear
The heavier sheets across, across, across,
In voluptuous bravery; so children pare
Skin from a wound half-healed, admiring loss.

A phrase, like a deep look, glows from this pale
Manila paper: now flurrying, as past clutch
As confetti for the street sweeper to nail.
The word that a moment since was to behold, to touch,
Collapses into an impalpable Braille.

Postcards resist squarely, stiff to defeat
The redoubled twitch would slice them like a knife;
As if each public view—park, river, or street—
Were alive and clinging to its private life:
All that the eyes have loved returning in retreat.

What's left then? Mincings like receipted bills.
Those lines where the ink throbbed like an artery,
So littled, would not serve a fire by way of spills.
Yet in the widowing wrist the pulse more stubbornly
Beats: the heart swears: memory salutes, and kills.

Ruth Pitter

Time's Fool

Time's fool, but not heaven's: yet hope not for any return.
The rabbit-eaten dry branch and the halfpenny candle
Are lost with the other treasure: the sooty kettle
Thrown away, become redbreast's home in the hedge, where the nettle
Shoots up, and bad bindweed wreathes rust-fretted handle.
Under that broken thing no more shall the dry branch burn.

Poor comfort all comfort: once what the mouse had spared
Was enough, was delight, there where the heart was at home;
The hard cankered apple holed by the wasp and the bird,
The damp bed, with the beetle's tap in the headboard heard,
The dim bit of mirror, three inches of comb:
Dear enough, when with youth and with fancy shared.

I knew that the roots were creeping under the floor,
That the toad was safe in his hole, the poor cat by the fire,
The starling snug in the roof, each slept in his place:
The lily in splendour, the vine in her grace,
The fox in the forest, all had their desire,
As then I had mine, in the place that was happy and poor.

An Old Woman Speaks of the Moon

She was urgent to speak of the moon: she offered delight
And wondering praise to be shared by the girl in the shop,
Lauding the goddess who blessed her each sleepless night
Greater and brighter till full: but the girl could not stop.

She turned and looked up in my face, and hastened to cry
How beautiful was the orb, how the constant glow
Comforted in the cold night the old waking eye:
How fortunate she, whose lodging was placed that so

She in the lonely night, in her lonely age,
She from her poor lean bed might behold the undying
Letter of loveliness written on heaven's page,
The sharp silver arrows leap down to where she was lying.

The dying spoke love to the immortal, the foul to the fair,
The withered to the still-flowering, the bound to the free:
The nipped worm to the silver swan that sails through the air:
And I took it as good, and a happy omen to me.

 _____

Louise Bogan

Medusa

I had come to the house, in a cave of trees,
Facing a sheer sky.
Everything moved, —a bell hung ready to strike,
Sun and reflection wheeled by.

When the bare eyes were before me
And the hissing hair,
Held up at a window, seen through a door.
The stiff bald eyes, the serpents on the forehead
Formed in the air.

This is a dead scene forever now.
Nothing will ever stir.
The end will never brighten it more than this,
Nor the rain blur.

The water will always fall, and will not fall,
And the tipped bell make no sound.
The grass will always be growing for hay
Deep on the ground.

And I shall stand here like a shadow
Under the great balanced day,
My eyes on the yellow dust, that was lifting in the wind,
And does not drift away.

Zone

We have struck the regions wherein we are keel or reef.
The wind breaks over us,
And against high sharp angles almost splits into words,
And these are of fear or grief.

Like a ship, we have struck expected latitudes
Of the universe, in March.
Through one short segment's arch
Of the zodiac's round
We pass,
Thinking: Now we hear
What we heard last year,
And bear the wind's rude touch
And its ugly sound
Equally with so much
We have learned how to bear.

Women

Women have no wilderness in them,
They are provident instead,
Content in the tight hot cell of their hearts
To eat dusty bread.

They do not see cattle cropping red winter grass,
They do not hear
Snow water going down under culverts
Shallow and clear.

They wait, when they should turn to journeys,
They stiffen, when they should bend.

They use against themselves that benevolence
To which no man is friend.

They cannot think of so many crops to a field
Or of clean wood cleft by an axe.
Their love is an eager meaninglessness
Too tense, or too lax.

They hear in every whisper that speaks to them
A shout and a cry.
As like as not, when they take life over their door-sills
They should let it go by.

Old Countryside

Beyond the hour we counted rain that fell
On the slant shutter, all has come to proof.
The summer thunder, like a wooden bell,
Rang in the storm above the mansard roof,

And mirrors cast the cloudy day along
The attic floor; wind made the clapboards creak.
You braced against the wall to make it strong,
A shell against your cheek.

Long since, we pulled brown oak-leaves to the ground
In a winter of dry trees; we heard the cock
Shout its unplaceable cry, the axe's sound
Delay a moment after the axe's stroke.

Far back, we saw, in the stillest of the year,
The scrawled vine shudder, and the rose-branch show
Red to the thorns, and, sharp as sight can bear,
The thin hound's body arched against the snow.

Song for the Last Act

Now that I have your face by heart, I look
Less at its features than its darkening frame
Where quince and melon, yellow as young flame,
Lie with quilled dahlias and the shepherd's crook.
Beyond, a garden. There, in insolent ease
The lead and marble figures watch the show

Of yet another summer loath to go
Although the scythes hang in the apple trees.

Now that I have your voice by heart, I look.

Now that I have your voice by heart, I read
In the black chords upon a dulling page
Music that is not meant for music's cage,
Whose emblems mix with words that shake and bleed.
The staves are shuttled over with a stark
Unprinted silence. In a double dream
I must spell out the storm, the running stream.
The beat's too swift. The notes shift in the dark.

Now that I have your voice by heart, I read.

Now that I have your heart by heart, I see
The wharves with their great ships and·architraves;
The rigging and the cargo and the slaves
On a strange beach under a broken sky.
O not departure, but a voyage done!
The bales stand on the stone; the anchor weeps
Its red rust downward, and the long vine creeps
Beside the salt herb, in the lengthening sun.

Now that I have your heart by heart, I see.

Henceforth, From the Mind

Henceforth, from the mind,
For your whole joy, must spring
Such joy as you may find
In any earthly thing,
And every time and place
Will take your thought for grace.

Henceforth, from the tongue,
From shallow speech alone,
Comes joy you thought, when young,
Would wring you to the bone,
Would pierce you to the heart
And spoil its stop and start.

Henceforward, from the shell,
Wherein you heard, and wondered

At oceans like a bell
So far from ocean sundered—
A smothered sound that sleeps
Long lost within lost deeps,

Will chime you change and hours,
The shadow of increase,
Will sound you flowers
Born under troubled peace—
Henceforth, henceforth
Will echo sea and earth.

Léonie Adams

The Figurehead

This that is washed with weed and pebblestone
Curved once a dolphin's length before the prow,
And I who read the land to which we bore
In its grave eyes, question my idol now,
What cold and marvelous fancy it may keep,
Since the salt terror swept us from our course,
Or if a wisdom later than the storm,
For old green ocean's tinctured it so deep;
And with some reason to me on this strand
The waves, the ceremonial waves have come,
And stooped their barbaric heads, and all flung out
Their glittering arms before them, and are gone,
Leaving the murderous tribute lodged in sand.

Janet Lewis

Remembered Morning
The axe rings in the wood,
And the children come,
Laughing and wet from the river;
And all goes on as it should.

I hear the murmur and hum
Of their morning forever.

The water ripples and slaps
The white boat at the dock;
The fire crackles and snaps.
The little noise of the clock
Goes on and on in my heart,
Of my heart parcel and part.

O happy early stir!
A girl comes out on the porch
And the door slams after her.
She sees the wind in the birch,
And then the running day
Catches her into its way.

Hildegarde Flanner

From *Sonnets in Quaker Language*

2

Thee sets a bell to swinging in my soul,
And though the sound is nebulous and dark,
Yet musical my thought unto its toll.
And seldom is my hush! and loud my hark!
Thee knows that in response continual
My heart is all ways resonant to thee,
Yet with how dim a sound antiphonal,
Like a lost wind that blows beneath the sea.
Can thee resolve confusion of my tears
Into a single silence of desire?
Can thee, when singing has gone cold with fears,
Put on more music and put on more fire?
If so, then I am cloister to a bell
That utters advent of a miracle.

6

Hearing a sound that may be thy return,
I set my heart upon the window sill.

By such a mortal lamp thee may discern
The tossing pathway on the hidden hill.
The leaves are stepping softly from the trees.
I listen. That was a bird sighed in her nest.
I lean and wonder if thee runs and sees
The lighted dream upon the dreamer's breast.
But no foot springs upon the silken air,
No strand of silence breaks to let thee by.
Thee does not come. But still I wait and stare
Then turn from the massive darkness with a cry.
For now the desolate owl with lonely shout
Descends the mountain and my light goes out.

Hawk Is a Woman

I saw a hawk devour a screaming bird,
Devour the little ounce sugared with song.
First bent and ate the pretty eyes both out,
One eye and twice, stooping to taste the pang.
Then her dripping tongue she cleaned, then
Into the winsome breast she plied her beak,
Took at a gulp the rosy heart, a pinch
Of too great innocence, drank the whole lark
Down, the inmost blood down, licked the lark down
With vicious dainty pick, oh the damned thief!
To break! into the beating bird! and tear
The veins out, out the joy, flesh out of life.
May hawk be hawked upon, I say,
May she be spied and nailed upon the ground
And feel herself divided and devoured
To ease the gullet of some casual fiend.
She, she! before her agony lapse quite,
Before her breast is eaten to her back,
May she, the very she, may that hawk hear
The ugly female laughter of a hawk.

Swift Love, Sweet Motor

And will they always be so tender, her
Face a kind of star to burn him up, she
Nearly there and wholly tremulous, his lap?
Where ecstasy lolls unabashed, his knee?

Will always run the road under the wheels,
The kiss of tire to boulevard complete,
The fuels of joy and speed flow brightly, make
Sunday combust in a miraculous heat?

Will ever just this perilous hot way
Survive to make them almost crash in bliss,
Just missing (where old panic licks his grin)
Black flowers and funerals of the abyss?

Question to question: and no answer mine.
Love rides locked to love whose motors pass
Leaving upon my traffic eye one token,
A gleam at fifty miles through shatterproof glass,

Her smile, a little honey-comb just broken.

Let Us Believe

Let us believe in the flesh, the hope made flesh,
For the soul is an exile without rest,
And the brain is a pack of apes in flight,
And the heart of the world is breaking in every breast.
Let us honor the flesh with faith extreme.
See, on this vicious day, how the brave blood,
How the frail racial bone, the mysterious marrow
Would fill with life the rotten sons of God.
Though death has overrun our desperate walls
And panic has us in a corner, cold,
Do hope, do cling: by the great atom, by the cell,
By the black centuries already old,
By the bright skull hid in the living face,
By the five-pointed magic of the hand,
Flesh, that pale prophet that survives all fates,
Will, if it matters, make a more human race.

This Day

This day when I lay my hope aside
Dawns with a single stone of light
That builds to a low meridian
Till noon, a bare pillar, is my own height,
As such I can measure it.

This place seems right to say good-bye,
Having only a centre, no east or west,
Where nothing is large and all is calm.
Its firmament is my own eye,
It fits the landscape of my palm.

Since time has majesty to be so meek,
And space comes tamely to the hand,
This person must do no less for sorrow,
This mourner must not be too grand
Nor strike on golden tablets beyond belief.
Let the pen lie where it has fainted,
The few black words it wrote
Were not set down to flatter grief.

 _____

Marya Zaturenska

The Descent of the Vulture

As he left the ship he saw this, only this
Painted in clear vision on the sunny air:
That it was pleasant and green on *terra firma* there,
But he heard a vulture scream over an abyss.

Green, smiling, solid the earth; the dazzling sky
Ripe for adventure, spilling good nature down;
Fortuna the giddy goddess in her flashing golden gown,
Distributing joy, fame, honors, and prosperity.

Adorable as always, her eyes seemed cooler, narrow,
As if too full of knowledge and desire,
And with slow, decorous steps she walked through a cloud of fire,
Smiling as the vulture devoured a sparrow.

Gallant, alert, erect, he surveyed the dangerous strand,
Kissed his hand to the goddess who looked farewell;
Lightning flashed, and thunder pealed like a bell, like a knell—
He was left forever in the fatal land.

Where neither beauty, presence, nor wit can bless
Nor intellect, affection, charm, prevail—

He saw the river dim, the crags darken, the last boat sail,
And the pleasant land become a wilderness.

The listening landscape heard but did not say
That the armed antagonists were waiting behind the tree,
Dark spreading tree, emblem of life and destiny
Under your shade no leaves dance, no nymphs play.

For warm flesh cannot compete with grass and stone,
Nor the bright face conquer against a world in arms;
All his adventure is done, but the fruitful sleepy farms,
Slumber in moonlight, till the evil bird has flown.

Stevie Smith

From *The Dedicated Dancing Bull and the Water Maid*

(Beethoven's Sonata in F Op. 17,
for Horn and Piano, played by
Dennis Brain and Dennis Matthews)

Hop hop, thump thump,
Oh I am holy, oh I am plump,
A young bull dancing on the baked grass glade,
And beside dances the water maid.
She says I must dance with her,
Why should I? I loathe her,
She has such a stupid way of singing
It does not amount to anything,
But she thinks it does, oh yes
She does not suppose she is spurious.
I wish I could be rid of the Water Maid
Or hid from her. Does she think she can make me afraid?
Ho ho, thump thump,
Oh I am elegant, oh I am plump,
As I wave my head my feet go thud
On the baked grass. Oh I am good.

Now night comes and I go into the wood shades
And the moon comes up and lights them as the day fades.

. . . . . .

Kay Boyle

Thunderstorm in South Dakota

All that blazing day, swift-breasted swallows, envious crows, grackles
    in trees,
Gathered in roadside conference. At dusk
Winged ants splattered the windshield, dying indelibly.
No ripped glove, no kleenex, could efface their gauze
From the glass. At night, on the black pass, the bereft
Sheep slept, and I, bereft, was awakened by fountains of light
Spraying over the granite monuments of clouds, over the towers and
    cornices,
Over this toppling architecture of storm,
And I wrote you:

"I am afraid of the uproar of this demolition,
And reach my hand out in the alien motel bed,
Seeking all that is absent, seeking the pulse
That skips so lightly in your wrist. I remember
The singular wisdom of your hands, their shape,
Their knowledge of many things, the narrow division of your fingers.
It is so different, this thundering of stone, this clamor, this that pounds
    at the window,
Drenching the beasts in their stretches of land on the South Dakota
    pass;
It is so different from the uncertain pace of your heart, from the far
    rain,
That is falling, falling, gentle as tears, in Ireland where you are."

The New Emigration

*(On reading a French reporter's
account of the clandestine crossings
from Spain)*

They cross the frontier as their names cross your pages,
Dark-eyed, slender throated, with tongues that have run
As mercury runs to the fever of sun. But now as I read, as I write,
They are crossing by moon, traps shut, guitars muted,
Fox-smell on the night, without passport or visa or money to ring. So
    they come
Through the trees. They are young, but they wear
Bleak masks of hunger, coats tight in the armpits, too short in the
    sleeve.
But hope can be cloak, can be shoes on the feet, can be lash
Out of bull-hide still tough in the dust when the trumpets are done.

The joke of it is they are not in the news. Not Koreans who follow
    torrent and stone
From northward to southward; not Germans who flux from east
    toward the west.
These quick-eyed, these young, who are musical-tongued, have blood
    that is lava
Pursuing the vein from lover to lover, Spaniard to Spaniard, dead man
    to son,
And no milestone to say it is here, the frontier.
    But the dead of wars and hunger rattling in their beds
    Are stilled in the brief, sweet moment that the thin-ribbed come
    Out of the province of Zamora, out of Asturias, Seville,
    Bearing in flight their country, bearing Spain,
    Leaving the soft-voweled names behind to genuflection; not to bend
    Elbow or knee again, but to cross before the altars of wild olive trees,
    Upright, like men.
    Here France is France, wide open in the dark,
    Who takes them in.

Does history state that all men seek the classical
Grave face of liberty, leave interchangeable footprints as they run,
Communicate identical dreams from man to son,
Whatever the continent or century? Listen. Men
Are as different as their climates are. The pride of some

Lies in the passage of firearms from palm to palm,
War after war, along an iron Rhine; in some
The honeycomb has hardened like an artery. But not in these
Whose presence states a frontier is that undetermined place
One comes upon alone at night, in life, and crosses
Even if afraid.

Phyllis McGinley

From *"I Know a Village"*

Occupation: Housewife

Her health is good. She owns to forty-one,
  Keeps her hair bright by vegetable rinses,
Has two well-nourished children—daughter and son—
  Just now away at school. Her house, with chintzes
Expensively curtained, animates the caller.
  And she is fond of Early American glass
Stacked in an English breakfront somewhat taller
  Than her best friend's. Last year she took a class

In modern drama at the County Center.
  Twice, on Good Friday, she's heard *Parsifal* sung.
She often says she might have been a painter,
  Or maybe writer; but she married young.
She diets. And with Contract she delays
The encroaching desolation of her days.

The 5:32

She said, If tomorrow my world were torn in two,
Blacked out, dissolved, I think I would remember
(As if transfixed in unsurrendering amber)
This hour best of all the hours I knew:
When cars came backing into the shabby station,
Children scuffing the seats, and the women driving
With ribbons around their hair, and the trains arriving,
And the men getting off with tired but practiced motion.

Yes, I would remember my life like this, she said:
Autumn, the platform red with Virginia creeper,

And a man coming toward me, smiling, the evening paper
Under his arm, and his hat pushed back on his head,
And wood smoke lying like haze on the quiet town,
And dinner waiting, and the sun not yet gone down.

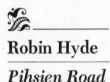

Robin Hyde

Pihsien Road

Old men in blue: and heavily encumbered
Old shoulders held by shadowy whips in sway,
Like ox and ass, that down this road have lumbered
All day: all the bright murderous day.
More than their stumbling footprints press this clay.

And light in air, pure white, in wonder riding,
Some crazy Phaeton these have never known
Holds by a lever their last awe, deciding
How flesh shall spurt from sinews, brain from bone—
Crushing desolate grain with a harder stone.

The Deserted Village

In the deserted village, sunken down
With a shrug of last weak old age, pulled back to earth,
All people are fled or killed. The cotton crop rots,
Not one mild house leans sideways, a man on crutches,
Not a sparrow earns from the naked floors,
Walls look, but cannot live without the folk they loved—
It would be a bad thing to awaken them.
Having broken the rice-bowl, seek not to fill it again.

The village temple, well built, with five smashed gods, ten whole ones,
Does not want prayers. Its last vain prayer bled up
When the women ran outside to be slain.
A temple must house its sparrows or fall asleep,
Therefore a long time, under his crown of snails,
The gilded Buddha demands to meditate.
No little flowering fires on the incense-strings
Startle Kwan-Yin, whom they dressed in satin—

Old women sewing beads like pearls in her hair.
This was a temple for the very poor ones:
Their gods were mud and lath: but artfully
Some village painter coloured them all.
Wooden dragons were carefully carved.
Finding in mangled wood one smiling childish tree,
Roses and bells not one foot high,
I set it back, at the feet of Kwan-Yin.
A woman's prayer-bag,
Having within her paper prayers, paid for in copper,
Seeing it torn, I gathered it up.
I shall often think, 'The woman I did not see
Voiced here her dying wish.
But the gods dreamed on. So low her voice, so loud
The guns, all that death-night, who would stoop to hear?'

Eve Langley

Native Born

In a white gully among fungus red
Where serpent logs lay hissing at the air,
I found a kangaroo. Tall, dewy, dead,
So like a woman, she lay silent there,
Her ivory hands, black-nailed, crossed on her breast,
Her skin of sun and moon hues, fallen cold.
Her brown eyes lay like rivers come to rest
And death had made her black mouth harsh and old.
Beside her in the ashes I sat deep
And mourned for her, but had no native song
To flatter death, while down the ploughlands steep
Dark young Camelli whistled loud and long,
"Love, liberty and Italy are all."
Broad golden was his breast against the sun.
I saw his wattle whip rise high and fall
Across the slim mare's flanks, and one by one
She drew the furrows after her as he
Flapped like a gull behind her, climbing high,
Chanting his oaths and lashing soundingly,

While from the mare came once a blowing sigh.
The dew upon the kangaroo's white side
Had melted. Time was whirling high around,
Like the thin woomera, and from heaven wide
He, the bull-roarer, made continuous sound.
Incarnate, lay my country by my hand:
Her long hot days, bushfires and speaking rains,
Her mornings of opal and the copper band
Of smoke around the sunlight on the plains.
Globed in fire bodies the meat-ants ran
To taste her flesh and linked us as we lay,
For ever Australian, listening to a man
From careless Italy, swearing at our day.
When, golden-lipped, the eagle-hawks came down
Hissing and whistling to eat of lovely her,
And the blowflies with their shields of purple brown
Plied hatching to and fro across her fur,
I burnt her with the logs, and stood all day
Among the ashes, pressing home the flame
Till woman, logs and dreams were scorched away,
And native with night, that land from where they came.

Celeste Turner Wright

Yugoslav Cemetery

Jackson, California

At Gettysburg full anonymity:
Number for him whose name is past recall;
The marker dwindles, and the turf appears
Scant for a soldier's wear. (Can this be all?)

But here each granite bears a photograph:
As from a window, personality—
A miniature wraith—is gazing out,
Rain on the cheek in wistful parody.

Slavic inscription cannot hide this pair,
Wholly themselves, too young for such a bed;

Miner who died of silicosis; wife
Thin-faced and dark, with braids about her head.

Quietly as their neighbors they persist,
Preserve their essence, hint their special pain;
We are intruding on their privacy,
These large-eyed mournful lovers in the rain.

Kathleen Raine

The Wilderness

I came too late to the hills: they were swept bare
Winters before I was born of song and story,
Of spell or speech with power of oracle or invocation,

The great ash long dead by a roofless house, its branches rotten,
The voice of the crows an inarticulate cry,
And from the wells and springs the holy water ebbed away.

A child I ran in the wind on a withered moor
Crying out after those great presences who were not there,
Long lost in the forgetfulness of the forgotten.

Only the archaic forms themselves could tell
In sacred speech of hoodie on gray stone, or hawk in air,
Of Eden where the lonely rowan bends over the dark pool.

Yet I have glimpsed the bright mountain behind the mountain,
Knowledge under the leaves, tasted the bitter berries red,
Drunk water cold and clear from an inexhaustible hidden fountain.

In Time

The beautiful rain falls, the unheeded angel
lies in the street, spreadeagled under the footfall
that from the divine face wears away the smile

whose tears run in the gutter, melting where
the stationary cars wait for departure;
the letter that says Ave is passed over

for at the ever-present place the angel waits,
passes through walls and hoardings, in dark porches
his face, wounded by us, for us and over us watches.

Written in Exile

There is a word at heart for the next of death,
The farthest from joy; if I could fathom it
I would from this most desolate and distant place, bless

The maker of distances, since what divides
Me from His presence is the extent of Heaven.
Were He less high, I could not be so far.

And my unrest fathoms the deep of peace,
And by my depth downcast, Lord, you are risen,
Your love's great realm, my separation measures.

Message From Home

Do you remember, when you were first a child,
Nothing in the world seemed strange to you?
You perceived, for the first time, shapes already familiar,
And seeing, you knew that you have always known
The lichen on the rock, fern-leaves, the flowers of thyme,
As if the elements newly met in your body,
Caught up into the momentary vortex of your living
Still kept the knowledge of a former state,
In you retained recollection of cloud and ocean,
The branching tree, the dancing flame.

Now when nature's darkness seems strange to you,
And you walk, an alien, in the streets of cities,
Remember earth breathed you into her with the air, with the sun's
   rays,
Laid you in her waters asleep, to dream
With the brown trout among the milfoil roots,
From substance of star and ocean fashioned you,
At the same source conceived you
As sun and foliage, fish and stream.

Of all created things the source is one,
Simple, single as love; remember
The cell and seed of life, the sphere

That is, of child, white bird, and small blue dragon-fly
Green fern, and the gold four-petalled tormentilla
The ultimate memory.
Each latent cell puts out a future,
Unfolds its differing complexity.
As a tree puts forth leaves, and spins a fate
Fern-traced, bird-feathered, or fish-scaled.
Moss spreads its green film on the moist peat,
The germ of dragon-fly pulses into animation and takes wing
As the water-lily from the mud ascends on its ropy stem
To open a sweet white calyx to the sky.
Man, with farther to travel from his simplicity,
From the archaic moss, fish, and lily parts,
And into exile travels his long way.

As you leave Eden behind you, remember your home,
For as you remember back into your own being
You will not be alone; the first to greet you
Will be those children playing by the burn,
The otters will swim up to you in the bay,
The wild deer on the moor will run beside you.
Recollect more deeply, and the birds will come,
Fish rise to meet you in their silver shoals,
And darker, stranger, more mysterious lives
Will throng about you at the source
Where the tree's deepest roots drink from the abyss.

Nothing in that abyss is alien to you.
Sleep at the tree's root, where the night is spun
Into the stuff of worlds, listen to the winds,
The tides, and the night's harmonies, and know
All that you knew before you began to forget,
Before you became estranged from your own being,
Before you had too long parted from those other
More simple children, who have stayed at home
In meadow and island and forest, in sea and river.
Earth sends a mother's love after her exiled son,
Entrusting her message to the light and the air,
The wind and waves that carry your ship, the rain that falls,
The birds that call to you, and all the shoals
That swim in the natal waters of her ocean.

Tu Non Se' in Terra,
Si Come Tu Credi ...

Not upon earth, as you suppose
tower these rocks that turn the wind,
for on their summits angels stand.

Nor from the earth these waters rise—
to quench not thirst, but ecstasy
the waterfall leaps from the sky.

Those nameless clouds that storm and swirl
about the mountain are the veil
that from these sightless eyes shall fall

when senses faint into the ground,
and time and place go down the wind.

The Human Form Divine

The human contours are so easily lost.
Only close your eyes and you seem a forest
Of dense vegetation, and the lurking beast

That in the night springs from the cover
Tears with tiger's mouth your living creatures,
A thousand innocent victims without name that suffer.

Science applies its insect-lenses to the form divine
As up the red river (all life comes from the sea)
Swim strange monsters, amoeboid erythrean spawn.

Rock-face of bone, alluvium of cartilage
Remote from man as the surface of the moon
Are vast and unexplored interior desert ranges,

And autonomous cells
Grow like unreaped fields of waving corn.
Air filters through the lungs' fine branches as through trees.

Chemistry dissolves the goddess in the alembic,
Venus the white queen, the universal matrix,
Down to molecular hexagons and carbon-chains,

And the male nerve-impulse, monition of reality,
Conveys the charge, dynamic of non-entity
That sparks across the void *ex nihilo.*

At the extreme of consciousness, prayer
Fixes hands and feet immobile to a chair,
Transmutes all heaven and earth into a globe of air,

And soul streams away out of the top of the head
Like flame in a lamp-glass carried in the draught
Of the celestial fire kindled in the solar plexus.

Oh man, oh Garden of Eden, there is nothing
But the will of love to uphold your seeming world,
To trace in chaos the contours of your beloved form!

Rose

Gather while you may
Vapour of water, dust of earth, rose
Of air and water and light that comes and goes:
Over and over again the rose is woven.

Who knows the beginning?
In the vein in the sun in the rain
In the rock in the light in the night there is none.
What moves light over water? An impulse
Of rose like the delight of girl's breasts
When the nipples bud and grow a woman
Where was a child, a woman to bear
A child unbegun (is there
Anywhere one? Are the people of dreams
Waiting—where?—to be born?) Does the green
Bud rose without end contain?
Within green sepals, green cells, you find none.
The crude
Moist, hard, green and cold
Petal on petal unfolding rose from nowhere.

But the perfect form is moving
Through time, the rose is a transit, a wave that weaves
Water, and petals fall like notes in order;
No more rose on ground unbecome
Unwoven unwound are dust are formless
And the rose is over but where
Labours for ever the weaver of roses?

Envoi

What has want to give plenty but knowledge of its own riches untold?
I found you wretched, and miserable, and poor, and blind, and naked,
And lent you, for a while, the golden kingdom I in you beheld.

Helen Sorrells

Mountain Corral

The gate was open; the fence under the aspens, fallen.
But horses were there, I knew it.
I went in to find them—transparent creatures
with ribs showing white as aspen bark
through their glistening hides.
One, with a broken star on his forehead,
came and laid his cool muzzle in my hand.

I thought this the presence of horses only,
and then I sensed the riders,
two girls clear as bright bottles
who leaned the blonde filament of their hair
in the horses' manes, a gesture for lovers,
a prophecy.
I could see it, like looking through water.

In the glass-white air the girls mounted.
Horses, girls,
sunlight shining through them,
stood still, a clarity of shining.
Then they cantered away,
taking the light with them.

To a Child Born in Time
of Small War

Child, you were conceived in my upstairs room,
my girlhood all around. Later I spent
nights there alone imploring the traitor moon
to keep me childless still. I never meant
to bear you in this year of discontent.

Yet you were there in your appointed place,
remnant of leaving, of a sacrament.
Child, if I loved you then, it was to trace
on a cold sheet your likeness to his absent face.

In May we were still alone. That month your life
stirred in my dark, as if my body's core
grew quick with wings. I turned away, more wife
than mother still, unwilling to explore
the fact of you. There was an orient shore,
a tide of hurt, that held my heart and mind.
It was as if you lived behind a door
I was afraid to open, lest you bind
my breaking. Lost in loss, I was not yours to find.

I swelled with summer. You were hard and strong,
making me know you were there. When the mail
brought me no letter, and the time was long
between the war's slow gains, and love seemed frail,
I fought you. You were error, judgment, jail.
Without you, there were ways I, too, could fight
a war. Trapped in your growing, I would rail
against your grotesque carriage, swollen, tight.
I would have left you, and I did in dreams of flight.

Discipline of the seasons brought me round.
Earth comes to term and so, in time, did we.
You are a living thing of sight and sound.
Nothing of you is his, you are all of me:
your sex, gray eye, the struggle to be free
that made your birth like death, but I awake
for that caught air, your cry. I try to see,
but cannot, the same lift his eyebrows take.
Child, if I love you now, it is for your own sake.

The Amputation

More than he mourned for walking he grieved for the presence
of the leg, and more than for the dancing he hadn't, for all
his nineteen years, done much of yet. It became to him
like a lost lover, all things because all lost—the diamond
part of his self, fleshed like roses. He cried in the night

for its substance, and felt it there! there! there!
Felt it itch, felt the complexity of its ankle, the satiny
socket; the authority of its heel; moved its toes and had to
touch the sudden stump in the darkest of darknesses
to know the truth.

Sometimes in dreams he had it back, the sunrise grass wet
and prickly under his bare feet. The leg was his friend,
his companion. He stitched it in place in dreams,
had it tattooed with his name. He balanced his big blond
weight on it and spun like a dervish. The joy of that!

Waking, loss engulfed him. Waking again and again, grief
burned him thin and hard. The leg lay still in its grave
and he acknowledged the grave at last. He learned to walk
on a stubborn, bloodless copy of his severed limb.
And not to think about it any more.

The Hand Analyst

It is all here in the palm of my hand, the way she reads it.
We are in a bar, and down the room in a family group
four nuns lost to a black leather bench lean the cloister
of their faces out of their own dusk to say blessing,
to sip Seven Up over ice,
                       and Jee-sus! the analyst says,
glaring at the pianist, he must think he's Rachmaninoff
in Carnegie Hall—I wish someone would complain
and then
back to my hands spread under that light she carries
—in search of truth?

Two margaritas apiece, and why not? We'd asked her to our
table, she a priestess of psychochirology wearing
oriental satin, to promise me money and intimate friends
and then it comes:
                    news of a slashing stranger who will
                    seek me out from the rumor-crying
                    lines of my hands and flay me with
                    two-edged words, but I am to withhold
                    all bleeding so he may not devastate
                    me, so I may still live

—this last she whispers—
then takes up her money and goes away
leaving me with the sword-tongued
visitor waiting in the blood pools
of the palms of these hands I use,
that I must keep.

From a Correct Address in a Suburb of a Major City

She wears her middle age like a cowled
gown, sleeved in it, folded high
at the breast,

charming, proper at cocktails
but the inner one raging
and how to hide her,

how to keep her leashed, contain
the heat of her, the soaring cry
never yet loosed,

demanding a chance before the years devour her,
before the marrow of her fine long legs
congeals and she

settles forever for this street, this house,
her face set to the world
sweet, sweet

above the shocked, astonished
hunger.

Constance Carrier

Pro Patria

On a green island in the Main Street traffic
is a granite arch to the dead of the Civil War—
in the Eastlake style, all cubes and tetrahedrons,
each end of the passage barred by an iron-lace door.

They are always locked, tho the space between is empty—
from door to door it isn't much over a yard:
break open one, you could almost touch the other.
Nobody knows what the locks were meant to guard.

East and west, the head of a blank-eyed lion
hisses an arc of spray to the pool below
with a faint persistent sound, an endless whisper
steady under the traffic's stop-and-go.

On top of the monument stands a gilded lady
casting a wreath forever into space:
her carven robes are decent and concealing:
there is no emotion graven on her face.

Words are cut in the stone above the arches—
THEY JOINED THE MORTAL STRUGGLE AND WENT DOWN—
and on every quoin is written the name of a battle
that bloodied creek or landing, bluff or town

now dry and hard in history and granite . . .
In summer the sun lies hot upon the stone,
and the bums and the drunks and the old men and the pigeons
take over the little island for their own.

The old men sit on a bench, with nuts and breadcrusts
for the birds to eat from their hands: the ne'er-do-wells
sprawl on the grass and drowse and boast and argue:
the drunks discourse like statesmen and oracles,

while the birds skim over their heads with a cardboard clatter
of wings, or mince on the pavement at their feet . . .
They are all of them tolerant of one another
in this world like a bubble, this island in the street.

The sun is warm, the lions hiss, and the faithful
loaf in their places, lazy and benign,
a little hierarchy who inherit
this plot of earth, this obsolescent shrine.

    .   .   .   .   .

Who can recall the day of that war's ending?
Think of our own time, then, the summer night

when the word came, and all the churchbells sounded
the end of the dark and the coming of the light.

How many times how many towns have seen it,
the light, the hope, the promise, after the dark—
seen it, and watched it flicker and ebb and vanish,
leaving no trace except some little park

where no one recalls that dream, that disillusion,
and a monument to death is only known
as a place where the harmless unambitious gather
and the doves come down for bread on the sun-warmed stone.

Commencement

Thro elm and maple and syringa branches
the almost-summer sunlight fills the air—
so bright itself, it blurs, it rims with brilliance
all Franklin Square.

The school's a tabernacle, gilded, holy,
half-seen thro the long tunnel of the trees:
the light, like honey, warm and melting, covers
our indolent ease.

Half-seen, a valedictory group of schoolgirls—
upon them, casual shadow, casual light
falling like prophecy, like revelation,
bewildering sight

in the moment before the moment of perception,
so we must turn, our eyelids heavy with sun,
to look at them, potential, undetermined,
until one

moves away from the others, with no backward
turning or glance, moves from the chequered shade
into the light, so swiftly, singly, surely
we are almost afraid

to take our eyes from her, from the self emerging
here on a May day noon, in the golden square—
and the other figures, when we look behind her,
vanished in air.

243

At Tripolis

Down mountain roads like scars across a fist,
thru whitewashed towns that clutched at cliff and crest,
we drove on, dusty with a fabulous dust,

and stopped for coffee at a village square
blinding in sunlight, but at half-past four
one side in shadow, cool against the glare.

Opposite, with its bronze doors, rose the church,
bright-white, sharp-towered, angle besting arch;
two awninged shopfronts underneath the porch,

the central doors black-draped. And as we sat,
a high bell clanged, and at the sound of it
suddenly spoke forth trumpet, drum, cornet—

in reverent assonance, the village band
circled the square, their ranks precisely lined,
the leader's baton decorous in his hand.

And after them an acolyte who held
a coffin-lid before him like a shield.
Then seven priests, and one of them in gold.

(Still overhead, the churchbell's antiphon
fell like a nervous intermittent rain
upon the brasses and their steady drone.)

Then seven townsmen holding fern-wreathed poles
from which hung great square purple satin scrolls
lettered in gilt. We spelled the syllables:

M A R I K A . . . And at last Marika comes,
heralded by the bell-notes and the drums,
heedless of dirge and deaf to holy hymns,

in a bright yellow coffin carried high,
covered with flowers, open to the sky,
white-haired, gaunt-featured, she is carried by.

Arch-matriarch whom every clan has known,
she lay there, and the landscape's face of stone
was not more strictly sculptured than her own.

Mourners walked after her. Around the square
everyone rose, even the alien pair
whom chance alone permitted to be there—

awkward intruders, witnessing a scene
they had no part of, yet that drew them in,
made them partake, until they might have been

kinsmen of her whose final grace was this:
to grant them respite from their rootlessness,
with her for symbol, her for synthesis.

Gene Derwood

After Reading
St. John the Divine

Moon's glow by seven fold multiplied, turned red,
Burned fierce by the coronal limbs at last
Out-leaping insulating space, a-blast
The searing heat sheeting round earth ahead
Of the scorched geoid's course; and I a-bed
Watching that increased flame and holding fast
To pulse and pillow. Worse! No shadow cast
By chair or cat. All people waking dead . . .

Earth lurches spacial waste; my room is hot;
That moon waxes her monstrous, brimstone disk;
Thick fear stretches before the febrile light;
Green fires pierce at my clenching eye's blind spot . . .
My buried soul, rising to face the risk,
With one pure deed restores the natural night.

Marguerite Young

Noah's Ark

When world is water and all is flood, God said,
And the ark is wavering on rising seas,

Windowed on waters, a prison of purple wood
Like to Noah, the ark of soul and body,

Then salvaged from corruption by flood, in mated blisses
Are the twin foxes, the ravens, the three pacific doves,
And are zebras in a golden cage,
The ram, the ewe, the paired gazelles of love,

And in union blessed, are saved for future time
The meek sparrows, and all things of their kind,
Both male and female: yet have I ever aged,
It is the corrupt world of the mind.

For though in the dark hold are harmonies
As the antelope moon-spotted, the ostriches light-eyed,
The dual lions sleeping, and copulating butterflies,
And arch-angel flare on this sensual tide,

And though do rabbits breed and multiply
In this dark cavern of this estranged dream,
And there do adders coil in marriage, spiders weave,
And all is the assurance of one scheme,

Yet God is the impotent old man, and withered,
And the imaginings of His heart, as that vain Noah
Whose limbs extend in a sterile brood
And heart is the hive of all imaginings now

Or tree where do cling the mimic moths like bark;
For God is loneliest, He is creation's flaw
And celibate, nor passenger of this uniting ark.
Unmated were the beautiful He knew

And loneliest, as His voice speaking from the clouds
When water covers over the waste of all
And idea of lilies implicit with the crowd
And dust implicit with lilies of His skull.

The Whales

And yet the southern whale does some time come
To sleep in a river or a sheltered cove
For a memory maketh the whale to turn toward home
And pasture under the green beech leaves of earth

And there, where shoreline is the only green mythos
Of the dry airs stinging, and the tenantless fields,
There does he lie moored in a profound peace
Even as picnickers long summer quest

Between dark mountains, under the green beech leaves,
Leaves seeming to him all mystery
And the farmer is a fugitive to waves
As is the heartbeat's creaking like a gate.

For the canyon sky is this adventure of skull,
An infant earth or aged earth in tears,
And the whale in his river is irresponsible
For the fate of lilies in valleys of our shadow

But is the vision unreasoned in his mind
As rainbow submerged in water, and water's moons, and suns,
And all the acres of that calm, and stars in wind,
And the green beech leaves like fountains over him

And no face of the shepherd or the shepherd's tear.
So if a shoreline curves on earth shoreline
Ours is bubble eye, and angel of the stratosphere
Nor the travesty of deadened trees in time

Under the marauding flight of the grey horned geese.
For there is an inland of that famed time also
And by a green immensity divides from us
The fable of butterflies in a lane of dust.

The Angels

O, where, where are the winter grounds of angels,
Where like the crested auklets do they nest
And the blue fox shall not discover their stony holes?
O, are there for the angels then such atolls

And archipelagoes as haven? Do they where the rose-breasted
Grosbeak is not extinct, do they dwell?
Or where the migratory redwing nested
Or the golden plover some time fed?

Are there for the angels such uninhabited islands where
The beautiful birds are not destroyed yet,

Reef or Easter islands, the soul's! or where the rare
Loon puts on his snowy plumage in the white air,

What islands of snowy angels as of the lone shearwater,
As of the laughing gull, what habitat of angel
O, whom no grebe and gold-eye, and no bird remember
But death is the flight of angel and golden plover.

Winter Scene

So earth's inclined toward the one invisible,
The prince of space, and yet he was disproved,
But this is her nuptial night, a cruel season
As limbless lizards coil together in love

And her whiteness veils over the dog-faced owl,
Whiteness veils over the frozen streams, the moon,
And the deer islanded without family,
Nuzzling cold tulips. Whiteness veils over the sea,

And the heart of the snail is beating slow.
But as an early bride, with heaven's rose
She is adorned, she is wound in seven veils
Even as a bride going forth to the bridegroom,

And her whiteness veils over the scarred fields.
She is celebrant for the failure of a theory,
And the white ptarmigan treads in the snow
                            among the low hills.

Frances Minturn Howard

Sampler From Haworth

His daughter Charlotte said to Mr. Brontë,
"Papa, I've been writing a book." "Have you, my dear?"
Deep in a sermon, Mr. Brontë let
The news float on the top of his attention,
The part that answered easily, without
Troubling the thought beneath. Embroidery
And painting china, even scribbling verse

On the romantic aspects of the tomb
Were all fit occupation for a female,
Though placed, in his mind, after baking bread,
Sweeping the rugless floors, making more comfortable
As was his daughters' duty, Mr. Brontë, père. Her father
Read on untroubled, even when he heard,
"—want you to read it." "I'm afraid," he said,
"It'll try my eyes too much." That settled it;
Victorian daughters never questioned these
Oracular pronouncements. But some words blew back
Which shattered harshly Mr. Brontë's peace.
"Printed," he heard, and put his paper down.
Composure crashed into a hundred bits
Of horrified conjecture. "My dear, the expense!
It's sure to be a loss. Who knows your name?"
Sputtered poor Mr. Brontë. Not her father, surely,
Eyeing his staid, reserved, and grey-eyed daughter
In shocked harassment, while the presses thundered
Her fame all over England. One can but admire
The imperviousness of this Victorian gentleman
To phantoms, whose gigantic shadows stalked
About his house, wild creatures of the moors
Grinned at his windows, howlings shook the room,
Terror and passion and pity and sudden death
Rattled their thunders over his unheeding ears,
Drinking his port, watching his daughters mend
Neatly, his cotton stockings. Decorous, prim,
His daughters battled werewolves of the air
And pressed their father's clothing. Slain by the same white sword
The iron maidens went down one by one,
No groan distressing Papa. O Victorian daughters,
In whose prim bosoms lawless passions raged,
Kept safe within a framed gentility—
Who scribbled with weak eyes by candlelight
After Papa was safely fed and bedded,
The housework done, the pain suppressed, the hope
Disowned, the passionate words confined to paper—
The sampler worked in savage virgins' blood.

Josephine Jacobsen

The Thief

She stole my pencil-case, red leather,
soft, and ten years my friend.
It zipped. Thirty-one pencils in it
long to short, like Aaron's rod
multiplied, held fountains in their spiral.
She was observed: too late I heard;
she sat, sniffled, sniffled, sat, and while I got
white paper out
she stole my case.

While I the ninny peered under chair legs
and slapped my pockets, she vanished like a wolf,
the droop-nosed sniffling gray-green bitch!
A torn kodak: (pony, child, and woman
whose light hand lifted beat off the sun from her eyes,)
was in the case.
Dust sugared the pony's hooves, the woman squinted in that sun
9000 days ago. I carried it with the pencils
and very precious it was. The thief
dropped her handkerchief over the case, dropped
that in her purse and vanished like a wolf—
the sniffling, shuffling, sadistic thief.

Now my pencils are gone—raped from the paper's touch—
Venus, Faber #2 and a yellow Mogul stub, mongrel-sharp,
that had Monte Alban and a tense noon
by those terrible stones, in its yellow shaft.
The Venus had a thing about the Wallendas
and how pyramids go down, or some
at least, and how when the safe hearts vicariously panicked
the clown called for quiet.
But the mongrel would have bayed
at a flight of birds—not the birds, but the flight—
mechanics of feather and current and the eyes escape.

Now a snuffling wretch with a mean quick thumb has scooped it—
my scarlet fetish that held possibility:

the dead July, and the pony's dusty twitch and the woman's
gesture;
and my performing pencils.
Manège horses, incognito,
straining against a mountain of junk in an August alley,
they will lie, in her service—they will limit
the butcher's guile.

She slipped into an elevator, silly, with her prize
and my poems locked in it.

O Dismas do not ask me to be mild—
to the mean gray wretch, the hag,
the pencil thief!

Reindeer and Engine

The reindeer
fastened to the great round eye
that glares along the
Finnish forest track
runs runs runs runs runs
before that blast of light, will die
but not look back

will not
look back, or aside, or swerve
into the black tall deep
good dark of the forests of winter
runs runs runs runs runs
from that light that thrust through his brain's nerve
its whitehot splinter.

The reindeer
has all the forests of Finland to flee
into, its snowy crows and owlly
hush; but over the icy ties
runs runs runs runs runs
from his white round i-
dée fixe until he dies.

To his west
is wide-as-the-moon, to his right
is deep-as-the-dark, but

lockt to his roaring light
runs runs runs runs runs
the fleeing flagging reindeer
from, into, the cold
        wheels'
          night.

Destinations

Home is mysterious: a place to die, a place to breed:
a rock, a streambed, a burrow. From far far far
a deadly magnet: violent unarguable rapid need.

The waste of waters, printless, the wastes of air, prepare
for them death, failure, but never death of destination:
the thread snapped in the labyrinth, the shifting of a star.

From the Brazilian water-pastures, in her homing passion
the green turtle travels fourteen hundred miles to find
(with tiny water-level eye) Ascension Island reared above her motion.

Eels. No eel in the western world but is reminded
in autumn of Sargasso: to its weeds and washes comes in the spring
to breed and to die: the elvers will return to do in kind.

The Manx sheerwater (monogamous as a wolf) flying
back back to his unidentifiable cliffy burrow; the al-
batross, the salmon: need I labor the point in fin, fur, wing?

The point is established. But if I swim, I sink, if I fly, I fall.
How do I know that over the terrible distances where you are I must
    arrive?
Well, the point is established. But the how, the how is not established
    at all.

But there is a question below the question of how I contrive
finally to reach you through the disasters of my weather;
I must come, and I come; so I accede, prevail, arrive.

This is the false arrival. O most fortunate fin and feather,
fortunate voyagers come where they had to go.
Now it turns out that this was a shelter, a shelter we leave together;
for elsewhere. And the shadows, pulsing, say "night", and the short
    wind says "snow".

Josephine Miles

Sale

Went into a shoestore to buy a pair of shoes,
There was a shoe salesman humming the blues
Under his breath; over his breath
Floated a peppermint lifesaver, a little wreath.

I said please I need a triple-A,
And without stopping humming or swallowing his lifesaver away
He gave one glance from toe to toe
And plucked from the mezzanine the very shoe.

Skill of the blessed, that at their command
Blue and breathless comes to hand
To send, from whatever preoccupation, feet
Implacably shod into the perfect street.

Find

Diligent in the burnt fields above the sea
The boy searches for what, sticks,
Cans; he walks like a rider
The rough and stumpy ground.

And finds all morning while the sun
Travels to crest, a blooming fullness of day,
Just one ant-paste spike, rusted.
Says the boy with relish, Poison.

Often at night his fears have told him these
Dooms to find in the hills, and his heart lightens
To find them there in fact, black as intended,
But small enough.

Summer

When I came to show you my summer cottage
By the resounding sea,
We found a housing project building around it,

Two stories being painted green row after row
So we were set in an alley.

But there is the sea I said, off the far corner
Through that vacant land;
And there the pile of prefabricating panels
And the cement blocks swiftly
Rose in the sand.

So darkened the sunlit alley.
Ovid, Arthur, oh Orion I said, run
Take Rags with you, send me back
News of the sea.
So they did, vanishing away off and shouting.

Civilian

The largest stock of armaments allows me
A reason not to kill.
Defense Department does the blasting for me
As soundly as I will.

Indeed, can cover a much wider area
Than I will ever score
With a single rifle sent me on approval
From a Sears Roebuck store.

Only the psycho, meaning sick in spirit,
Would aim his personal shot
At anybody; he is sick in spirit
As I am not.

Oedipus

The gang wanted to give Oedipus Rex a going away present.
He had been a good hard-working father and king.
And besides it is the custom in this country
To give gifts on departure.

But we didn't know what to give Oedipus; he had everything.
Even in his loss, he had more than average.
So we gave him a travelling case, fitted, which we personally
Should have liked to receive.

The Campaign

My Packard Bell was set up in the vacant lot near the stump
Of the old peach tree. Before it, a love-seat
In tan and green told us what comfort said.
And many looked over us, or sat on the ground, why not?
There certainly were not enough ashtrays for everybody.

And from there it began.
All down the dingle through the mustard ran the voices,
All down the shale in the sunlight ran the faces,
A board fence on the left and a board fence on the right,
Because after all this was private property.

And this is what they said:
He was a child of the people and he will be a man of the people.
He read the Bible at his mother's knee
And that Bible has followed him
All the days of his life.

This is what they said:
The sovereign state of Alabama
Gives you a leader of the people for the people
All the days of his life.
Equal educational opportunity, political opportunity, economic
    opportunity,
Ability, honesty, integrity, widows and orphans.

Canal Zone deems it a privilege
To second the nomination of that great
All the days of his life.
This is what they said. This is what Cooper Blane
Representing the sovereign state of New Jersey said.

Now all the apples in our apple orchard
Are ripening toward fall
And on our poles the beans are greening fast
The pods with sun alert.

And stubble in the field keeps springing yet
In fresh weed, white puffs of daisy weed,
The cat after the gophers
And the breeze brisk.

The Women Poets in English

Round the ears of Packard Bell brisks the breeze
Blows the volume loud and away,
Puffs of volume pile up in the fence corners
Where the cat is active.

What do we understand?
First of all, we know the speakers are speaking the English language.
We can tell that from our love-seat, and others agree.
Second, they are both loud, lively both, and there are two of them.
Who are you for?

Now enters from the upper left, the hill slope,
A dog. After the cat.
For a while we miss the whole campaign,
But later the dog comes round for friendship.
Pats him the taxpayer and the tax receiver.

Now enters from the upper right a fisherman.
He leans to hear what's sounding on the screen
Then wordlessly he fades
Down the green sidepatch and the cliff steps
To the roaring bay, leaving no vote behind.

Ladies and gentlemen, when I spoke to you last
In Pawtucket, Maine, the tide was coming in
With a long roar against the shingle of the world.
And ladies and gentlemen I say to you
Vote now against corruption, calumny,
Crime, evil, and corruption,
For the tide is coming in
With a long foreign roar against the world.
Against Winthrop Rockefeller, fair play,
Farm money, cartels, bourbon, and the fifth districts of the world.

Slowly comes up the moon over Lottie's rabbit shed,
Fencing into the sky its bars of protest,
But the vote midwest moves at another cycle
Of midnight desperate.

South Dakota five no,
Robert J. Martin of the fifth district, no.
And at the four hundred and eightieth slogan
The yes and the yes that will survive the midnight.

One sure thing is
That the tough tubes on this little old Packard Bell
Jiggling and jumping in the twi- and moonlight,
Hot as hornets in the excitement,
Won't set the beans on fire, and won't
Harm the cat, and won't
Even warm us where we sit and listen,
But will burn away
Lively as bugs in the midsummer
To get the last yes and no in the midsummer
On record to the moon's blanched countenance.
Who are you for?

Brenda Chamberlain

Lament

My man is a bone ringed with weed.
Thus it was on my bridal night:
That the sea, risen to a green wall
At our window, quenching love's new delight,
Stood curved between me and the midnight call
Of him who said I was so fair
He could drown for joy in the salt of my hair.
We sail, he said,
Like the placid dead
Who have long forgotten the marriage-bed.

On my bridal night
Brine stung the window.
Alas, on every night since then
These eyes have rained
For him who made my heart sing
At the lifting of the latch;
For him who will not come again
Weary from the sea.

The wave tore his bright flesh in her greed:
My man is a bone ringed with weed.

Dead Ponies

There is death enough in Europe without these
Dead ponies on the mountain.
They are the underlining, the emphasis of death.
It is not wonderful that when they live
Their eyes are shadowed under mats of hair.
Despair and famine do not gripe so hard
When the bound earth and sky are kept remote
Behind clogged hairs.

The snows engulfed them, pressed their withered haunches flat,
Filled up their nostrils, burdened the cage of their ribs.
The snow retreated. Their bodies stink to heaven,
Potently crying out to raven hawk and dog;
Come! Pick us clean; cleanse our fine bones of blood.

They were never lovely save as foals,
Before their necks grew long, uncrested;
But the wildness of the mountain was in their stepping,
The pride of Spring burnt in their haunches,
They were tawny as the rushes of the marsh.

The prey-birds have had their fill, and preen their feathers:
Soft entrails have gone to make the hawk arrogant.

May Sarton

At Lindos

"What are ruins to us,
The broken stones?"
They made for the sea,
These elementals
Possessed by Poseidon.
"And what is Athene?"
The sun flamed around them.
The waters were clear green.

What compelled us
To face the harsh rock?

Why did we choose
The arduous stairways?
There lay the crescent
Of white sand below us,
And the lucky swimmers.

But at last we came out,
Stood high in the white light,
And we knew you, Athene,
Goddess of light and air,
In your roofless temple,
In your white and gold.
We were pierced with knowledge.
Lucidity burned us.
What was Poseidon now,
Or the lazy swimmers?
We looked on a flat sea
As blue as lapis.
We stood among pillars
In a soaring elation.

We ran down in triumph,
Down the jagged stairways
To brag to the bathers,
But they rose up to meet us
Mysterious strangers
With salt on their eyelids,
All stupid and shining.

So it is at Lindos,
A place of many gods.

Anne Ridler

Nothing Is Lost

Nothing is lost.
We are too sad to know that, or too blind;
Only in visited moments do we understand:
It is not that the dead return—
They are about us always, though unguessed.

This pencilled Latin verse
You dying wrote me, ten years past and more,
Brings you as much alive to me as the self you wrote it for,
    Dear father, as I read your words
    With no word but Alas.

Lines in a letter, lines in a face
Are faithful currents of life: the boy has written
His parents across his forehead, and as we burn
    Our bodies up each seven years,
    His own past self has left no plainer trace.

Nothing dies.
The cells pass on their secrets, we betray them
Unknowingly; in a freckle, in the way
    We walk, recall some ancestor,
    And Adam in the colour of our eyes.

Yes, on the face of the newborn,
Before the soul has taken full possession,
There pass, as over a screen, in succession
    The images of other beings:
    Face after face looks out, and then is gone.

Nothing is lost, for all in love survive.
I lay my cheek against his sleeping limbs
To feel if he is warm, and touch in him
    Those children whom no shawl could warm,
    No arms, no grief, no longing could revive.

Thus what we see, or know,
Is only a tiny portion, at the best,
Of the life in which we share; an iceberg's crest
    Our sunlit present, our partial sense,
    With deep supporting multitudes below.

Backgrounds to Italian Paintings: Fifteenth Century

Look between the bow and the bowstring, beneath
The flying feet of confederate angels,
    Beyond old Montefeltro's triumph seat—
    There the delectable landscape lies

Not furtive, but discreet:
It is not hiding, but withholds the secret.
What do the calm foreground figures know of it?
(Suffering martyrdom, riding a triumph
With a crowd of nymphs and Loves about the car)
What do they know of the scenes wherein they are?

The knees of the hills rise from wreaths of sleep,
The distant horsemen glimmer; the pigment fading
Has turned the juniper-green to brown;
And there the river winds away for ever.

We ourselves have walked those hills and valleys
Where the broom glows and the brittle rock-rose,
Combes are cool with chestnut and plains with poplar:
The juniper there was green—we have been
There, but were not given the secret,
Did not find our rest.

So give this land a stranger's look at best.

Later the landscape stole the picture, the human
Figures were banished, and with the figures vanished
From every natural scene the look of secrets.
So it seems that the figures held the clue.
Gaze at the story boldly as children do—
The wonder awaits you, cornerwise, but never
Full in the face; only the background promises,
Seen through the purple cones at the edge of the eye
And never to be understood:
The sleep-wreathed hills, the ever-winding river.

Muriel Rukeyser

Night Feeding

Deeper than sleep but not so deep as death
I lay there dreaming and my magic head
remembered and forgot.   On first cry I
remembered and forgot and did believe.

I knew love and I knew evil:
woke to the burning song and the tree burning blind,
despair of our days and the calm milk-giver who
knows sleep, knows growth, the sex of fire and grass,
renewal of all waters and the time of the stars
and the black snake with gold bones.

Black sleeps, gold burns;   on second cry I woke
fully and gave to feed and fed on feeding.
Gold seed, green pain, my wizards in the earth
walked through the house, black in the morning dark.
Shadows grew in my veins, my bright belief,
my head of dreams deeper than night and sleep.
Voices of all black animals crying to drink,
cries of all birth arise, simple as we,
found in the leaves, in clouds and dark, in dream,
deep as this hour, ready again to sleep.

Boy With His Hair Cut Short

Sunday shuts down on this twentieth-century evening.
The El passes. Twilight and bulb define
the brown room, the overstuffed plum sofa,
the boy, and the girl's thin hands above his head.
A neighbor radio sings stocks, news, serenade.

He sits at the table, head down, the young clear neck exposed.
watching the drugstore sign from the tail of his eye;
tattoo, neon, until the eye blears, while his
solicitous tall sister, simple in blue, bending
behind him, cuts his hair with her cheap shears.

The arrow's electric red always reaches its mark,
successful neon! He coughs, impressed by that precision.
His child's forehead, forever protected by his cap,
is bleached against the lamplight as he turns head
and steadies to let the snippets drop.

Erasing the failure of weeks with level fingers,
she sleeks the fine hair, combing: "You'll look fine tomorrow!
You'll surely find something, they can't keep turning you down;

the finest gentleman's not so trim as you!" Smiling, he raises
the adolescent forehead wrinkling ironic now.

He sees his decent suit laid out, new-pressed,
his carfare on the shelf. He lets his head fall, meeting
her earnest hopeless look, seeing the sharp blades splitting,
the darkened room, the impersonal sign, her motion,
the blue vein, bright on her temple, pitifully beating.

Jean Garrigue

Old Haven

Directions that you took
Which told me how I could
Amid those cultured streets describe
My rude impulse to you,
Now turn within my head,
Signs tangled while I sought
Good milkmen who could set me straight.

As those on bicycles
Who asked me was I lost
And mouldy houses that concurred
With cornices to bless,
All proved such lesson of
Love's reassuring depths.

The churches of the place
And dear, pastured squares
Like museum objects borrowed
An ancient air to please
Till dim old gentlemen
Like robin goodmen winked
And sprightly dogs were unicorns.

Now absent from you, dear,
My fatuous joy declares
How love may change a city, give
Glee to horses pulling

Loads, to gutters virtue
And to salesmen, grace.

For smile so sweetly those
Tottering cupolas, old
Curbs in my enamoured thought (where
Spongy Florida steals
The stale New England air),
I ponder on love's strength,

So cunning when direct,
So roguish when sincere!
If dogs may charm because you're there,
Drugstores infatuate,
And meanest citizens
Like saints from niches step
To guide me to your goodness and to luck.

Now Snow Descends

Now snow descends as if I'd gapped a grave
And all my heart is visible like death.
So you are gone who beggar all you gave
By still outvying what of you I have.
So you are gone and I am all your grave
Who long as longs the body for its soul
To turn the time which was its last, control,
Compose the sweetness that so ran,
And envy not the time that will not come,
Control, compose, and so then die again!

The snow now hastens to its formal rest.
So you are gone and I'm alone with ills.
Despair now seeks me as great longing starts.
Despair to know what I'm unworthy of,
Despair to know what changes as I breathe
So each farewell must seem its last and I
The laggard with what's both too quick and dear,
Left here with what now mutates in your sphere
Your lately joys become my harsh red north.

All this surrounds me like great stones,
Great stones the snow has covered delicately.

But if they move ... I sit in darkness here
Until past pang, past common pang, and care,
I'm hunted to this last extremity:
To make one instant that you gave a life
Or by one word upon your cold soft mouth
Elucidate the action of your soul
By that one rose whose language is your myth.
(O snow that makes the wind too visible
And dares to tell enigmas of its wrath!)

 _____

Jean Burden

Poem Before Departure

This place moves from me
like a slow tide pulling out
against the moon.
It does not matter if I push up earth
against the door,
or turn the key within the lock;
even as I lean,
the tree trembles in the wood,
the pebble flies within the rock.

Or if I stay like a crouched animal
within,
I watch the walls move back,
grow membrane-thin;
leaves sprayed against the pane
blur a little at the edge;
vines pale and loosen on the sill.

It does not matter that I prop beneath the knob
tables, chairs.
Something recedes
that once was still;
what was mobile, stares.

The time is soon,
though I, longing to be caught by root
or weed,

resist departure as a kind of death.
Something began and ended here.

One morning, whether I dare or do not dare,
I shall look up, unroofed, to sky;
I shall gaze through timber
that once I leaned my fear against—
and knock on air.

Barbara Howes

Out Fishing

We went out, early one morning,
Over the loud marches of the sea,
In our walnut-shell boat,
Tip-tilting over that blue vacancy.

Combering, coming in,
The waves shellacked us, left us breathless, ill;
Hour on hour, out
Of this emptiness no fish rose, until

The great one struck that twine-
Wrapped flying-fish hard, turned and bolted
Off through the swelling sea
By a twist of his shoulder, with me tied fast; my rod

Held him, his hook held me,
In tug-of-war—sidesaddle on the ocean
I rode out the flaring waves,
Rode till the great fish sounded; by his submersion

He snapped the line, we lost
All contact; north, south, west, my adversary
Storms on through his world
Of water: I do not know him: he does not know me.

Danaë

Golden, within this golden hive
Wild bees drone,

As if at any moment they may
Swarm and be gone
From the arched fibres of their cage,
Lithe as whalebone.

Over a pasture, once, I saw
A flock of small
Martins flying in concert, high
Then wheeling, fall;
Like buckshot pent in a string bag
They dotted all

That sky-patch, holding form in their flight,
A vase poured,
Their breathing shape hung in the air—
Below, the road
Fled secretly as quicksilver:
My eyes blurred.

All things come to their pinnacle
Though landscapes shift,
Women sit in the balance, as
Upon a knife;
Irony cuts to the quick—is this
Life or new life?

They sit their years out on a scale,
The heavy yoke
Of their heavy stomachs grounding them—
Or else come back
To barrenness with each full moon;
Minds go slack

Longing, or dreading, that a new
Form will take shape.
(The martins' swarming is a brush-stroke
On the landscape,
Within their white-gold, fleshly hall
The wild bees wake.)

Homing at close of day, they meet
This moment: now:
Love calls from its subterranean passage,

The bed they know
May support agony or joy—
To bed they go.

Isabella Gardner

Cock-a-Hoop

How struts my love my cavalier
How crows he like a chanticleer
How softly I am spurred my dear;
Our bed is feathered with desire
And this yard safe from fox and fire.
But spurless on the dunghill, dead,
The soldier's blood is rooster red,
His seed is spent and no hen fed,
Alas no chick of this sweet cock
Will speak for Christ at dawn o'clock.

That "Craning of the Neck"

The Primary word is I-Thou. The
primary word I-Thou can only be
spoken with the whole being. The
primary word I-It can never be spoken
with the whole being.—Martin Buber

Birthdays from the ocean one desert april noon
I rode through the untouching and no-odored air
astride an english saddle on a western mare
through the resisting tow-colored grass and the dune-
less sand. Under me swam a stream strange in that dried
country. A "great blue heron" stood still in the tide-
less water and when I saw him there my heart daz-
zled. I whispered the mare to move quietly as
Indians move, I reined her with a catpaw hand
and my breathless feet crouched into the stirrups and
I prayed her through cactus mesquite and cattlebones
to the water's edge where the tall bird fished the stones.
The listening heron expanded with despair

unloosed unwilling wings, heaved from water into air.
O he hated to fly he flapped with a splayed pain-
ful motion. Deliberate as a weathervane
he plodded through the air that touched the fishful water.
I followed him silently giving no quarter
all that afternoon. He never flew far from me
we kept meeting past each cape and estuary
but he always heaved doggedly out of touch. I
only wanted to stare myself into him to try
and thou him till we recognized and became each
other. We were both fishing. But I could not reach
his eye. He fled in puzzled ponderous pain
and I last rode home, conspicuous as Cain,
yet ashamed of a resigned demeaning pity
that denied us both. I returned to the city
and visited the zoo, fished on a concrete shore,
took children to aquariums, and rode no more.

I found that the encyclopedia says "A
gregarious bird . . ." No one spoke that desert day,
not one word. That fisher who heaved to dodge my eye
has damned himself an It and I shall never fly.

Barbara Guest

Direction

Let us give up our trips
to pace to and fro here as easily
the foreignness of these leaves
the untranslatable silences, the echoes
of a tower, difficult winds,
as well here sail our barges.

Friend of the static hour
I take your hand across the borders.

Haven't we with our skills
lost important elements
of our luggage performing in lonely

hotels? The seacoasts are cruel
in winter the sand is a waste
cry to my tongue the sand it is like
my heart which I have buried in it
now there is a posture lying there
you can recognize it. I have only
two hearts, I need this orphaned
one here at home which is
the Scandinavia of all Russias.

The light is not idle, it is full of rapid
changes we can call voyages
if we like, moving from room to room.

How representative of us this thoughtful
weather that has travelled the water
to reach us, the touch of a certain side
of the skin when we open the window.

Our eyes are viewing monuments
constantly, the angry sculpture
of the facade it is also a journey
to the center where the rock is uncut.
Climbing it tests our strength, our bruises
are so many cities, the blood we shed
is ours, so I say we can belong
nowhere else, here is the counter
of our wounds and our delicacies.

On our own soil that is an excavation
desolate as the place whose name
we must never pronounce.

 _____

Ruth Stone

The Burned Bridge

Sister was wedged beside the wicker basket,
Slats of hot midsummer striped her dress,
Speckled dust in shifting sun and shadow.

The trolley lurched to leeward, seemed to press
Our bodies backward in a flowered meadow,
Tossed mama's brown hair sculptured in a puff.
Father rose and reeling from our side
Interviewed the trenchant motorman. How rough
The whitecaps glittered beyond the marsh;
Our pulses leaped at the stench of kelp and the harsh
Scream of the cormorant skimming the trolley wire.
Halfway on the clanging headlong ride
The trolley crossed a bridge charred black from fire
And reason impaled me, even through mama's smile
And the arc of the motorman's tobacco juice.
"There, there," soothed mama; "The deuce!" said father.
But knowing better, I cried.
Though we went on for mile after summer mile
And arrived as we always did at the rank seaside,
All that held me up seemed wholly mad.
Not even the hidden drop-off, or bloated death
In the luminous choppy water, diverted my sad
Foreboding, or the derelict lighthouse in whose shade we lunched.

At sunset sister slept like a rosy anchor
Fastening parents to bench, and while they bunched
The tide rolled softly landward like her breath;
While I sat listening, wretched, without rancor,
Submissive on the bench beside the track.
Knowing, this time, the burned bridge would break,
I clearly saw my parents committed to folly.
Mama, for all her airs, could but clean and bake.
Now father, as in a nightmare, would take us back;
And hooting around the bend came the feckless trolley.

My Son
Having lost my leather purse
Stuffed with all those unpaid bills and trading stamps,
I live with two dogs who sleep on my bed.
I have forgotten who owes who;
More, the lamps wabble, the wiring is bad.
True, there were epigrams which cost me five years of my life;
Nail clippers, address books

Crammed with poems and telephone numbers.
The list of contents cannot classify
My hatchet wounds.
Dismembered.
Part of me is gone;
Concrete proof of responsibility,
Identification, driver's license.
Friends say, where are your numbers?
What will you put in your zipper?
Have you searched the ground?
Who is to be informed in case you are drowned?
The essential family has become myself. A son who might have been
Pays the penalty of oblivion. Who is he?
He sleeps in the old pouch; an unfinished poem
Lying along some roadside where exercising frogs
Rest on his mother's leather
And his father is nowhere to be found.

Bernice Ames

Country of Water

Sleep is a country of water
found in abandoned bodies.
Some motion missing from day
shakes the limbs of their essence
frees the last cornered reflection
sea-wracks the psyche
a dragged stone in the stream.

Words tumble darkness
their flat edges lost
and faces go with them
catch in the dreams' undertow
a torn seaweed drifting.
Each dream pushes another ahead
and pulls one to follow.

All the turbulence shored
by the banks of the body

all the lives lived behind closed eyes
run in sleep-dark veins.

Just before waking
in the light sleep of leaves over water
sleep and dream are one.
Then sun draws the water
from discarded limbs.
In a sweet reluctance
the shallows are crossed.
All the borders are known.

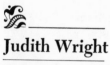

Judith Wright

Storm

On the headland's grassed and sheltered side,
out of the wind I crouch and watch
while driven by the seaward ship-destroying storm
races of insane processional breakers come.
A long-dead divine authority reflows the tide
at evening, and already the gnawed hill of beach
alters and shrinks. The waves cry out: Let us be done.

Let us be done with the long submission, the whips
that hurl us for ever on time's frigid stone
mouthing our ever-repeated plea for an answer and getting none.
Let us break free, smash down the land's gate
and drown all questions under a black flood.
Hate, then, the waves cry; hate.

And round each headland of the world, each drenching rock,
crowding each wild spray-drop, as in the womb's calm lying,
they beat and whirl on the waves, the invisible legion
of momentary crystals, less-than-a-second's-tick
lives, love's first and everywhere creation;
so small, so strong, that nothing of this mad rock-torn
surge and violence, not the storm's final desperation
touches them,
busy in the unhurt stillness, breeding and dying.

South of My Days

South of my days' circle, part of my blood's country
rises that tableland, high delicate outline
of bony slopes wincing under the winter;
low trees blue-leaved and olive; outcropping granite—
clean, lean, hungry country. The creek's leaf-silenced,
willow-choked, the slope a tangle of medlar and crab-apple,
branching over and under, blotched with a green lichen;
and the old cottage lurches in for shelter.

O cold the black-frost night. The walls draw in to the warmth
and the old roof cracks its joints; the slung kettle
hisses a leak on the fire. Hardly to be believed that summer
will turn up again some day in a wave of rambler roses,
thrust its hot face in here to tell another yarn—
a story old Dan can spin into a blanket against the winter.
Seventy years of stories he clutches round his bones.
Seventy summers are hived in him like old honey.

Droving that year, Charleville to the Hunter,
nineteen-one it was, and the drought beginning;
sixty head left at the McIntyre, the mud round them
hardened like iron; and the yellow boy died
in the sulky ahead with the gear, but the horse went on,
stopped at the Sandy Camp and waited in the evening.
It was the flies we seen first, swarming like bees.
Came to the Hunter, three hundred head of a thousand—
cruel to keep them alive—and the river was dust.

Or mustering up in the Bogongs in the autumn
when the blizzards came early. Brought them down; we brought them
down, what aren't there yet. Or driving for Cobb's on the run
up from Tamworth—Thunderbolt at the top of Hungry Hill,
and I give him a wink. I wouldn't wait long, Fred,
not if I was you; the troopers are just behind,
coming for that job at the Hillgrove. He went like a luny,
him on his big black horse.
                    Oh, they slide and they vanish
as he shuffles the years like a pack of conjuror's cards.
True or not, it's all the same; and the frost on the roof
cracks like a whip, and the back-log breaks into ash.

Wake, old man. This is winter, and the yarns are over.
No one is listening.
                    South of my days' circle
I know it dark against the stars, the high lean country
full of old stories that still go walking in my sleep.

The Hawthorn Hedge

How long ago she planted the hawthorn hedge—
she forgets how long ago—
that barrier thorn across the hungry ridge;
thorn and snow.

It is twice as tall as the rider on the tall mare
who draws his reins to peer
in through the bee-hung blossom. Let him stare.
No one is here.

Only the mad old girl from the hut on the hill,
unkempt as an old tree.
She will hide away if you wave your hand or call;
she will not see.

Year-long, wind turns her grindstone heart and whets
a thornbranch like a knife,
shouting in winter "Death"; and when the white bud sets,
more loudly, "Life."

She has forgotten when she planted the hawthorn hedge;
that thorn, that green, that snow;
birdsong and sun dazzled across the ridge—
it was long ago.

Her hands were strong in the earth, her glance on the sky,
her song was sweet on the wind.
The hawthorn hedge took root, grew wild and high
to hide behind.

Woman to Man

The eyeless labourer in the night,
the selfless, shapeless seed I hold,
builds for its resurrection day—

silent and swift and deep from sight
foresees the unimagined light.

This is no child with a child's face;
this has no name to name it by;
yet you and I have known it well.
This is our hunter and our chase,
the third who lay in our embrace.

This is the strength that your arm knows,
the arc of flesh that is my breast,
the precise crystals of our eyes.
This is the blood's wild tree that grows
the intricate and folded rose.

This is the maker and the made;
this is the question and reply;
the blind head butting at the dark,
the blaze of light along the blade.
Oh hold me, for I am afraid.

Woman to Child

You who were darkness warmed my flesh
where out of darkness rose the seed.
Then all a world I made in me:
all the world you hear and see
hung upon my dreaming blood.

There moved the multitudinous stars,
and coloured birds and fishes moved.
There swam the sliding continents.
All time lay rolled in me, and sense,
and love that knew not its beloved.

O node and focus of the world—
I hold you deep within that well
you shall escape and not escape—
that mirrors still your sleeping shape,
that nurtures still your crescent cell.

I wither and you break from me;
yet though you dance in living light,

I am the earth, I am the root,
I am the stem that fed the fruit,
the link that joins you to the night.

The Surfer

He thrust his joy against the weight of the sea,
climbed through, slid under those long banks of foam—
(hawthorn hedges in spring, thorns in the face stinging).
How his brown strength drove through the hollow and coil
of green-through weirs of water!
Muscle of arm thrust down long muscle of water.
And swimming so, went out of sight
where mortal, masterful, frail, the gulls went wheeling
in air, as he in water, with delight.

Turn home, the sun goes down; swimmer, turn home.
Last leaf of gold vanishes from the sea-curve.
Take the big roller's shoulder, speed and swerve.
Come to the long beach home like a gull diving.

For on the sand the grey-wolf sea lies snarling;
cold twilight wind splits the waves' hair and shows
the bones they worry in their wolf-teeth. O, wind blows,
and sea crouches on sand, fawning and mouthing;
drops there and snatches again, drops and again snatches
its broken toys, its whitened pebbles and shells.

Sanctuary

The road beneath the giant original trees
sweeps on and cannot wait. Varnished by dew,
its darkness mimics mirrors and is bright
behind the panic eyes the driver sees
caught in headlights. Behind his wheels the night
takes over: only the road ahead is true.
It knows where it is going; we go too.

Sanctuary, the sign said. Sanctuary—
trees, not houses; flat skins pinned to the road
of possum and native-cat; and here the old tree stood
for how many thousand years? that old gnome-tree
some axe-new boy cut down. Sanctuary, it said:

but only the road has meaning here. It leads
into the world's cities like a long fuse laid.

Fuse, nerve, strand of a net, tense
bearer of messages, snap-tight violin-string,
dangerous knife-edge laid across the dark,
what has that sign to do with you? The immense
tower of antique forest and cliff, the rock
where years accumulate like leaves, the tree
where transient bird and mindless insect sing?
The word the board holds up is Sanctuary,
and the road knows that notice-boards make sense,

but has no time to pray. Only, up there,
morning sets doves upon the power-line.
Swung on that fatal voltage like a sign
and meaning love, perhaps they are a prayer.

Ann Stanford

The Riders

For Eunice

We made castles of grass, green halls, enormous stem-lined rooms
and sailed in trees.
Close to the backyard fence
We dug a cave.
We never finished it,
But there was plenty of time for moving that last foot or two of earth,
It was an eternity till Christmas.

Do you remember the yellow fields
We tussled through, small mustard petals clinging?
And the hikes on Saturday up to the grove of oaks?
Plenty of time then, and dark came down before we were home.
They were out calling and searching.

There was a winter year and a summer year.
The last was for beaches.
Salt wind over the gaudy pier,

And things moved faster.
You on the yellow horse, I on the dun.
One way the sea, the battleship,
The pier, the fishers leaning by the rail,
The ferris wheel,
And turning still
The shoddy mermaid painted on the wall.
Up and down we laughed and caught the rings.
And one was gold for summer.

Then summer was gone, and the horse bunched warm ripples
Trotting through orchards down to the practice ring.
His eyes were like suns, when he changed his gait
Faster and faster till the trees blurred and the sky
And there were only posts and the wind and the packed earth
And the warm beast gathering and springing.
How to get off, how to escape!
At last I fell, but it was no better.

The earth turned under my back
Swift, swift, we turned out of day to night to day again,
Light and shadow from a picket fence.

And the planet whirled on the sun, a swift carousel.

Our heads grow gray, our children laugh in the long grasses.

The Beating

The first blow caught me sideways, my jaw
Shifted. The second beat my skull against my
Brain. I raised my arm against the third.
Downward my wrist fell crooked. But the sliding

Flood of sense across the ribs caught in
My lungs. I fell for a long time,
One knee bending. The fourth blow balanced me.
I doubled at the kick against my belly.

The fifth was light. I hardly felt the
Sting. And down, breaking against my side, my
Thighs, my head. My eyes burst closed, my
Mouth the thick blood curds moved through. There

Were no more lights. I was flying. The
Wind, the place I lay, the silence.
My call came to a groan. Hands touched
My wrist. Disappeared. Something fell over me.

Now this white room tortures my eye.
The bed too soft to hold my breath,
Slung in plaster, caged in wood.
Shapes surround me.

No blow! No blow!
They only ask the thing I turn
Inside the black ball of my mind,
The one white thought.

Night of Souls

I saw each soul as light, each single body
With his life's breath kindled and set like flame
Before his nostrils. All creatures visible—
Small beings moving in the midnight grasses,

Light in the thoroughfares underfoot
The mole's house hung with the mole's breath
As with candles, and the busy air
Clouded with light.

It is no longer midnight, for the sea
Rustles translucent waters, windows letting out
The glow of all its denizens, colored as through
Cathedral glass, the night sky dark
Save where a lost gull drops like a meteor
Into the phosphorous waves.

The linnets chirp as in daylight. The owl dazzles himself.
Silent and still, wondering by the glare of his mother
The new colt shines.
Light betrays the young deer in the thicket

On this night of the lighting of spirits
All quiet, all visible
Till the lantern of man comes up over the hill,
Shades out those other beams like a bare sun rising.

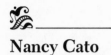

Nancy Cato

Independence

*I will think of the leech-gatherer on
the lonely moor.* —Wordsworth

How the red road stretched before us, mile on mile
Narrowing into the distance, straight as though ruled
On yellow paper, away to the lilac hills
Low on the horizon. Above them the storm-clouds piled
In a sky blue as though bruised; yet all ahead
Was glowing in an unearthly wash of light—
Dry roly-poly and saltbush lit to beauty,
The sky a menace, but the wide plains bright.

And there in that lonely place an ancient swagman,
Traveller, bagman, sundowner, what you will—
His rolled-up blankets slung aslant his shoulders,
Billy dangling, his back to the line of hills
And the coming storm: as mysterious in that place
(With his hat set straight and his grey beard blowing)
As a small ship glimpsed a moment far from land.
Where did he come from, where could he be going?

I shall never know, for we had to race the rain
That turns the blacksoil plains to a gluey mud
Bogging to the axles. Only a wave of the hand,
But still the imagination glows, the blood
Stirs at the memory of that symbolic stranger
Glimpsed in a moment of vision and swiftly gone:
Man and his independent spirit, alone
On the vast plains, with night and rain coming on.

Edith Marcombe Shiffert

Manners

In the pleasant pastime of temple viewing
smile and say oh as each treasure is revealed.
Stand back and look up at rooflines often.

Toss a small coin in the offering boxes
and bow respectfully where others bow.
At the end, bow also to the guiding priest and say thank you,
and walk away slowly, looking back at the buildings again.

Quiet amazement is appreciated as a response
or one simple question, such as, "What wood are the pillars made of?"
Actually, just being there is enough,
and looking peaceful, and wanting to go slowly.

In front of the greatest treasure,
whether carved Buddha, an old scroll, a wall painting,
or a group of rocks on the moss,
to just kneel silent for ten minutes, happily,
as though no greater bliss could be asked for,
is ample for all to be satisfied

and they may leave you there, alone with your joy
in a dark corner, or on a veranda edge,
peering through the gloom past rainbow curtains
to glimpses of images while you breathe in vague smoke
of incense and candles, or watching the austere garden,
until it seems no one else comes there and the time is inexhaustable.

Monkeys on Mt. Hiei

They came hurrying across the mountain highway,
the monkeys,
and from the car window we had only three oranges
to toss out in sections to a hundred.

Each baby clung tightly to a mother's chest,
joggled, upside down, as she ran toward us.

Neither sacred nor human,
liking commercial foods,
certainly thinly covered from cold by their fur,
none deserts the tribe
and the tribe does not leave its high ridge.

We keep remembering the brown eyes
looking up into ours,
unemotional but waiting.
Did they show what serenity might be,
each face calm
even while accepting that one would be the one
to snatch a given bit of food
although another almost had it?

Yesterday it snowed up there on the red foliage
and on the ancient huge enduring cedar trees.
From the city we look up at the white ridges.

The Shadow of a Branch

I think of things like the shadow of a branch
brushed back and forth on the wall
vanishing in an instant when a light is lit.

And of beams of light
slanting through water to its bottom
without a thing added nor lost.

Such additions and movements
as a cloud coming gradually over the moon and then
in a subtraction of uncountable parts evaporating.
And of exploded fragments of a spaceship shattered on the moon.

Life in the hand is a fish
in a solitary pool—and then more fish.
And leaves falling into the pool, and slime they become.

Between expansion and shrinkage crickets keep sounding
and we say it is October, it gets colder.
The color of flaming increases until it is all black and white
like a vast ruin, still, with birds.

Gwendolyn Brooks

From *The Womanhood*

I

the children of the poor

1

People who have no children can be hard:
Attain a mail of ice and insolence:
Need not pause in the fire, and in no sense
Hesitate in the hurricane to guard.
And when wide world is bitten and bewarred
They perish purely, waving their spirits hence
Without a trace of grace or of offense
To laugh or fail, diffident, wonder-starred.
While through a throttling dark we others hear
The little lifting helplessness, the queer
Whimper-whine; whose unridiculous
Lost softness softly makes a trap for us.
And makes a curse. And makes a sugar of
The malocclusions, the inconditions of love.

2

What shall I give my children? who are poor,
Who are adjudged the leastwise of the land,
Who are my sweetest lepers, who demand
No velvet and no velvety velour;
But who have begged me for a brisk contour,
Crying that they are quasi, contraband
Because unfinished, graven by a hand
Less than angelic, admirable or sure.
My hand is stuffed with mode, design, device.
But I lack access to my proper stone.
And plenitude of plan shall not suffice
Nor grief nor love shall be enough alone
To ratify my little halves who bear
Across an autumn freezing everywhere.

VI

the rites for Cousin Vit

Carried her unprotesting out the door.
Kicked back the casket-stand. But it can't hold her,
That stuff and satin aiming to enfold her,
The lid's contrition nor the bolts before.
Oh oh. Too much. Too much. Even now, surmise,
She rises in the sunshine. There she goes,
Back to the bars she knew and the repose
In love-rooms and the things in people's eyes.
Too vital and too squeaking. Must emerge.
Even now she does the snake-hips with a hiss,
Slops the bad wine across her shantung, talks
Of pregnancy, guitars and bridgework, walks
In parks or alleys, comes haply on the verge
Of happiness, haply hysterics. Is.

XI

One wants a Teller in a time like this.

One's not a man, one's not a woman grown.
To bear enormous business all alone.

One cannot walk this winding street with pride,
Straight-shouldered, tranquil-eyed,
Knowing one knows for sure the way back home.
One wonders if one has a home.

One is not certain if or why or how.
One wants a Teller now: —

Put on your rubbers and you won't catch cold.
Here's hell, there's heaven. Go to Sunday School.
Be patient, time brings all good things—(and cool
Strong balm to calm the burning at the brain?)—
Behold
Love's true, and triumphs, and God's actual.

The Last Quatrain of the Ballad of Emmett Till

after the murder,
after the burial

Emmett's mother is a pretty-faced thing;
    the tint of pulled taffy.
She sits in a red room,
    drinking black coffee.
She kisses her killed boy.
    And she is sorry.
Chaos in windy grays
    through a red prairie.

Ruth Herschberger

The Huron

I swam the Huron of love, and am not ashamed,
It was many saw me do it, scoffing, scoffing,
They said it was foolish, winter and all,
But I dove in, greaselike, and swam.
And came up where Erie verges.
I would say for the expenditure of love,
And the atrophy of longing, there is no cure
So swift, so sleek, so fine, so draining
As a swim through the Huron in the wintertime.

The Lumberyard

We watched our love burn with the lumberyard,
Bats in their wheeling showed our crazèd sense,
We stood in fields where weeds with chiggers scrambled,
And stood the heat flush in our face, immense.

Softly the crowd acclaimed the devastation,
And we, we smiled to see the embers twist,
Tottering towers and poles with flashing wires.
We shifted feet when shifting structures kissed.

Up in the sky the stars were red sparks shuttling,
Planes with a scouter's appetite hung by.
And at our backs the Negro huts were lit
With yellow mist, a ghostly gayety.

Sound above all: the cracking and the crocked,
As bones that, whetted by the warmer flames,
Edged into death, until the crimson glow
Vanquished the knotted amber boards, the names.

All banished, all decided, all cast in;
Far back beyond, the trees made silver white
By steaming flames, rose as cold piles of cloud
To cool this mirror of the blazing night.

And we beheld, we watched, as drunk as all,
And gladdened when the bursting peaked and sprung,
Rejoiced to see the threat of fire win,
And sang to see the worthy timbers wrung.

We watched our love burn with the lumberyard,
Magnificent the sight, the sin, the shame,
The vice profusely lavished; wheeled the bats
Silent as we, but crazed, crazed as the flame.

May Swenson

Frontispiece

In this book I see your face and in your face
your eyes holding the world and all else besides
as a cat's pupils rayed and wide
to what is before them and what more alive
ticks in the shadows flickers in the waves

Your hair in a slow stream curves
from your listening brow
to your ear shaped like a sea-thing found
in that water-haunted house where murmurs
your chaste-fierce name   The vow

that corners your mouth
compelled you to that deep between words and acts
where they cross as sand with salt
There spills the layered light
your sockets lips and nostrils drank

before they sank
On stages of the sea the years tall
tableaus build   The lighthouse you commanded
the room the oak and mutable Orlando
reoccur as the sea's pages to land's mind   The wall

the steep and empty slate
your cane indented until you laid it as a mark
above where the tide would darken
is written in weed and shell how you were sane
when walking you wrapped your face

in the green scarf
the gray
and then the black
The waves carve your hearse and tomb
and toll your voyage out again again

Death Invited

Death invited to break his horns
on the spread
cloth. To drop his head
on the dragged flag on the sand.
Death's hooves slipping
in blood, and a band
of blood down the black side.
Death's tongue, curved in the open mouth
like a gray horn, dripping
blood. And
six colored agonies decking the summit
of his muscled pride.
Death invited to die.

The head
of death, with bewildered raging eye,

flagged down,
dragged down to the red
cloth on the sand.
Death invited to stand,
legs spread,
on the spot of the cape.
To buckle stubborn knees and lie
down in blood on the silken shape.
Beg blindness come to the sun-pierced eye.

The sword, sunk at the top of the shoulder's pride—
its hilt a silver cross—drawn forth now lets
hot radiant blood slide
from bubbling nostrils
through cloth to thirsty ground.

Yearning horns found
fleeing cloth and bloodless pillow,
substance none. Arrogant thighs,
that swiped and turned death by,
now, close as love, above lean lunging,
filling the pain-hot eye.
That stares till it turns to blood.
With the short knife dug
quick!
to the nape.
And the thick
neck drops on the spot of the cape.

Chains are drawn
round the horns, whose points are clean.
Trumpets shout.
New sand is thrown
where death's blood streamed.
Four stout,
jingling horses with gilded hooves
tug death out.

Life is awarded ears and flowers.
Pelted with hats and shoes, and praise,
glittering life, in tight pink thighs,
swaggers around a rotunda of screams and *Oles*.

Death is dragged from the ring,
a clumsy hide,
a finished thing—
back to his pen.
The gate swings shut.

The gate swings wide.
Here comes trotting, snorting death
let loose again.

Flying Home From Utah

Forests are branches of a tree lying down,
its blurred trunk in the north.
Farms are fitted pieces of a floor,

tan and green tiles that get smoother,
smaller, the higher we fly.
Heel-shaped dents of water I know are deep

from here appear opaque, of bluish glass.
Curl after curl, rivers are coarse locks
unravelling southward over the land;

hills, rubbed felt, crumpled bumps
of antlers pricking from young bucks' heads.
Now towns are scratches here and there

on a wide, brown-bristled hide.
Long roads rayed out from the sores of cities
begin to fester and crawl with light—

above them the plane is a passing insect
that eyes down there remark, forget
in the moment it specks the overcast.

It climbs higher. Clouds become ground.
Pillows of snow meet, weld into ice.
Alone on a moonlit stainless rink

glides the ghost of a larva, the shadow
of our plane. Lights go on
in the worm-belly where we sit;

it becomes the world, and seems to cease
to travel—only vibrates, stretched out tense
in the tank of night.

The room of my mind replaces the long, lit room.
I dream I point my eye over a leaf
and fascinate my gaze upon its veins:

A sprawled leaf, many-fingered, its radial
ridges limber, green—but curled,
tattered, pocked, the brown palm

nibbled by insects, nestled in by worms:
One leaf of a tree that's one tree of a forest,
that's the branch of the vein of a leaf

of a tree. Perpetual worlds
within, upon, above the world, the world
a leaf within a wilderness of worlds.

The Willets

One stood still, looking stupid. The other,
beak open, streaming a thin sound,
held wings out, took sideways steps,
stamping the salt marsh. It looked threatening.
The other still stood wooden, a decoy.
He stamp-danced closer, his wings arose,
their hinges straightened,
from the wedge-wide beak the thin sound
streaming agony-high. In fear she wouldn't
stand? She stood.
Her back to him pretended—was it welcome,
or only dazed admission of their fate?
Lifting, he streamed a warning from his beak,
and lit upon her,
trod upon her back, both careful feet.
The wings held off his weight.
His tail pressed down, slipped off. She
animated. And both went back to fishing.

Four-Word Lines

Your eyes are just
like bees, and I
feel like a flower.
Their brown power makes
a breeze go over
my skin. When your
lashes ride down and
rise like brown bees'
legs, your pronged gaze
makes my eyes gauze.
I wish we were
in some shade and
no swarm of other
eyes to know that
I'm a flower breathing
bare, laid open to
your bees' warm stare.
I'd let you wade
in me and seize
with your eager brown
bees' power a sweet
glistening at my core.

On Its Way

Orange on its way
to ash. Anger that a night

will quench. Passion
in its honey swell

pumpkin-plump before the rot.
Bush of fire

everywhere. Fur of hillside
running flame. Rush of heat

to rosehip cheek. Ripeness
on its way to frost.

Glare of blood
before the black. Foxquick

pulse. The sun a den.
Heartkill. And the gold

a gun. It is death
that tints the leaves.

Gwen Harwood

Father and Child

I. Barn Owl

Daybreak: the household slept.
I rose, blessed by the sun.
A horny fiend, I crept
out with my father's gun.
Let him dream of a child
obedient, angel-mild—

old No-sayer, robbed of power
by sleep. I knew my prize
who swooped home at this hour
with daylight-riddled eyes
to his place on a high beam
in our old stables, to dream

light's useless time away.
I stood, holding my breath,
in urine-scented hay,
master of life and death,
a wisp-haired judge whose law
would punish beak and claw.

My first shot struck. He swayed,
ruined, beating his only
wing, as I watched, afraid
by the fallen gun, a lonely
child who believed death clean
and final, not this obscene

bundle of stuff that dropped,
and dribbled through loose straw

tangling in bowels, and hopped
blindly closer. I saw
those eyes that did not see
mirror my cruelty

while the wrecked thing that could
not bear the light nor hide
hobbled in its own blood.
My father reached my side,
gave me the fallen gun.
'End what you have begun.'

I fired. The blank eyes shone
once into mine, and slept.
I leaned my head upon
my father's arm, and wept,
owl-blind in early sun
for what I had begun.

II. Nightfall

Forty years, lived or dreamed:
what memories pack them home.
Now the season that seemed
incredible is come.
Father and child, we stand
in time's long-promised land.

Since there's no more to taste
ripeness is plainly all.
Father, we pick our last
fruits of the temporal.
Eighty years old, you take
this late walk for my sake.

Who can be what you were?
Link your dry hand in mine,
my stick-thin comforter.
Far distant suburbs shine
with great simplicities.
Birds crowd in flowering trees,

sunset exalts its known
symbols of transience.

Your passionate face is grown
to ancient innocence.
Let us walk for this hour
as if death had no power

or were no more than sleep.
Things truly named can never
vanish from earth. You keep
a child's delight for ever
in birds, flowers, shivery-grass—
I name them as we pass.

'*Be your tears wet?*' You speak
as if air touched a string
near breaking-point. Your cheek
brushes on mine. Old king,
your marvellous journey's done.
Your night and day are one

as you find with your white stick
the path on which you turn
home with the child once quick
to mischief, grown to learn
what sorrows, in the end,
no words, no tears can mend.

Marcia Lee Masters

At My Mother's Bedside

Bring now the last flower in to warm this room
That has no fires,
No beauty but the face,
Sorrowed in sleep.

I remember how she gathered flowers,
Bending blithely in the fields,
How she surfed the country pitchers with Queen Anne's Lace.
In the city, she brought in almond blossoms, lilacs,
From the small yard,
And put them in a copper vase, rich as the gongs of China.

And then, in fringe and satin
And her great pearls,
Stood by the mantel, welcoming
Masefield, Lindsay, Tagore.

Here, in this stern white place,
Where voices whisper, like trees in snow,
I think of her glory when I was little,
When waiting by the blurred window,
I saw her come joyous and strong,
Fresh with the love of friends,
Down the cold street, up the hazardous steps of winter.

Then she wore her hair high,
Not drained from her brow,
But golden and swirled,
Like a seashell.
And her hands, turning up lamps,
Had the bright pride of rings.

Later, the glow from the hearth
Made the room sway, pushing back shadows,
While she played, and we danced to Strauss Waltzes,
Which Father begged for his muse.

I remember her voice in the Michigan orchard,
Calling across the leaves,
When she descended the ladder—
Summer was heaped in her skirt: apples, and pears,
And the deep grass whinnied with flurries of bees.

Often, she rose at dark,
Taking her daughters with her,
Walking to town to meet the boat,
Bearing some writer from far seas of his fame;
Seven miles past swamplands, farmlands, and cornfields.
As we came down the hills—the lake sprang with light,
And the sun plunged its scythe into the wheat.

She stood so straight on the pier—
With the verve of an uncut tulip.

Now, in these alien walls
Only a few pale flowers are left,

Shedding their strength on the clockless dresser,
And no more will grow,
No other season come after;
The fruit is all picked, and the bees are scattered.

And I wish that the chill would take leave of the sky,
And the sunset appear, and wrap her in shades of velvet,
Saffron and plum as the gown she wore
Coming home from some splendor in my childhood.

 ———————

Joan Finnigan

From *May Day Rounds: Renfrew County*

The stoop on the log-house is brown with sweet rain-rot
like the boards around an old pump   and the woman is afraid
she comes out of the daylight darkness of the little old house
like an ewe reflecting house-fire in her eyes   retreats
messages shouted back into the house   welfare is like sex
without love   it may be withdrawn at any time without reason
or notice   and then she moves to greet us   wiping her hands
on her faded apron   she is very afraid that we have come
to take something away   to make less in this single room
of cracked and worn linoleum and things without places
peeling unpainted   broken unmended   torn irreparable
work beyond woman's hands   and a nest of three hot irons
on the wood-stove for the week's wash   a man named Job
coughs behind the curtain and moves his feet restlessly in bed
the woman stands skitterish in the middle of the kitchen—
Jordan's voice reaches out to help—"How's your husband, Mrs.
      Clarke?"
"Oh, no better, I'm afraid. He's keepin' no better at all, at all" - - -
(Christ the Martyr, here is thy servant of the hot-stove
hands wring over this wretched fortune and hearken an old pain
going back into the childhood nails of our hands and feet)
"The children are all at school"   "Oh, yes, indeed, indeed - - -"
"And how are they doing?"   "Oh, none too badly, I guess - - -"
she switches the frying pans of green bacon on the stove

297

the woman has only two biting teeth and an ironing-board back
age beyond all chronological reckoning including
this day's addition of fear   but something opens her pores
and flashes an earlier self now   it is when she finds
that we have not come to take anything away   "Oh, yes.
the Clarkes have been here a hundred years," she says
"that's my husband's family   three generations   did you see
the Century Sign on the gate?   the lawyer told us
one-hundred-and-twenty years   SHE HAS A MOMENT OF PRIDE
"I hear you grow apples here the size of pumpkins?"
she has ANOTHER moment standing by her cook-stove
with a battered array of potato-pots scoured and at-the-ready
"yes, yes, the Spy Apples like it here on the side
of the hill beside Lake Doré and our maple syrup was good
this year, too   let me give you some"   (she wants to reward us
for calling on her and not taking anything away)
we demur   she insists   and brings out a twelve-ounce whisky
      bottle
full of the sweet spirits of the tall svelte vats
warm days and cold nights make love and sap come trickling down
we move towards her garden now   shelved along the small panes
a hundred-and-twenty years of moonlight and sunlight
falling on the floor and the faces of babies   school-boys
brides   mothers   dancers   cursers   lovers   wailers
givers   takers   weepers   singers   workers   coffin-bearers
fathers   sisters   brothers   second-cousins   users   accusers
here this sainted shrine of scarlet geraniums and sweet pink clover
shoddies the room further and lights up her eyes   reaches out
and illuminates the manure piles   defies this stony heritage
the man coughs behind the curtain   he has nothing to say
all his prayers have gone unanswered   the three irons nest
hot on the cook-stove   the eldest son   aged twenty-one
is trapped here on this invisible farm   he is the sacrifice
on the mountain   alone in the barn he lets the cattle
have it with a pitch-fork

Mona Van Duyn

The Gardener to His God

*"Amazing research proves simple
prayer makes flowers grow many times
faster, stronger, larger."*
—*Advertisement in* The Flower Grower

I pray that the great world's flowering stay as it is,
that larkspur and snapdragon keep to their ordinary size,
and bleedingheart hang in its old way, and Judas tree
stand well below oak, and old oaks color the fall sky.
For the myrtle to keep underfoot, and no rose
to send up a swollen face, I pray simply.

There is no disorder but the heart's. But if love goes leaking
outward, if shrubs take up its monstrous stalking,
all greenery is spurred, the snapping lips are overgrown,
and over oaks red hearts hang like the sun.
Deliver us from its giant gardening, from walking
all over the earth with no rest from its disproportion.

Let all flowers turn to stone before ever they begin to share
love's spaciousness, and faster, stronger, larger
grow from a sweet thought, before any daisy
turns, under love's gibberellic wish, to the day's eye.
Let all blooms take shape from cold laws, down from a cold air
let come their small grace or measurable majesty.

For in every place but love the imagination lies
in its limits. Even poems draw back from images
of that one country, on top of whose lunatic stemming
whoever finds himself there must sway and cling
until the high cold God takes pity, and it all dies
down, down into the great world's flowering.

Denise Levertov

What Were They Like?

(*Questions and Answers*)

1) Did the people of Viet Nam
use lanterns of stone?
2) Did they hold ceremonies
to reverence the opening of buds?
3) Were they inclined to rippling laughter?
4) Did they use bone and ivory,
jade and silver, for ornament?
5) Had they an epic poem?
6) Did they distinguish between speech and singing?

1) Sir, their light hearts turned to stone.
It is not remembered whether in gardens
stone lanterns illumined pleasant ways.
2) Perhaps they gathered once to delight in blossom,
but after the children were killed
there were no more buds.
3) Sir, laughter is bitter to the burned mouth.
4) A dream ago, perhaps. Ornament is for joy.
All the bones were charred.
5) It is not remembered. Remember,
most were peasants; their life
was in rice and bamboo.
When peaceful clouds were reflected in the paddies
and the water-buffalo stepped surely along terraces,
maybe fathers told their sons old tales.
When bombs smashed the mirrors
there was time only to scream.
6) There is an echo yet, it is said,
of their speech which was like a song.
It is reported their singing resembled
the flight of moths in moonlight.
Who can say? It is silent now.

Living

The fire in leaf and grass
so green it seems
each summer the last summer.

The wind blowing, the leaves
shivering in the sun,
each day the last day.

A red salamander
so cold and so
easy to catch, dreamily

moves his delicate feet
and long tail. I hold
my hand open for him to go.

Each minute the last minute.

Psalm Concerning the Castle

Let me be at the place of the castle.
Let the castle be within me.
Let it rise foursquare from the moat's ring.
Let the moat's waters reflect green plumage of ducks, let the shells of
    swimming turtles break the surface or be seen through the rippling
    depths.
Let horsemen be stationed at the rim of it, and a dog, always alert on
    the brink of sleep.
Let the space under the first storey be dark, let the water lap the stone
    posts, and vivid green slime glimmer upon them; let a boat be kept
    there.
Let the caryatids of the second storey be bears upheld on beams that are
    dragons.
On the parapet of the central room, let there be four archers, looking
    off to the four horizons. Within, let the prince be at home, let him
    sit in deep thought, at peace, all the windows open to the loggias.
Let the young queen sit above, in the cool air, her child in her arms;
    let her look with joy at the great circle, the pilgrim shadows, the
    work of the sun and the play of the wind. Let her walk to and
    fro. Let the columns uphold the roof, let the storeys uphold the
    columns, let there be dark space below the lowest floor, let the

castle rise foursquare out of the moat, let the moat be a ring and
the water deep, let the guardians guard it, let there be wide lands
around it, let that country where it stands be within me, let me
be where it is.

Julia Randall

Rockland

Masters, be kind to the old house that must fall,
Burn, or be bulldozed. The apples have grown small
And the ivy great here. The walk must be moved once more
Beyond the holly. Do not use the side door,
The lilies have broken the step. If you fix it,
They will break it again; they live under the stone.
There is blown glass
In three windows; hold them up with a stick.
The smoke is always thick
With the first fire. The Landseer in the attic
Was tacked there when I came. There is a snake
With a red tongue in the terrace; he has never been known
To hurt. The worst leak
Is in the bedroom ceiling. So. It was a good house
For hands to patch, a boon to August eyes. And when
The moon lay on the locusts, and the stream
Croaked in the bottom, muted by high grass,
Small rustlings in the woodlot, birdcries, was
A minister like music. Should I say
This—with the apple tree—was Sirmio,
This—with the two-year parsley—Twickenham,
Aldworth, or Abbotsford, I would only mean
We lease one house in love's divided name.

To William Wordsworth
From Virginia

I think, old bone, the world's not with us much.
I think it is too difficult to see,
But easy to discuss. Behold the bush.

His seasons out-maneuver Proteus.
This year, because of the drought, the barberry
Is all goldflakes in August, but I'll still say
To the First Grade next month, "*Now* it is Fall.
You see the leaves go bright, and then go small.
You see October's greatcoat. It is gold.
It will lie on the earth to keep the seed's foot warm.
Then, Andrew Obenchain, what happens in June?"
And Andrew, being mountain-bred, will know
Catawba runs too deep for the bus to get
Across the ford—at least it did last May,
And school was out, and the laundry wouldn't dry,
And when the creek went down, the bluebells lay
In Hancock's pasture-border, thick as hay.

What do they tell the First Grade in Peru,
I wonder? All the story: God is good,
He counts the children, and the sparrow's wing.
God loved William Wordsworth in the spring.
William Wordsworth had enough to eat.
Wye was his broth, Helvellyn was his meat,
And English was his cookstove. And where did words
Come from, Carlyle Rucker? Words that slide
The world together. Words that split the tide
Apart for Moses (not for Mahon's bus),
Words that say, the bushes burn for us—
Lilac, forsythia, orange, Sharon rose—
For us the seasons wheel, the lovers wait,
All things become the flesh of our delight,
The evidence of our wishes.

                                    Witch, so might
I stand beside the barberry and dream
Wisdom to babes, and health to beggar men.
And help to David hunting in the hills
The Appalachian fox. By words, I might.
But, sir, I am tired of living in a lake
Among the watery weeds and weedy blue
Shadows of flowers that Hancock never grew.
I am tired of my wet wishes, of running away
Like all the nymphs, from the droughty eye of day.

Run, Daphne. Run, Europa, Io, run!
There is not a god left underneath the sun
To balk, to ride, to suffer, to obey.
Here is the unseasonable barberry.
Here is the black face of a child in need.
Here is the bloody figure of a man.
Run, Great Excursioner. Run if you can.

Janet Frame

Telephonist

Her sense of humor has no gold stop
or sweetly flowing channel.
Her heavy feet plough tweed
through a silk and lace paddock of earth,
upturning pink daisies and hoppity mice
with no by your leave or remedial poem.

She can laugh with any farmer,
her arms akimbo, her mouth braying
the yokel burden of a woman
who slaps daylight on the back
who walks in her lace country
with every flea-bitten shaggy dog.

Yet for eight hours each day
in the swiveling city of concrete
the talking wire commands her loud mouth.
She becomes the vital link, the braying ass
bearing news of life and death
to the hungry starstruck city.

The Foxes

Within the purple graph of the Hokonuis, the dark
peak of Milford, my memory of Wyndham is drawn to scale.
I see the weathered gray sheep pens, their gates askew,
still standing not used now, scattered with old sheep dirt
like shriveled berries of a deadly nightshade

that lead me to suppose a spreading sheep tree grew here.
I cannot remember. The widest tree was the sky. Also,
deadly nightshade is poisonous, and sheep are not, are they?

The trains used to pass here. Wyndham station is closed now
and the railway lines like iron thorns are lifted
from their sleeper beds. The stranded station hangs
a sheltering verandah over no human traveler
for the track is overgrown with grass and it is grass, rooted on the
    platform,
stay-at-home, that meets only the wind passing through
with hospitality of plaintive moan and sigh
instead of the usual cup of tea and meat pie.

Sunday and topdressed the spring hills prosper with grass
the home paddocks with plump ewes and night-mushrooming
lambs, pink underneath, proudly declared
in the national interest, edible. The sheep, like subsidized legends,
    thrive,
their keepers too, but my childhood Wyndham has stayed
secure in its mutinous dream, unchanged since I knew
the railway house by the railway line and was five,
starting school, walking through long grass where the foxes lived.

Vassar Miller

The Quarry

What are you, then, my love, my friend, my father,
My anybody-never-mine? Whose aim
Can wing you with a knowledge-bullet, tame
You long enough to term you fur or feather?
Labeled one species, you become another
Before I have pronounced your latest name.
My fingers itching after you, like flame
Melting to frost, you vanish into neither.

Face, mind, heart held in honor for your sake,
Magical creature none can ever snare,
Are but the trails you beat, the arcs you make,

305

Shy animal the color of the air,
Who are the air itself, the breath ashake
Among the leaves—the bird no longer there.

Beat Poem by an Academic Poet

Birds, birds, birds
burst from the trees, from a feeble beginning
like a bundle of sticks lit under a pot
crackling and sputtering
to the great gorgeous bonfire of sunrise
exploding far overhead
like a high hallelujah.

Birds! their wings
tickling my stomach instead of butterflies
wavering wanly; in bones, belly, blood, flapping,
Get up, get up,
till I do, chanting, by God and by glory
if you can't lick 'em, join 'em,
though body weeps dry tears.

Maxine Kumin

The Sound of Night

And now the dark comes on, all full of chitter noise.
Birds huggermugger crowd the trees,
the air thick with their vesper cries,
and bats, snub seven-pointed kites,
skitter across the lake, swing out,
squeak, chirp, dip, and skim on skates
of air, and the fat frogs wake and prink
wide-lipped, noisy as ducks, drunk
on the boozy black, gloating chink-chunk.

And now on the narrow beach we defend ourselves from dark.
The cooking done, we build our firework
bright and hot and less for outlook

than for magic, and lie in our blankets
while night nickers around us. Crickets
chorus hallelujahs; paws, quiet
and quick as raindrops, play on the stones
expertly soft, run past and are gone;
fish pulse in the lake; the frogs hoarsen.

Now every voice of the hour—the known, the supposed, the strange,
the mindless, the witted, the never seen—
sing, thrum, impinge, and rearrange
endlessly; and debarred from sleep we wait
for the birds, importantly silent,
for the crease of first eye-licking light,
for the sun, lost long ago and sweet.
By the lake, locked black away and tight,
we lie, day creatures, overhearing night.

Morning Swim

Into my empty head there come
A cotton beach, a dock wherefrom

I set out, oily and nude
Through mist, in chilly solitude.

There was no line, no roof or floor
To tell the water from the air.

Night fog thick as terry cloth
Closed me in its fuzzy growth.

I hung my bathrobe on two pegs.
I took the lake between my legs.

Invaded and invader, I
Went overhand on that flat sky.

Fish twitched beneath me, quick and tame.
In their green zone they sang my name

And in the rhythm of the swim
I hummed a two-four-time slow hymn.

I hummed *Abide With Me.* The beat
Rose in the fine thrash of my feet,

Rose in the bubbles I put out
Slantwise, trailing through my mouth.

My bones drank water; water fell
Through all my doors. I was the well

That fed the lake that met my sea
In which I sang *Abide With Me*.

The Presence

Something went crabwise
across the snow this morning.
Something went hard and slow
over our hayfield.
It could have been a raccoon
lugging a knapsack,
it could have been a porcupine
carrying a tennis racket,
it could have been something
supple as a red fox
dragging the squawk and spatter
of a crippled woodcock.
Ten knuckles underground
those bones are seeds now
pure as baby teeth
lined up in the burrow.

I cross on snowshoes
cunningly woven from
the skin and sinews of
something else that went before.

 _____

Carolyn Kizer

The Great Blue Heron

M. A. K., September, 1880–
September, 1955

As I wandered on the beach
I saw the heron standing

Sunk in the tattered wings
He wore as a hunchback's coat.
Shadow without a shadow,
Hung on invisible wires
From the top of a canvas day,
What scissors cut him out?
Superimposed on a poster
Of summer by the strand
Of a long-decayed resort,
Poised in the dusty light
Some fifteen summers ago;
I wondered, an empty child,
"Heron, whose ghost are you?"

I stood on the beach alone,
In the sudden chill of the burned.
My thought raced up the path.
Pursuing it, I ran
To my mother in the house
And led her to the scene.
The spectral bird was gone.
But her quick eye saw him drifting
Over the highest pines
On vast, unmoving wings.
Could they be those ashen things,
So grounded, unwieldy, ragged,
A pair of broken arms
That were not made for flight?
In the middle of my loss
I realized she knew:
My mother knew what he was.

O great blue heron, now
That the summer house has burned
So many rockets ago,
So many smokes and fires
And beach-lights and water-glow
Reflecting pin-wheel and flare:
The old logs hauled away,
The pines and driftwood cleared
From that bare strip of shore

Where dozens of children play;
Now there is only you
Heavy upon my eye.
Why have you followed me here,
Heavy and far away?
You have stood there patiently
For fifteen summers and snows,
Denser than my repose,
Bleaker than any dream,
Waiting upon the day
When, like grey smoke, a vapor
Floating into the sky,
A handful of paper ashes,
My mother would drift away.

Hera, Hung From the Sky

I hang by my heels from the sky.
The sun, exploded at last,
Hammered his wrath to chains
Forged for my lightest bones.
Once I was warmed to my ears,
Kept close; now blind with fire!
What a child, taking heat for delight
So simply! Scorched within,
I still burn as I swing,
A pendulum kicking the night,
An alarum at dawn, I deflect
The passage of birds, ring down
The bannering rain. I indict
This body, its ruses, games,
Its plot to unseat the sun.
I pitted my feminine weight
Against God, his terrible throne.
From the great dome of despair,
I groan, I swing, I swing
In unconstellated air.

I had shared a sovereign cloud:
The lesser, the shadowy twin
To my lord. All woman and weight

Of connubial love that sings
Within the cabinet's close
And embracing intimacy.
I threw it all to the skies
In an instant of power, poise—
Arrogant, flushed with his love,
His condescending praise;
From envy of shine and blaze,
Mad, but beautifully mad,
Hypnotized by the gaze
Of self into self, the dream
That woman was great as man—
As humid, as blown with fame,
So great I seemed to be!
I threw myself to the skies
And the sky has cast me down.
I have lost the war of the air:
Half-strangled in my hair,
I dangle, drowned in fire.

Columns and Caryatids

I

The Wife:
"I am Lot's pillar, caught in turning,
Bellowing, resistant, burning
With brine. Fine robes laced with sand,
Solid, soon to be hollowed by tongues of kine."

Solid, solitary salt lick, she
Is soon to be shaped by wind, abstracted,
Smoothed to a sex-shape only.
Large and lonely in the plain,
Rain melting her slowly.

So proud shoulder dips with compliance
Never in life. God's alliance with weather
Eroding her to a spar, a general grief-shape,
A cone, then an egg no bigger than a bead.

"I saw Sodom bleed, Gomorrah smoke.
Empty sockets are a joke of that final vision.

Tongueless, I taste my own salt, taste
God's chastisement and derision."

II

The Mother:
"I am God's pillar, caught in raising
My arms like thighs, to brace the wall.
Caught by my own choice,
I willed myself to hold this ceiling.

"He froze me at the moment of decision.
Always I wished to bear weight,
Not in my belly where the seed would light.
That globe is great with stone.
But, over me, the weight of endless function,
My thick trunk set for stress,
My face, showing calmly through guano
No strain, my brain sloped by marble curls
To wedge the architrave.

"The world is a womb.
Neither I nor the foetus tire of our position.
My ear is near God, my temples to his temple.
I lift and I listen. I eat God's peace."

III

The Lover:
"I am your pillar that has fallen.
And now, for centuries of rest
I will regard my breast, my calm hills,
My valley for the stars to travel."

Stripped of all ornament she lies,
Looted alike by conquerors and technicians,
Her curling fingers for an emperor's flower,
Her trinkets in barbarians' museums.
They dust away, but she endures, and smiles,
Accepting ravage as the only tribute
That men can pay to gods, that they would dint them
To raise or decorate themselves, themselves are dinted,
The bruise upon the sense of generations.

So boys will turn from sleep and search the darkness,
Seeking the love their fathers have forgotten.
And they will dream of her who have not known her,
And ache, and ache for that lost limb forever.

Elizabeth Jennings

The Storm House

The wind is shaking this house,
This new house, nine storeys high and no one guessing
Such newness could ever be broached. The storm has done it,
The only natural sound in the whole city.

Along the river the boats are hooting farewell
And lights are coming on in the dingy streets.
Somebody, far-off, kicks a can and then
Returns to his separateness, his only gesture
Echoing down the street against the storm.

This moderate skyscraper is full of sickness,
A hospital houses a hundred different ailments.
The wind grows strong, winding a noisy bandage
Around the building; human sounds are unheard.

And if you cried, you would have to cry so loudly
That the wind was stilled a moment as if a hand,
In godlike supplication, laid peace upon it,
But the gods we invoke are quiet here as our prayers.

The Interrogator

He is always right.
However you prevaricate or question his motives,
Whatever you say to excuse yourself
He is always right.

He always has an answer;
It may be a question that hurts to hear.
It may be a sentence that makes you flinch.
He always has an answer.

He always knows best.
He can tell you why you disliked your father,
He can make your purest motive seem aggressive.
He always knows best.

He can always find words.
While you fumble to feel for your own position
Or stammer out words that are not quite accurate,
He can always find words.

And if you accuse him
He is glad you have lost your temper with him.
He can find the motive, give you a reason
If you accuse him.

And if you covered his mouth with your hand,
Pinned him down to his smooth desk chair,
You would be doing just what he wishes.
His silence would prove that he was right.

Fountain

Let it disturb no more at first
Than the hint of a pool predicted far in a forest,
Or a sea so far away that you have to open
Your window to hear it.
Think of it then as elemental, as being
Necessity,
Not for a cup to be taken to it and not
For lips to linger or eye to receive itself
Back in reflection, simply
As water the patient moon persuades and stirs.

And then step closer,
Imagine rivers you might indeed embark on,
Waterfalls where you could
Silence an afternoon by staring but never
See the same tumult twice.
Yes come out of the narrow street and enter
The full piazza. Come where the noise compels.
Statues are bowing down to the breaking air.

Observe it there—the fountain, too fast for shadows,
Too wild for the lights which illuminate it to hold,

Even a moment, an ounce of water back;
Stare at such prodigality and consider
It is the elegance here, it is the taming,
The keeping fast in a thousand flowering sprays,
That builds this energy up but lets the watchers
See in that stress an image of utter calm,
A stillness there. It is how we must have felt
Once at the edge of some perpetual stream,
Fearful of touching, bringing no thirst at all,
Panicked by no perception of ourselves
But drawing the water down to the deepest wonder.

Anne Sexton

For My Lover, Returning
to His Wife

She is all there.
She was melted carefully down for you
and cast up from your childhood,
cast up from your one hundred favorite aggies.

She has always been there, my darling.
She is, in fact, exquisite.
Fireworks in the dull middle of February
and as real as a cast-iron pot.

Let's face it, I have been momentary.
A luxury. A bright red sloop in the harbor.
My hair rising like smoke from the car window.
Littleneck clams out of season.

She is more than that. She is your have to have,
has grown you your practical, your tropical growth.
This is not an experiment. She is all harmony.
She sees to oars and oarlocks for the dinghy,

has placed wild flowers at the window at breakfast,
sat by the potter's wheel at midday,
set forth three children under the moon,
three cherubs drawn by Michelangelo,

done this with her legs spread out
in the terrible months in the chapel.
If you glance up, the children are there
like delicate balloons resting on the ceiling.

She has also carried each one down the hall
after supper, their heads privately bent,
two legs protesting, person to person,
her face flushed with a song and their little sleep.

I give you back your heart.
I give you permission—

for the fuse inside her, throbbing
angrily in the dirt, for the bitch in her
and the burying of her wound—
for the burying of her small red wound alive—

for the pale flickering flare under her ribs,
for the drunken sailor who waits in her left pulse,
for the mother's knee, for the stockings,
for the garter belt, for the call—

the curious call
when you will burrow in arms and breasts
and tug at the orange ribbon in her hair
and answer the call, the curious call.

She is so naked and singular.
She is the sum of yourself and your dream.
Climb her like a monument, step after step.
She is solid.

As for me, I am a watercolor.
I wash off.

Lament

Someone is dead.
Even the trees know it,
those poor old dancers who come on lewdly,
all pea-green scarfs and spine pole.
I think . . .
I think I could have stopped it,
if I'd been as firm as a nurse

or noticed the neck of the driver
as he cheated the crosstown lights;
or later in the evening,
if I'd held my napkin over my mouth.
I think I could ...
if I'd been different, or wise, or calm,
I think I could have charmed the table,
the stained dish or the hand of the dealer.
But it's done.
It's all used up.
There's no doubt about the trees
spreading their thin feet into the dry grass.
A Canada goose rides up,
spread out like a gray suede shirt,
honking his nose into the March wind.
In the entryway a cat breathes calmly
into her watery blue fur.
The supper dishes are over and the sun
unaccustomed to anything else
goes all the way down.

The Nude Swim

On the southwest side of Capri
we found a little unknown grotto
where no people were and we
entered it completely
and let our bodies lose all
their loneliness.

All the fish in us
had escaped for a minute.
The real fish did not mind.
We did not disturb their personal life.
We calmly trailed over them
and under them, shedding
air bubbles, little white
balloons that drifted up
into the sun by the boat
where the Italian boatman slept
with his hat over his face.

Water so clear you could
read a book through it.
Water so buoyant you could
float on your elbow.
I lay on it as on a divan.
I lay on it just like
Matisse's *Red Odalisque.*
Water was my strange flower.
One must picture a woman
without a toga or a scarf
on a couch as deep as a tomb.

The walls of that grotto
were everycolor blue and
you said, "Look! Your eyes
are seacolor. Look! Your eyes
are skycolor." And my eyes
shut down as if they were
suddenly ashamed.

Adrienne Rich

The Trees

The trees inside are moving out into the forest,
the forest that was empty all these days
where no bird could sit
no insect hide
no sun bury its feet in shadow
the forest that was empty all these nights
will be full of trees by morning.

All night the roots work
to disengage themselves from the cracks
in the veranda floor.
The leaves strain toward the glass
small twigs stiff with exertion
long-cramped boughs shuffling under the roof
like newly discharged patients

half-dazed, moving
to the clinic doors.

I sit inside, doors open to the veranda
writing long letters
in which I scarcely mention the departure
of the forest from the house.
The night is fresh, the whole moon shines
in a sky still open
the smell of leaves and lichen
still reaches like a voice into the rooms.
My head is full of whispers
which tomorrow will be silent.

Listen. The glass is breaking.
The trees are stumbling forward
into the night. Winds rush to meet them.
The moon is broken like a mirror,
its pieces flash now in the crown
of the tallest oak.

Orion

Far back when I went zig-zagging
through tamarack pastures
you were my genius, you
my cast-iron Viking, my helmed
lion-heart king in prison.
Years later now you're young

my fierce half-brother, staring
down from that simplified west
your breast open, your belt dragged down
by an oldfashioned thing, a sword
the last bravado you won't give over
though it weighs you down as you stride

and the stars in it are dim
and maybe have stopped burning.
But you burn, and I know it;
as I throw back my head to take you in
an old transfusion happens again:
divine astronomy is nothing to it.

Indoors I bruise and blunder,
break faith, leave ill enough
alone, a dead child born in the dark.
Night cracks up over the chimney,
pieces of time, frozen geodes
come showering down in the grate.

A man reaches behind my eyes
and finds them empty
a woman's head turns away
from my head in the mirror
children are dying my death
and eating crumbs of my life.

Pity is not your forte.
Calmly you ache up there
pinned aloft in your crow's nest,
my speechless pirate!
You take it all for granted
and when I look you back

it's with a starlike eye
shooting its cold and egotistical spear
where it can do least damage.
Breathe deep! No hurt, no pardon
out here in the cold with you
you with your back to the wall.

Abnegation

The red fox, the vixen
dancing in the half-light among the junipers,
wise-looking in a sexy way,
Egyptian-supple in her sharpness—
what does she want
with the dreams of dead vixens,
the apotheosis of Reynard,
the literature of fox-hunting?
Only in her nerves the past
sings, a thrill of self-preservation.
I go along down the road

to a house nailed together by Scottish
Covenanters, instinct mortified
in a virgin forest,
and she springs toward her den
every hair on her pelt alive
with tidings of the immaculate present.
They left me a westernness,
a birthright, a redstained, ravelled
afghan of sky.
She has no archives,
no heirlooms, no future
except death
and I could be more
her sister than theirs
who chopped their way across these hills
—a chosen people.

Sylvia Plath

The Bee Meeting

Who are these people at the bridge to meet me? They are the
    villagers—
The rector, the midwife, the sexton, the agent for bees.
In my sleeveless summery dress I have no protection,
And they are all gloved and covered, why did nobody tell me?
They are smiling and taking out veils tacked to ancient hats.

I am nude as a chicken neck, does nobody love me?
Yes, here is the secretary of bees with her white shop smock,
Buttoning the cuffs at my wrists and the slit from my neck to my
    knees.
Now I am milkweed silk, the bees will not notice.
They will not smell my fear, my fear, my fear.

Which is the rector now, is it that man in black?
Which is the midwife, is that her blue coat?
Everybody is nodding a square black head, they are knights in visors.
Breastplates of cheesecloth knotted under the armpits.

The Women Poets in English

Their smiles and their voices are changing. I am led through a bean-
field.

Strips of tinfoil winking like people,
Feather dusters fanning their hands in a sea of bean flowers,
Creamy bean flowers with black eyes and leaves like bored hearts.
Is it blood clots the tendrils are dragging up that string?
No, no, it is scarlet flowers that will one day be edible.

Now they are giving me a fashionable white straw Italian hat
And a black veil that moulds to my face, they are making me one of
    them.
They are leading me to the shorn grove, the circle of hives.
Is it the hawthorn that smells so sick?
The barren body of hawthorn, etherizing its children.

Is it some operation that is taking place?
It is the surgeon my neighbours are waiting for,
This apparition in a green helmet,
Shining gloves and white suit.
Is it the butcher, the grocer, the postman, someone I know?

I cannot run, I am rooted, and the gorse hurts me
With its yellow purses, its spiky armoury.
I could not run without having to run forever.
The white hive is snug as a virgin,
Sealing off her brood cells, her honey, and quietly humming.

Smoke rolls and scarves in the grove.
The mind of the hive thinks this is the end of everything.
Here they come, the outriders, on their hysterical elastics.
If I stand very still, they will think I am cow parsley,
A gullible head untouched by their animosity,

Not even nodding, a personage in a hedgerow.
The villagers open the chambers, they are hunting the queen.
Is she hiding, is she eating honey? She is very clever.
She is old, old, old, she must live another year, and she knows it.
While in their fingerjoint cells the new virgins

Dream of a duel they will win inevitably,
A curtain of wax dividing them from the bride flight,

The upflight of the murderess into a heaven that loves her.
The villagers are moving the virgins, there will be no killing.
The old queen does not show herself, is she so ungrateful?

I am exhausted, I am exhausted—
Pillar of white in a blackout of knives.
I am the magician's girl who does not flinch.
The villagers are untying their disguises, they are shaking hands.
Whose is that long white box in the grove, what have they accomplished,
     why am I cold?

Tulips

The tulips are too excitable, it is winter here.
Look how white everything is, how quiet, how snowed-in.
I am learning peacefulness, lying by myself quietly
As the light lies on these white walls, this bed, these hands.
I am nobody; I have nothing to do with explosions.
I have given my name and my day-clothes up to the nurses
And my history to the anaesthetist and my body to surgeons.

They have propped my head between the pillow and the sheet-cuff
Like an eye between two white lids that will not shut.
Stupid pupil, it has to take everything in.
The nurses pass and pass, they are no trouble,
They pass the way gulls pass inland in their white caps,
Doing things with their hands, one just the same as another,
So it is impossible to tell how many there are.

My body is a pebble to them, they tend it as water
Tends to the pebbles it must run over, smoothing them gently.
They bring me numbness in their bright needles, they bring me sleep.
Now I have lost myself I am sick of baggage—
My patent leather overnight case like a black pillbox,
My husband and child smiling out of the family photo;
Their smiles catch onto my skin, little smiling hooks.

I have let things slip, a thirty-year-old cargo boat
Stubbornly hanging on to my name and address.
They have swabbed me clear of my loving associations.

323

The Women Poets in English

Scared and bare on the green plastic-pillowed trolley
I watched my tea-set, my bureaus of linen, my books
Sink out of sight, and the water went over my head.
I am a nun now, I have never been so pure.

I didn't want any flowers, I only wanted
To lie with my hands turned up and be utterly empty.
How free it is, you have no idea how free—
The peacefulness is so big it dazes you,
And it asks nothing, a name tag, a few trinkets.
It is what the dead close on, finally; I imagine them
Shutting their mouths on it, like a Communion tablet.

The tulips are too red in the first place, they hurt me.
Even through the gift paper I could hear them breathe
Lightly, through their white swaddlings, like an awful baby.
Their redness talks to my wound, it corresponds.
They are subtle: they seem to float, though they weigh me down,
Upsetting me with their sudden tongues and their colour,
A dozen red lead sinkers round my neck.

Nobody watched me before, now I am watched.
The tulips turn to me, and the window behind me
Where once a day the light slowly widens and slowly thins,
And I see myself, flat, ridiculous, a cut-paper shadow
Between the eye of the sun and the eyes of the tulips,
And I have no face, I have wanted to efface myself.
The vivid tulips eat my oxygen.

Before they came the air was calm enough,
Coming and going, breath by breath, without any fuss.
Then the tulips filled it up like a loud noise.
Now the air snags and eddies round them the way a river
Snags and eddies round a sunken rust-red engine.
They concentrate my attention, that was happy
Playing and resting without committing itself.

The walls, also, seem to be warming themselves.
The tulips should be behind bars like dangerous animals;
They are opening like the mouth of some great African cat,

And I am aware of my heart: it opens and closes
Its bowl of red blooms out of sheer love of me.
The water I taste is warm and salt, like the sea,
And comes from a country far away as health.

The Moon and the Yew Tree

This is the light of the mind, cold and planetary.
The trees of the mind are black. The light is blue.
The grasses unload their griefs on my feet as if I were God,
Prickling my ankles and murmuring of their humility.
Fumy, spiritous mists inhabit this place
Separated from my house by a row of headstones.
I simply cannot see where there is to get to.

The moon is no door. It is a face in its own right,
White as a knuckle and terribly upset.
It drags the sea after it like a dark crime; it is quiet
With the O-gape of complete despair. I live here.
Twice on Sunday, the bells startle the sky—
Eight great tongues affirming the Resurrection.
At the end, they soberly bong out their names.

The yew tree points up. It has a Gothic shape.
The eyes lift after it and find the moon.
The moon is my mother. She is not sweet like Mary.
Her blue garments unloose small bats and owls.
How I would like to believe in tenderness—
The face of the effigy, gentled by candles,
Bending, on me in particular, its mild eyes.

I have fallen a long way. Clouds are flowering
Blue and mystical over the face of the stars.
Inside the church, the saints will be all blue,
Floating on their delicate feet over the cold pews,
Their hands and faces stiff with holiness.
The moon sees nothing of this. She is bald and wild.
And the message of the yew tree is blackness—blackness and silence.

Marge Piercy

Letter to Be Disguised
as a Gas Bill

Your face scrapes my sleep tonight
sharp as a broken girder.
My hands are empty shoppingbags.
Never plastered on the walls of subway night
in garish snake-lettered posters of defeat.
I was always stomping on your toes eager to stick
clippings that should have interested you into the soup.
I told and retold stories weeping mascara on your shirt.
If I introduced a girl she would sink fangs in your shin
or hang in the closet for months, a sleazy kimona.
I brought you my goathaired prickheavy men to bless
while they glowered on your chairs turning green as Swiss hats.
I asked your advice and worse, took it.
I was always hauling out the dollar watch of my pride.
Time after time you toted me home in a wheelbarrow drunk
with words sudsing, dress rumpled and randomly amorous
teasing you like an uncle made of poles to hold clotheslines up.
With my father you constantly wished I had been born
a boy or a rowboat or a nice wooden chest of drawers.
In the morning you delivered clanking chronicles of my faults.
Now you are respectable in Poughkeepsie.
Every couple of years I call you up
and your voice thickens with resentment and shame.
It is all done, it is quiet and still
a piece of old cheese too hard to chew.

I list my own faults now ledger upon ledger
yet it's you I cannot forgive who have given me up.
Are you comfortable in Poughkeepsie with Vassar and IBM?
Do you stoke up your memory on cold mornings?
My rector, I make no more apologies,
I say my dirt and chaos are more loving
than your cleanliness and I exile no one,

this smelly old hunting dog you sent to the vet's
to be put away, baby, put to sleep with all her fleas.
You murdered me out of your life.
I do not forgive, I hate it, I am not resigned.
I will howl at every hydrant for thirty years.

 _____

Lucille Clifton

The Way It Was
mornings
I got up early
greased my legs
straightened my hair and
walked quietly out
not touching

in the same place
the tree   the lot
the poolroom   Deacon Moore
everything was stayed

nothing changed
(nothing remained the same)
I walked out quietly
mornings

in the '40s
a nice girl
not touching
trying to be white

The Lost Baby Poem
the time i dropped your almost body down
down to meet the waters under the city
and run one with the sewage to the sea
what did i know about waters rushing back
what did i know about drowning
or being drowned

you would have been born into winter
in the year of the disconnected gas
and no car   we would have made the thin
walk over Genesee Hill into Canada wind
to watch you slip like ice into strangers' hands
you would have fallen naked as snow into winter
if you were here i could tell you these
and some other things

if i am ever less than a mountain
for your definite brothers and sisters
let the rivers pour over my head
let the sea take me for a spiller
of seas   let black men call me stranger
always   for your never named sake

Shirley Kaufman

Beetle on the Shasta Daylight

for Reggie Kriss

Hills moved. I watched their shadows
riding by like names said
only once. The oaks turned round
and leaves ran past my head.

It was all reeling back where
the old disasters hung between
locked doors stitching the air,
unheard, as if they'd never been.

And the sun came falling through
the window of the train; it filled
my lap, slid down my arms into
the aisle, a blazing river spilled

inside. I found her in the shallow
light, wearing her skeleton
strapped smooth over her belly,
wallowing on her back, alone.

Some little Pequod spitting, mastheads
tufted with joints like unfleshed frogs,
lame as a butterfly spread
on a pin. And from the thrashing legs

hooks caught at nothing, casting
and casting in the air, her
bent and beaded feelers lashing
until the threads would have to tear.

Pharaohs watched her push her dung ball
on the sand the way the sun
rolled slowly over heaven, saw
how she hatched her children

out of that roundness, called her Life.
They made her image out of stone,
greener than stems, to celebrate
the ornamental lake a queen

had built, to mark a lion hunt
or even marriage. They sent
her gleaming in the tombs of all
the dead so they might rise again.

I didn't touch her; slipping a marker
from my book under her back,
I turned my wrist down gently, set her
right. A piece of the whole shook

world turned up. Alive! She was
amazed to flex herself, to feel
the sun along her side like juice,
to have her front legs wheel

her forward, arched in a priestly
benediction. Oh she was tight. She served
her concentrated self, and neatly.
Her eyes glittered out of her head.

Lightly she went and steady down
the aisle. Not any landscape she
remembered. Yet she was sure of home,
composed her dark wherever she might be

creeping. I waved her well. Saw
that she left no furrow in the floor.
But someone got up, swelling out
of his seat and raised his foot, before

my hand could drop, and put it down
and passed into the next car
and was gone. There was no sound
but the train's sound. Far

down the tracks, the sun rolled over.
I had to sit there after that
and look at California moving
backward, pressing my face flat

against the glass until it froze
to my skin. All afternoon
I looked out at the hills, those
trees with the light crawling down

their branches like white beetles
and the sky lurching among
the leaves, the shape of it tilting
at me crushed under the sun.

Always She Moves From Me

Always she moves from me,
climbs over the bridge, singing
with other swift daughters, leans
into shadows, calling her image
to rise from the water.

A flight in one direction,
where the long paths littered
with sun end, and the rocks
warm to the light, the alternate
touch of her running feet.

Wanting my self again, not lost
but at a distance, dark
among trees, I stumble uneven
ground. My shadow the color
of old leaves and slow

to find her, thick with my own
mother. If she could hear me
through the upstream air that hums
between us, I would repeat
my old articulate love,

but she hears only the plum tree
knock like a clapper in a gong
of blue, thighs deep in lilies,
and the branches closing
behind her where she goes.

Margaret Atwood

Eden Is a Zoo

I keep my parents in a garden
among lumpy trees, green sponges
on popsickle sticks. I give them a lopsided
sun which drops its heat
in spokes the colour of yellow crayon.

They have thick elephant legs,
quills for hair and tiny heads;
they clump about under the trees
dressed in the clothes of thirty years
ago, on them innocent as plain skin.

Are they bewildered when they come across
corners of rooms in the forest,
a tin cup shining like pearl,
a frayed pink blanket, a rusted shovel?

Does it bother them to perform
the same actions over and over,
hands gathering white flowers
by the lake or tracing designs in the sand,
a word repeated till it hangs carved

forever in the blue air?

Are they content?

Do they want to get out?

Do they see me looking at them
from across the hedge of spikes
and cardboard fire painted red
I built with so much time
and pain, but
they don't know is there?

Mary Oliver

The Grandmothers

They moved like rivers in their mended stockings,
Their skirts, their buns, their bodies grown
Round as trees. Over the kitchen fires
They hoarded magics, and the heavy bowls
Of Sunday bread rose up faithful as light.
We smiled for them, although they never spoke.
Silent as stones, they merely stared when birds
Fell in the leaves, or brooms wore out, or children
Scraped their knees and cried. Within my village,
We did not think it odd or ask for words;
In their vast arms we knew that we were loved.
I remember their happiness at the birth of children.
I remember their hands, swollen and hard as wood;
And how sometimes in summer when the night
Was thick with stars, they gathered in the garden.
Near sleep, I watched them as they poured the wine,
Hung paper lanterns in the alien birches.
Then one would take a tiny concertina
And cradle it against her mammoth apron,
Till music hung like ribbons in the trees
And round my bed. Oh, still within my dreams,

Softly they gather under summer stars
And sing of the far Danube, of Vienna,
Clear as a flight of wild and slender girls!

The Diviners

Their black truck rattled up the dusty hill;
They braked it, smoking, by the kitchen door
And shambled out: two men from Arkansas.
Booted and lean, they spoke a mountain drawl
Half song, half sleep, and laughed like men who know
Some marvelous joke they do not think to share.
Laughing, they cut two branches from a tree
And stripped the bark away. They did not seem
To notice how we snickered at their heels.
There were no rites; they only turned and moved
Slowly along the edge of the wild field.
A few larks fluttered up. Somewhere they paused, —
And suddenly we could not make a sound;
The sun kept beating at our eyes, and then
The peeled sticks dipped, and rapped upon the ground.

One by one they called and put the sticks
Into our hands, and led us through the field.
Some of us said we felt a kind of nudge,
But all of us walked blindly past the line
Where water lay, like ropes of buried light.
They drove away, half singing and half sleeping.
The sticks lay silent in the tangled grass,
And there we stood, confused, between two worlds.
We dug into the ground, hoping to find
Nothing. But the buried water rose
Out of the earth and tumbled down the field
As, overhead, we felt the darkness close.

Through Ruddy Orchards

Through ruddy orchards now the grip of stems
Gives,—how easily!—and plunging bright,
—How furthering the thing to fall so bright!—
To earth comes back the fruit
With flavors of the light.

Through ruddy orchards, watch, where so much now
Is burnished to a health by the wild sun,
The falling and the falling . . . But these
That lurch in the wind and hold, what shall they be?
Why, they will wilt upon the tree,
The sun will take its golden back;
They will swing there, wry and wrinkled,
Till the white frost turns them black.

Through ruddy orchards, then, streams the deep wind—
The rife and lusty lungs of autumn wind; —
Then, cracked on rocks and bruised to brown,
Or sweet in caverns of the grass,
Or this, or that; but down, but down!

BIOGRAPHICAL
NOTES

Anonymous. "Eadwacer" (ca. 800) and "The Wife's Lament" (ca. 900) are among the poems preserved in the *Exeter Book* at Exeter Cathedral, Devonshire, England.

"The Flower and the Leaf," a poem of 595 lines, was written about 1450 and first published in Speght's edition of Chaucer and other poets, 1598. In it, the narrator, a woman, dreams that she watches two groups of knights and ladies at an entertainment, and at the end questions one of them, a lady in white, about the meaning of what she has seen. John Dryden, believing this to be a work of Chaucer, translated it into modern English. W. W. Skeat in his *Supplement to the Works of Geoffrey Chaucer*, 1899, reprints this work and "The Assembly of Ladies" in the original Middle English, together with his argument for feminine authorship of both.

"The Assembly of Ladies" bears many similarities to "The Flower and the Leaf" but is of a later date—Skeat places it during the last quarter of the fifteenth century. Again the author appears as a female character in the story. This poem of 756 lines was first published by Thynne in 1532 in *The Workes of Geffray Chaucer newly printed, with dyvers workes which were never in print before.*

MARIE DE FRANCE (fl. latter half twelfth century). All that is known about Marie must be deduced from her book. The *Lays* are in the Anglo-Norman dialect of the twelfth century and dedicated to a king, presumably King Henry II of England, whose wife was Eleanor of Aquitaine, a patron of poets. The stories are based on lays Marie herself had heard recited by minstrels, perhaps in Brittany.

JULIANS BARNES (fl. fifteenth century). Her *Boke of Huntyng* is contained in the *Boke of St. Albans*, published at the monastery of St. Albans, Hertfordshire, in 1486. Wynken de Worde, reprinting the *Boke* in 1496, changed her name to Bernes. An eighteenth-century writer suggested that her name was Berners, thereby connecting her to a noble family of

335

Hertfordshire or Essex whose name was sometimes spelled Bernes; a nine-teenth-century writer added that she was prioress of the Sopwell Nunnery of Hertfordshire. Other than the similarity of name, there is no basis for these later statements; there is no record of such a prioress at the Nunnery. Julians Barnes may have lived in the South of Yorkshire or the North or Northeast Midlands, for that is the location of the dialect in which her book is written. She used a French treatise, Twiti's *Craft of Venery*, as her source. *The Boke of Huntyng* was popular enough to be reprinted twenty times by the end of the sixteenth century.

MARGERY BREWS (d. ca. 1495). Daughter of Sir Thomas Brews of Topcroft, Norfolk. In 1477 married John Paston III. Her letters to her future husband are preserved among the correspondence kept by the Paston family over several generations. Buried in White Friars, Norwich.

QUEEN ELIZABETH OF YORK (1465–1503). Daughter of King Edward IV and Elizabeth Woodville. Born at Westminster Palace. Upon the death of her two brothers in the Tower, she became heir to the throne of her father, though Richard III became king. Her marriage to Henry of Richmond, who overthrew Richard and became King Henry VII, united the houses of York and Lancaster. Known for her gentleness, good-ness, and beauty. Mother of Henry VIII and of Margaret, who married the king of Scotland and became ancestor of the Stuart line.

QUEEN ANNE BOLEYN (1507–1536). Daughter of Sir Thomas Boleyn and Elizabeth Howard, daughter of the Earl of Surrey. Spent the years 1514 to 1522 at the court of France. In 1533 became the second wife of Henry VIII. Mother of Queen Elizabeth I. Beheaded for alleged adultery, although she protested herself innocent of the charge. "O Death, Rock Me Asleep" has been also attributed to her brother, Lord Rochford.

ANNE ASKEW (1520–1546). Daughter of Sir William Askew, Kelsey, Lincolnshire. Encouraged in Biblical studies by her tutor. After being turned out by her husband, who disapproved of her frequent reading of the Bible and absence from confession, she went to London with her two children. Condemned for her unorthodox religious views, she was burned at the stake at Smithfield during the reign of Henry VIII. The playwright and reformer, John Bale, who had fled to Marburg, Hesse, there published Anne Askew's own account of her examinations, in 1547.

QUEEN ELIZABETH I (1533–1603). Daughter of King Henry VIII and Anne Boleyn, granddaughter of Queen Elizabeth of York. Educated by tutors, among them the humanist Roger Ascham. As did many educated people of her day, Elizabeth composed and translated poetry. Most of her original poems deal with actual situations. Only one of her verse translations was published during her life—a version of the Thirteenth Psalm, printed at the end of her translation of Margaret of Navarre's *Godly Meditation of the Soul*, 1548. She also translated Petrarch's *Triumph of Eternity*, Seneca's *Hercules Oetaeus*, and, in 1593, Boethius' *Consolation of Philosophy*. All her poems and translations are collected by Leicester Bradner in *The Poems of Queen Elizabeth,* 1964.

ISABELLA WHITNEY (fl. 1567–1573). A gentlewoman. Sister of the poet Geoffrey Whitney. Presumed author of *The Copie of a Letter, lately written in Meeter by a yonge gentlewoman: to her unconstant lover. With an admonition to al yong Gentilwomen, and to all other mayds in general to beware of mennes flattery,* 1567. Also wrote *A Sweet Nosgay or Pleasant Posye containing a hundred and ten Phylosophicall Flowers,* 1573.

ANNE HOWARD, Duchess of Arundel (1557–1630). Born Anne Dacre, married Philip Howard, Earl of Arundel. Through her influence, her husband became a Roman Catholic in 1584. In 1585 he was fined and imprisoned for life; he died in the Tower, 1595. After her husband's arrest, Anne Howard lived in comparative poverty. "In sad and ashy weeds I sigh" was written on the cover of a letter and is believed to be an elegy on the death of her husband.

MARY SIDNEY HERBERT, Countess of Pembroke (1561–1621). Daughter of Sir Henry Sidney and Mary Dudley, daughter of the Duke of Northumberland. Sister of Sir Philip Sidney. Spent her childhood at Penshurst, Kent, and later in Ludlow Castle, Wales. Married Henry Herbert, Earl of Pembroke, 1577. Was a patron of men of letters, including Edmund Spenser, Ben Jonson, Nicholas Breton, Samuel Daniel, John Davies of Hereford, Gabriel Harvey, Abraham Fraunce, and others. Sir Philip Sidney began his pastoral romance the *Arcadia* at the Countess's request during his stay with her at Wilton in 1580. Probably the pair began their joint translation of the Psalms at this time also. Mary Herbert also translated Philip Mornay's *Discourse of Life and Death* which was published in 1592 with her translation of Robert Garnier's *Antonie.* The *Psalms,* of which Sir Philip translated numbers 1–43 and Mary Herbert translated 44–150, were not published until 1823.

ELIZABETH MELVILL, Lady Culross (fl. 1603). Daughter of Sir James Melvill of Halhill. Married Colvill of Culross. Her book *Ane Godlie Dreame,* published at Edinburgh in 1603, went through several Anglicized versions, one being printed as late as 1644. The excerpt used here is taken from the Edinburgh edition of 1606.

LUCY HARINGTON, Countess of Bedford (d. 1627). Daughter of Sir John Harington, Baron Harington of Exton. Married Edward Russell, Earl of Bedford, 1594. A patron of poets, she is repeatedly mentioned by the men of letters of her day, including Ben Jonson, John Donne, Samuel Daniel, Michael Drayton, and George Chapman. Her only surviving poem, an elegy beginning "Death, be not proud," was long thought to have been written by Donne.

LADY ELIZABETH CAREY (1585?–1639). Daughter of Lawrence Tanfield, later Lord Chief Baron of the Exchequer. She taught herself

The Women Poets in English

to read French, Spanish, Italian, Latin, and Transylvanian, and at an early age translated the epistles of Seneca and Abraham Ortelius's *Le Miroir du Monde*. In 1602 married Sir Henry Carey, later Viscount Falkland, and accompanied him to Dublin in 1622 when he became Lord Deputy of Ireland. There she set up workshops to train beggar children in trades. Returned to England in 1625 and became a Catholic convert. Estranged from her husband, she lived in poverty for the remainder of her life. Buried in Queen Henrietta Maria's chapel. Known for her learning, she was honored in the dedications of Michael Drayton's *England's Heroicall Epistles* (1587), John Davies of Hereford's *Muses Sacrifice* (1612), and John Marston's *Works*, 1633. Her own works include a play set in Sicily (c. 1602), now lost: *The History of the Life, Reign, and Death of Edward II. King of England . . . Written by E. F. in the year 1627* (London, 1680) attributed to her; *The Tragedie of Mariam the Faire Queene of Jewry*, written perhaps as early as 1603 (London, 1613), reprinted by The Malone Society, 1914. *The Lady Falkland: Her Life. From a MS. in the Imperial Archives at Lille* (London, 1861) was written by her daughter(s).

MARY SIDNEY WROTH, Countess of Montgomery (fl. 1621). Daughter of Robert Sidney, Earl of Leicester, younger brother of Sir Philip Sidney. Married Sir Robert Wroth at the age of eighteen. Was often at court after her marriage. King James often visited her husband's estate at Durrants. She was a patron of poets. On Twelfth Night, 1604–5, she acted at Whitehall in Ben Jonson's *Masque of Blackness*. Jonson dedicated to her several poems and his play *The Alchemist*. Chapman, Wither, and other poets dedicated works to her. On the death of her husband, 1614, she was left with large debts. She wrote *The Countess of Montgomeries Urania* as a financial venture. The *Urania* is a prose romance, interspersed with poems, but it goes beyond its model the *Arcadia* in adding dialogue and subplots which tend toward realism.

RACHEL SPEGHT (fl. 1617–1621). Author of two books: *A Mouzell for Melastomus, the Cynicall Bayter of, and foule mouthed Barker against Evahs Sex. Or an Apologeticall Answere to that Irreligious and Illiterate Pamphlet made by Jo. Sw. . . . The Arraignement of Women*, 1617; and *Mortalitie's Memorandum, with a Dreame Prefixed, imaginarie in manner, reall in matter*, 1621.

DIANA PRIMROSE (fl. 1630). Called "the Noble Lady Diana Primrose" on the title page of her book. She addressed her poem to "all noble ladies and gentle-women." The index to John Nichols' *The Progresses and Public Processions of Queen Elizabeth*, London, 1823, lists the name Diana Primrose under that of Anne Clifford, Countess of Pembroke, but he gives no reason for the identification. Anne Clifford was the wife of Philip Herbert, Earl of Pembroke and Montgomery. She was educated by the poet Samuel Daniel. Much of her life was spent in gaining title to the estates of her father, George Clifford, Earl of Cumberland. Because she was a woman, her right to the estates was in doubt, though she was the only surviving heir.

338

ANNE BRADSTREET (1612–1672). Born probably in Northamptonshire, England. Spent her youth in Lincolnshire, where her father, Thomas Dudley, was steward to the Earl of Lincoln. Came to the Massachusetts Bay Colony in 1630 with her father's family and her husband, Simon Bradstreet. Lived in Boston, Newtown (Cambridge), Ipswich, and North Andover. Was the first dedicated poet to settle in America. Her first book *The Tenth Muse Lately Sprung Up in America* was published in London, 1650; John Foster, a Boston printer, brought out a second edition, with revisions and additional poems, in 1678. *The Works of Anne Bradstreet in Prose and Verse*, 1867, edited by John Harvard Ellis, contains her complete canon.

ANNE COLLINS (fl. 1653). Apparently an invalid. Her *Divine Songs and Meditacions*, 1653, exists in a unique copy in the Huntington Library. A selection from the book was published by the Augustan Reprint Society in 1961.

MARGARET CAVENDISH, Duchess of Newcastle (1624–1674). Daughter of Sir Thomas Lucas, became maid of honor to Queen Henrietta Maria in 1643 and accompanied her in exile in France. Married William Cavendish. Lived in Paris, Rotterdam, and Antwerp until the Restoration. Known as an eccentric. Wrote twelve volumes of poetry, plays, essays, letters, and philosophical opinions. Her works include *Poems and Fancies*, 1653; *Sociable Letters*, 1664; *The Life of William Cavendish, Duke of Newcastle*, 1667; and an autobiographical sketch in *Nature's Pictures*, 1656. She is buried in Westminster Abbey.

KATHERINE PHILIPS (1631–1664). Daughter of a London merchant. Married James Philips, a Welsh Puritan and parliamentary leader. Her home in Cardigan, Wales, was the center for a "society of friendship" in which members took pseudonyms. She was known as "Orinda," her husband as "Antenor." *The Letters of Orinda to Poliarchus*, 1705, describe the society. Her translation of Corneille's *Pompey* was acted in Dublin. Orinda numbered among her friends Henry Lawes, the composer, Bishop Jeremy Taylor, and Henry Vaughan, to whose *Poems*, 1651, her earliest verses were prefixed. Taylor addressed a discourse on friendship to her; Dryden praised her; Abraham Cowley mourned her death in a long Pindaric ode. Her *Poems* were published in a pirated edition, 1664, and in her own edition, 1667.

APHRA BEHN (1640–1689). Born in Wye, Kent, apparently spent some time in Surinam, Guiana, probably in 1663–1664. Married briefly to a man named Behn. The first unquestioned facts of her life relate to her mission as a spy in the Netherlands for Charles II in 1666; she borrowed the money to return home, and, unable to pay it back, was imprisoned for debt. On her release, she became the first woman to earn her living by writing. She wrote seventeen plays, twelve novels, several translations, and a collection of poems, as well as poems to be sung during the plays. Buried in Westminster Abbey. BOOKS: include: *Poems upon Several*

Occasions, 1684. Plays: *The Amorous Prince*, 1671; *Abdelazer*, 1677; *The Rover*, 1677; *Sir Patient Fancy*, 1678; *The Feigned Courtesans*, 1679; *The Roundheads*, 1682; *The City Heiress*, 1682; *The Lucky Chance*, 1687. Novels: *Oroonoko*, 1688; *The Fair Jilt*, 1688; *The Unfortunate Bride*, 1698; *The Adventure of the Black Lady*, 1698; *The Dumb Virgin*, 1700. Editor: *Miscellany*, 1685.

JOAN PHILIPS (fl. 1679) wrote under the pseudonym "Ephelia." Author of *Female Poems on Several Occasions*, 1679 (second edition, 1682), which includes a poem of tribute to Aphra Behn, and of *Advice to His Grace*, ca. 1681–82.

ANNE KILLIGREW (1660–1685). Daughter of clergyman and dramatist Henry Killigrew, Chaplain to the Duke of York. She became Maid of Honour to Mary of Modena, Duchess of York, sharing this office with Anne Finch, Countess of Winchelsea. Known as a painter as well as a poet. Upon her untimely death, her father gathered a memorial edition of her poems, which included, as preface, John Dryden's famous ode to her memory. BOOK: *Poems*, 1686; reprinted, 1967.

MARY LEE, Lady Chudleigh (1656–1710). Daughter of Richard Lee of Winslade, Devonshire. Unhappily married to Sir George Chudleigh of Ashton. Her first publication was *The Ladies' Defence*, signed by her initials, in answer to a sermon preached by John Sprint. It was followed by other poems and essays. Some of her letters may be found in Richard Gwinnett's *Honourable Lovers*, 1732. BOOKS: *The Ladies' Defence: Or, the Bride-Woman's Counsellor Answered: A Poem in a Dialogue between Sir John Brute, Sir Wm. Loveall, Melissa, and a Parson*, 1701, unauthorized edition, 1709; *Poems on Several Occasions*, 1703; *Essays upon several Subjects*, 1710.

ANNE FINCH, Countess of Winchelsea (1661–1722). Daughter of Sir William Kingsmill, of Sidmonton, Southampton. Married Heneage Finch. With Anne Killigrew was Maid of Honour to the second wife of James, Duke of York. Pope and Rowe complimented her in their verse under the names of "Ardelia" and "Flavia." She is known now chiefly as a forerunner of romanticism. Her poem on the "Spleen" appeared in 1701 in Gildon's *Miscellany*. Her *Miscellany Poems, written by a Lady*, were published in 1713. More complete is *The Poems of Anne, countess of Winchilsea, from the original edition of 1713 and from unpublished manuscripts*, edited by Myra Reynolds, 1903.

JANE BRERETON (1685–1740) was the daughter of Thomas Hughes of Bryn-Griffith, Flintshire. She wrote under the name of "Melissa."

LADY MARY WORTLEY MONTAGU (1689–1762). Daughter of Evelyn Pierrepont, later Duke of Kingston. Self-educated, but encouraged in her studies by her uncle and by Bishop Burnet. She corresponded with Mary Astell, a champion of women's rights, and with Anne Wortley Montagu, whose brother she afterwards married. Her beauty and wit made her prominent at court. When her husband was appointed ambassador to Constantinople Lady Mary accompanied him; on her return she brought back the practice of inoculation for smallpox. She engaged in a famous literary feud with Alexander Pope. In 1739 she went abroad and remained there until shortly before her death. She is best known for her vivid letters. Her *Town Eclogues* were published in a pirated edition as *Court Poems,* 1716. Her *Letters* appeared in various editions beginning in 1763. A complete edition is *The Works of Lady Mary Wortley Montagu,* 1803.

CONSTANTIA GRIERSON (1706?–1733). Born at Kilkenny, Ireland. Her father encouraged her in her studies. At eighteen, studied obstetrics with Dr. Van Lewen, father of Laetitia Pilkington. Soon after married George Grierson, a Dublin printer, who obtained a patent as king's printer in Ireland. Mrs. Grierson knew Hebrew, Greek, Latin, and French; was a friend of Swift, Thomas Sheridan, and Patrick Delaney. Edited Latin classics, principally Terence, and Tacitus, and was editing Sallust at the time of her death. Her only poem extant is that printed in Mary Barber's *Poems on Several Occasions,* 1734. She is mentioned in the *Memoirs* of Laetitia Pilkington.

LAETITIA PILKINGTON (1712–1750). Born in Dublin, daughter of Dr. Van Lewen, a physician. Married Matthew Pilkington, a parson. She was a friend of Swift, and her reminiscences are a chief source of information on his later years. Separated from her husband, she went to London where she was assisted by Colley Cibber and Samuel Richardson. In 1748 imprisoned for debt, but released through the intervention of Cibber, who encouraged her to write her *Memoirs,* 1748. In that year her play "The Turkish Court, or the London Prentice," was acted in Dublin. She kept a bookshop in London for a short time. Returned to Dublin, where she died. BOOKS: *Memoirs of Mrs. Laetitia Pilkington, written by herself, Wherein are occasionally interspersed all her Poems, with Anecdotes of several eminent persons living and dead,* 1748; third edition, with an additional volume by her son, 1754; *The Celebrated Mrs. Pilkington's Jests, or the Cabinet of Wit and Humour,* 1751.

JANE ELLIOT [or Jean] (1727–1805). Daughter of Sir Gilbert Elliot. Born at Minto House, Teviotdale, Scotland. Wrote "The Flowers of the Forest" as the result of a wager with her brother. Lived in Edinburgh from 1782–1804, returning to Teviotsdale in her last year. She is not known to have written any other poem.

ANN MURRY (fl. 1778–1799). Author of *Mentoria: or the Young Ladies Instructor,* 1778, and *The Sequel to Mentoria,* 1799. Her volume, *Poems on Various Subjects,* 1779, contains a long list of subscribers.

PHILLIS WHEATLEY (ca. 1753–1784). Brought from Africa to Boston, Massachusetts, as a slave in 1761, when she was about seven. Her homeland is unknown; she spoke little of it, except for a remembrance of her mother pouring out water as a libation to the rising sun. She was purchased by John Wheatley, a tailor, as a servant for his wife Mary. Mary Wheatley gave her as good an education as most girls in Boston received and encouraged her talent for writing poetry. Between 1770–1773 she accompanied one of the Wheatleys to England, and was introduced to members of English society by the Countess of Huntingdon. In 1776 she was received by General Washington. Married John Peters, 1778, after which she suffered from poverty and increasing ill-health. BOOKS: *Poems on Various Subjects, Religious and Moral*, London, 1773. *The Poems of Phillis Wheatley*, edited by Julian D. Mason, Jr., 1966, contains her complete works.

ANNA GORDON BROWN (1747–1810). Lived in Falkland, Scotland. Known as a foremost reciter of the ancient ballads, many of which she learned from an aunt. Mrs. Brown practiced the reciting of ballads as an oral art, and her versions underwent change and development over the years. Her ballads are preserved in Francis James Child's *The English and Scottish Popular Ballads*, 1882–1898. In his introduction, Child says: "No Scottish ballads are superior in kind to those recited in the last century by Mrs. Brown, of Falkland."

CHARLOTTE SMITH (1749–1806). Born in London. Daughter of Nicholas Turner, a gentleman of wealth, she spent her youth at Bignor Park in Sussex. Married at sixteen to Benjamin Smith, son of a London merchant. Benjamin's extravagance caused his bankruptcy and a stay of six months in debtor's prison; much of that time Charlotte spent with him. To raise money, she had her *Elegiac Sonnets and Other Essays* published at her own expense, 1784. The couple, again in trouble with creditors, spent the winter of 1785 in Normandy, where their tenth child was born. There Charlotte produced her first work in prose—a translation of *Manon L'Escaut;* it was attacked by the critic George Steevens and she withdrew it from publication. She continued to write to support her children, producing over twenty books—novels, translations, books for young people, letters, and poems. Sir Walter Scott admired her novels and wrote a long critique of them. BOOKS: *Elegiac Sonnets and Other Essays*, 1784 (11 editions by 1851); *The Emigrants*, a poem, 1793. *Beachy Head, with other poems*, 1807. Novels: *Emmeline*, 1788; *Celestina*, 1791; *Desmond*, 1792; *The Old Manor House*, 1793. Other: *Conversations, Introducing Poetry*, 1804.

HENRIETTA ONEIL (1758–1793). Daughter of Charles, Viscount Dungarvon. Married John Oneil, of County Antrim, Ireland. Two of her poems are preserved in the work of her friend, Charlotte Smith: "Ode to the Poppy" in Smith's *Desmond;* and "Verses . . ." in the second edition of Smith's *Poems*.

LADY ANNE LINDSAY (1750–1825). Daughter of James Lindsay, Earl of Balcarres. Her balled "Auld Robin Gray" was published anonymously in 1771. In 1797, accompanied her husband when he became colonial secretary at the Cape of Good Hope. Remained until 1802. From 1807 until her death her house in Berkeley Square was a literary center. Her letters to Henry Dundas, then Secretary for War and the Colonies, were published in 1901 under the title *South Africa a Century Ago.*

JOANNA BAILLIE (1762–1851). Born at the manse of Bothwell, on the Clyde, Scotland. In 1784 left Scotland for London and settled in Hampstead. In 1790 published a volume of verses, but her major effort was in the drama. She attempted to "delineate the strange passions of the mind" in a series of plays, in three volumes appearing between 1798 and 1812. She wrote other plays as well. *Family Legend* ran successfully, though briefly, in Edinburgh in 1810; *De Montfort,* acted by John Kemble and Sarah Kemble Siddons, played in London in 1809. The cottage in Hampstead was the center of a brilliant literary circle. Her works are collected in *Dramatic and Poetical Works,* 1851.

CAROLINA OLIPHANT, Lady Nairne (1766–1845). Born into an ancient Jacobite family of Gask, Perthshire, Scotland. Married Major William Nairne. Wrote Jacobite songs, and humorous and pathetic ballads, which were published anonymously. She brought out a collection of national airs, with words to accompany them, called *The Scottish Minstrel,* to which she contributed a large number of songs under the initials "B. B."—"Mrs. Bogan of Bogan." Her poems were published posthumously as *Lays from Strathearn,* 1846.

ANNE RADCLIFFE (1764–1823). Born Anne Ward in London. In 1787 married William Radcliffe, editor-proprietor of the *English Chronicle.* Though not the first to write Gothic novels of terror and suspense, she established their vogue. She also added to the form a rational explanation of the apparently supernatural mysteries. BOOKS: *Poems,* 1834. Novels: *The Castles of Athlin and Dunbayne,* 1789; *The Sicilian Romance,* 1790; *The Romance of the Forest,* 1791; *The Mysteries of Udolpho,* 1794; *The Italian, or the Confessional of the Black Penitents,* 1797; *Gaston de Blondeville,* 1826.

FELICIA HEMANS (1793–1835). Born in Liverpool, daughter of George Browne, a merchant of Irish descent. Lived in Wales for a number of years after 1806. Married Alfred Hemans, a captain in the militia. By age twenty-five had published two volumes of poems as well as *The Restoration of Works of Art to Italy,* 1816; *Modern Greece,* 1817; and *Translations from Camoëns and Other Poets,* 1818. Her play *The Vespers of Palermo* ran at Edinburgh in 1824. She was a friend of Sir Walter Scott and visited Wordsworth in the Lake country. Her works have been several times collected since 1839, most recently in *Poetical Works,* 1914.

ELIZABETH BARRETT BROWNING (1806–1861). Spent her youth in the country near the Malvern Hills. From girlhood she was devoted to literature; without formal education, she managed to gain from her brother's tutor a knowledge of Greek, Latin, and modern languages. In 1819 a fall caused an injury to her spine, which kept her an invalid until shortly before her marriage to Robert Browning in 1846. The couple settled in Casa

The Women Poets in English

Guidi, Florence, which remained their home, except for occasional visits to France and England, until Mrs. Browning's death. Elizabeth Barrett Browning was a champion of the Italian struggle for freedom from Austria; she also wrote against child labor and slavery. BOOKS: *An Essay on the Mind and Other Poems*, 1826; *Prometheus Bound, and Miscellaneous Poems*, 1833; *The Seraphim, and Other Poems*, 1838; *Poems*, 1844; *Sonnets from the Portuguese*, 1850; *Casa Guidi Windows*, 1851; *Aurora Leigh*, 1857; *Poems before Congress*, 1860; *Last Poems*, 1862.

HELEN SELINA SHERIDAN, Lady Dufferin (1807–1867). One of three accomplished sisters, granddaughters of the playwright Richard Brinsley Sheridan. Her mother was a novelist; her sister, Caroline Norton, also became a writer. Spent part of her childhood at the Cape of Good Hope, where her father was colonial secretary. After his death, the family lived at Hampton Court Palace. Married Price Blackwood, heir to the Irish title of Baron Dufferin. After his death in 1841, lived in retirement. In 1863, her comedy *Finesse* played in Haymarket, London. Her *Poems and Verses* were published by her son in 1894.

FANNY KEMBLE (1809–1893). One of a noted family of English actors. Born in London, educated chiefly in France. Made her debut as an actress as Juliet at Covent Garden; achieved great popularity. Accompanied her father to the United States in 1832 and married a planter, Pierce Butler. Divorced in 1849, returned to London and the stage. Her play *Francis the First* was unsuccessfully produced in 1832. Her journals and reminiscences contain material important to the social and dramatic history of the period. BOOKS: *Poems*, 1844; *Plays*, 1863. Journals and reminiscences: *A Year of Consolation*, 1847; *Journal*, 1835; *Journal* (life on a Georgia plantation), 1863; *Records of a Girlhood*, 1878; *Records of Later Life*, 1882; *Notes on some of Shakespeare's Plays*, 1882; *Far Away and Long Ago*, 1889; *Further Records*, 1891.

LADY JOHN SCOTT (1810–1900). The name used by Alicia Anne Spottiswood, writer of Scottish songs. She wrote the popular version of the old ballad, "Annie Laurie." Her *Songs and Verses* were published in 1904.

CHARLOTTE BRONTË (1816–1855). Daughter of Patrick Brontë, an Irish clergyman, curate at Hartshead-cum-Clifton, Yorkshire, subsequently rector of Haworth, near Bradford, on the Yorkshire moors. There she and her sisters spent their time reading, writing, and walking over the moors except for a year at the Clergy Daughters' School at Cowan's Bridge, afterwards immortalized in *Jane Eyre*. In 1831 attended Miss Margaret Wooler's School, returning home after a year to tutor her sisters; became a governess with Miss Wooler, 1835–1838. In 1842 attended the Pensionnat Heger in Brussels as a pupil; returned as instructor at the Pensionnat for the year 1843. In 1846 had the volume of *Poems* by "Currer, Ellis, and Acton Bell" published. *Jane Eyre* was published under the name "Currer Bell" in 1847. After the publication of *Shirley*, 1849, Charlotte Brontë became acquainted with many prominent writers; Elizabeth Gaskell visited the rectory at Haworth and in 1857 published *The Life of Charlotte Brontë.* In 1854, she married her father's curate, and died the following year of illness following childbirth. BOOKS: *Poems by Currer, Ellis, and Acton Bell,* 1846. Novels: *Jane Eyre,* 1847; *Shirley,* 1849; *Villette,* 1853; *The Professor,* 1857; *Emma,* 1860.

EMILY BRONTË (1818–1848). Born at Hartshead, Yorkshire. Spent most of her life at Haworth, Yorkshire, where her father was rector. Educated at home, save for a year at the Clergy Daughters' School at Cowan's Bridge, three months at Miss Wooler's School, and eight months with Charlotte at the Pensionnat Heger in 1842. Her single novel *Wuthering Heights* was published in 1847. Always aloof and shy, she left little correspondence or other material for the biographer beyond her novel and her poems. Her poems have been collected several times, most recently in *Complete Poems,* 1951.

ANNE BRONTË (1820–1849). Born at Hartshead, Yorkshire; spent most of her life at Haworth, except for a few months at Miss Wooler's School at Roe Head, 1835, and a brief career as a governess, 1839–1845. BOOKS: *Poems by Currer, Ellis, and Acton Bell,* 1846; *Complete Poems,* 1920. Novels: *Agnes Grey,* 1847; *The Tenant of Wildfell Hall,* 1848.

JULIA WARD HOWE (1819–1910). Born in New York City. Daughter of Samuel Ward, a banker, and Julia Rush Cutler Ward, a poet. Educated by private tutors in music and languages. Married Dr. Samuel Gridley Howe, a philanthropist. Lectured, did editorial work, preached occasionally in the Unitarian Church. Advocated abolition, prison reform, world peace, and worked for the advancement of women. One of the founders of the American Woman-Suffrage Association. She wrote poetry, drama, biography, essays, books of travel, and memoirs. Best known for "The Battle Hymn of the Republic" which appeared in the *Atlantic,* February, 1862. Was the first woman elected to the American Academy of Arts and Letters. BOOKS: *From Sunset Ridge: Poems Old and New,* 1898. Biography and memoirs: *A Memoir of Dr. Samuel G. Howe,* 1876; *Margaret Fuller,* 1883; *Sketches of Representative Women of New England,* 1905; *Reminiscences,* 1899. *The Walk with God,* 1919. Essays and speeches: *Julia Ward Howe and the Woman Suffrage Movement,* edited by Florence Howe Hall, 1913.

DORA GREENWELL (1821–1882). Born at Greenwell Ford, Durham, England. Lived there until 1848, afterward in London. Her first publication was a volume of poems, 1848. Also wrote essays; one, published in the *North British Review,* asked for an extension of the work open to educated women. BOOKS: *Stories That Might Be True, with Other Poems,* 1850; *Carmina Crucis,* 1869; *Songs of Salvation,* 1873; *The Soul's Legend,* 1873; *Camera Obscura,* 1876. Prose: *A Present Heaven,* 1855; *The Patience of Hope,* 1860; *Essays,* 1866; *Life of Lacordaire,* 1867; *Two Friends,* 1867; *Colloquia Crucis,* 1871; *Liber Humanitatis: Essays on Spiritual and Social Life,* 1875.

The Women Poets in English

CHRISTINA ROSSETTI (1830–1894). Born in London, the youngest child of Gabriele Rossetti, Italian poet and refugee from Naples, who became professor of Italian at King's College, London. Sister of the painter and poet Dante Gabriel Rossetti; her serious beauty made her his favorite model in paintings of the Virgin. In 1850 contributed seven poems to *The Germ*, the pre-Raphaelite magazine. Helped her mother run a day-school in Somerset, 1853–1854. After a return to London in 1854, her father died, and the family lived in poverty. In 1862 she published *Goblin Market*, her earliest mature book, which contains much of her finest writing. She was an exceedingly devout Anglican, and in 1866 rejected a suitor whom she loved because his religion was too "undefined." In 1871 she became ill with "Grave's Disease" and remained a recluse for the rest of her life. BOOKS: *Goblin Market and Other Poems*, 1862; *The Prince's Progress*, 1866; *Sing-Song* (for children), 1872; *A Pageant*, 1881; *Verses*, 1893; *New Poems*, 1896. Prose: *Commonplace*, 1870; *Seek and Find*, 1879; *Time Flies*, 1885; *The Face of the Deep*, 1892.

EMILY DICKINSON (1830–1886). Born in Amherst, Massachusetts. Daughter of Edward Dickinson, a laywer, Congressman, and treasurer of Amherst College. In 1847 attended South Hadley Female Seminary, now Mount Holyoke College, but returned in less than a year to Amherst, where she lived the rest of her life. Began writing poetry in the 1850s; her period of greatest productivity was in the early 1860s. She sought the critical help of Thomas Wentworth Higginson, who later became her editor. Only seven poems were published during her lifetime; her first book appeared in 1890. Volumes containing additional poems appeared at intervals until 1945. The poems in this anthology represent the earliest published versions of the poems, which remain the most familiar to readers. BOOKS: *The Complete Poems of Emily Dickinson*, 1960. *The Letters of Emily Dickinson*, 1958.

MATHILDE BLIND (1841–1896). Born in Mannheim, Germany, came to England when she was eight. Her step-father, Karl Blind, was a political writer, one of the exiled leaders of the Baden revolt of 1848. Her first book *Poems*, 1867, appeared under the pseudonym Claude Lake. *The Heather on Fire*, 1886, grew out of her indignation over evictions in the Highlands. Other long poems were *The Prophecy of St. Oran*, 1881, and *The Ascent of Man*, 1888, an epic on Darwin's theory of evolution. BOOKS: *The Poetical Works of Mathilde Blind*, 1900. Translation: *The Old Faith and the New* (D. F. Strauss), 1873.

EMMA LAZARUS (1849–1887). Born in New York City. Educated by tutors. Much of her early work appeared in *Lippincott's Magazine*. Her *Admetus and Other Poems* (1871) was dedicated to Ralph Waldo Emerson, whom she later visited at Concord. Shocked by the pogroms against the Jews in Russia, she devoted much of the last decade of her life to the cause of Jewish nationalism. Her famous sonnet "The New Colossus," written to help raise contributions for the pedestal for the Statue of Liberty, is engraved on a tablet at its base. BOOKS: *Admetus and Other Poems*, 1871;

346

Songs of a Semite, 1882; *By the Waters of Babylon,* 1887. Translation: *Poems and Ballads of Heinrich Heine.* 1881. Other: *Alide,* 1874; *Emma Lazarus, Selections from her Poetry and Prose,* 1944.

ETHNA CARBERY (1866–1902). Pseudonym of Anna Johnston MacManus. Born in Ballymena, in the north of Ireland. Married Seumas MacManus. Her poems were first published in the journal *The United Irishman.* With their overtones of Gaelicism and strong nationalism, they were important in the early days of the Irish literary movement. BOOK: *The Four Winds of Eirinn,* 1926.

MARY ELIZABETH COLERIDGE (1861–1907). Educated at home in London. In 1881 her first essays published in periodicals; her first novel published, 1893. Her verse remained in manuscript until Robert Bridges persuaded her to publish a volume, *Fancy's Following,* 1896, which was privately printed in a limited edition. Continued to write novels, essays, and verse for the rest of her life. Most of her time devoted to helping working women in London, by lecturing on literature at the Working-Women's College and teaching in their homes. Her poems were published posthumously in 1907. BOOKS: *Collected Poems,* 1954. Prose: *The Seven Sleepers of Ephesus,* 1893; *The King with Two Faces,* 1897; *Non Sequitur,* 1900; *The Fiery Dawn,* 1901; *The Shadow on the Wall,* 1904; *The Lady on the Drawing-Room Floor,* 1906; *Life of Holman Hunt,* 1907; *Gathered Leaves* (extracts from her letters and diaries), 1910.

MICHAEL FIELD. Pseudonym for Katharine Harris Bradley (1846–1914) and Edith Emma Cooper (1862–1913). Katharine Bradley was born in Birmingham, England; educated by private tutors and briefly at Newnham College, Cambridge, and at the College de France, Paris. About 1865 joined her older sister's household, which included the child Edith Emma Cooper. Thereafter the aunt and niece were companions. In 1878 the family moved to Bristol, where the two poets attended University College. In 1878 Katharine Bradley published *The New Minnesinger* under the name Arran Leigh; in 1881 the first of many collaborations appeared under the title *Bellerophón* by Arran and Isla Leigh. The first volume under the name Michael Field contained the tragic dramas *Callirhoë* and *Fair Rosamund,* which appeared in 1884. They were followed by twenty-five other tragedies over the next thirty years. In 1890 the first of eight volumes of lyrics were published. From Bristol the poets moved to Reigate in 1888 and in 1899 to a small house in Richmond, where they spent the remainder of their lives, except for frequent visits to the continent and places used as the settings for their plays. Among their friends were Robert Browning, George Meredith, Herbert Spencer, Oscar Wilde, George Moore, and Bernard Berenson. The two poets became Roman Catholics in 1907. Their last books, marked by religious faith and the knowledge of approaching death, were written separately, though they too bore the collaborative name. The poet T. Sturge Moore, as their literary executor, published a portion of their journal and some letters in 1933. BOOKS: *Long Ago,* 1890; *Sight and Song,* 1892; *Underneath the Bough,* 1893; *Wild Honey,* 1908; *Poems of Adoration*

The Women Poets in English

(Edith Cooper), 1912; *Mystic Trees* (Katharine Bradley), 1913; *A Selection From the Poems of Michael Field,* 1923; *Works and Days From the Journal of Michael Field,* 1933.

ALICE MEYNELL (1847–1922). Grew up in Italy. Educated by her father, Thomas James Thompson. The examples of Elizabeth Barrett Browning and Christina Rossetti inspired her to write poetry in her youth. Her first book, *Preludes,* 1875, won the praise of George Eliot, John Ruskin, D. G. Rossetti, and Robert Browning. Wilfred Meynell read her sonnets, sought an introduction, and became her husband in 1877. For many years, she wrote little poetry, but devoted herself to her large family and to humanitarian causes—prevention of cruelty to animals, improvement of conditions in slums, extension of suffrage and industrial and professional rights to women. She rescued Francis Thompson from poverty and opium. Encouraged by W. H. Henley she began to write reviews and essays; contributed a weekly column to the *Pall Mall Gazette.* In her later years she turned again to poetry. BOOKS: Collections: *The Poems,* 1940. *Poems,* 1948. Prose: *Essays,* 1914. *Hearts of Controversy,* 1917; *The Second Person Singular, and Other Essays,* 1921; *John Ruskin,* 1900; *London Impressions,* 1898.

MARY AUSTIN (1868–1934). Born in Carlinville, Illinois; educated there at Blackburn College. Taught in California, where she became a friend and chronicler of Indian tribes. In 1900, settled in Carmel, California, one of the founders of the literary colony which included Jack London and George Sterling. Her first book, *Land of Little Rain,* 1903, brought her immediate recognition. Lived in New York; in 1918 settled in Santa Fe. Wrote articles and novels on social problems and feminism, but her best work was in interpreting the American Indians, their songs, and contributions to American life. BOOKS: *The American Rhythm,* 1923; *The Children Sing in the Far West,* 1928. Novels: *The Basket Woman,* 1904; *The Flock,* 1906; *Lost Borders,* 1909; *Woman of Genius,* 1912; *26 Jayne Street,* 1920; *A Small Town Man,* 1922; *The Land of Journey's Ending,* 1924. Play: *The Arrow Maker,* 1911. Autobiography: *Earth Horizon,* 1932.

BEATRICE RAVENEL (1870–1956). Born in Charleston, South Carolina. Educated at Miss Kelly's Female Seminary in Charleston and attended Radcliffe College, 1889–1892 and 1895–1897. In Cambridge she was an editor for the *Harvard Monthly* and one of a group which included Norman Hapgood and the poets William Vaughn Moody and Trumbull Stickney. Returned to Charleston, where she married Frank Ravenel in 1900. About 1915 she began writing poetry, prose fiction, and editorials on foreign affairs for national magazines and for the Columbia, S.C., *State.* The founding of the Poetry Society of South Carolina in 1920–21 helped to direct her poetry into the new patterns. She met Amy Lowell in 1922; thereafter the two corresponded. BOOKS: *The Arrow of Lightning,* 1926. *The Yemassee Lands: Poems of Beatrice Ravenel,* 1969.

CHARLOTTE MEW (1870–1928). Born in London and passed most of her life in Bloomsbury. Contributed verse, essays, and stories to such periodicals as *The Yellow Book, The Englishwoman, The Nation,* and *The New Statesman.* Her first collection of seventeen poems was issued by The Poetry Bookshop in 1917. Through the efforts of Thomas Hardy, who much admired her work, she was awarded a Civil List pension. BOOKS: *The Farmer's Bride,* 1917; *The Rambling Sailor,* 1929.

WILLA CATHER (1873–1947). Born in Winchester, Virginia, moved early to Red Cloud, Nebraska. Taught by her grandmothers to read Latin and classics at home, she went on to the University of Nebraska. Worked on *Pittsburgh Leader* as copy, music, and drama editor, taught school, became managing editor of *McClure's* magazine. Retired to write short stories and novels, one of which received the Pulitzer prize in 1922. Made frequent visits to the Southwest, setting for many of her stories. Her poems foreshadow the themes of her novels. BOOKS: *April Twilights,* 1903. Novels: *Alexander's Bridge,* 1912; *O Pioneers!,* 1913; *Song of the Lark,* 1915; *My Ántonia,* 1918; *One of Ours,* 1922; *A Lost Lady,* 1923; *Death Comes for the Archbishop,* 1927; *Shadows on the Rock,* 1931; *Sapphira and the Slave Girl,* 1940. Short stories: *The Troll Garden,* 1905; *Youth and the Bright Medusa,* 1920; *Lucy Gayheart,* 1935. Essays: *Not Under Forty,* 1936.

AMY LOWELL (1874–1925). Born in Brookline, Massachusetts, a member of an historic family, was educated by her mother and in private schools. She became a dominating figure in American poetry during the last decade of her life, particularly after her emergence as leader of the imagist poets. Imagism did not limit her, however, and she went on to experiment with other forms, including polyphonic prose and translations from and imitations of the Chinese. Her eighth book of poetry, *What's O'clock* (1925), won the Pulitzer Prize. BOOKS: *The Complete Poetical Works of Amy Lowell,* 1955. Criticism: *Tendencies in Modern American Poetry,* 1917; *Poetry and Poets,* 1930. Biography: *John Keats* (2 vols.), 1925.

ADELAIDE CRAPSEY (1878–1914). Born in Rochester, New York, graduated from Vassar, 1901. Taught history and literature at a preparatory school in Wisconsin. In 1905 studied archaeology in Rome. Taught school in Connecticut; became instructor in poetics at Smith College in 1911. She invented the *cinquain,* a five-line poem suggested by the Japanese *haiku* and *tanka.* BOOKS: *Verse,* 1915 (*New Edition,* 1934). Criticism: *A Study in English Metrics,* 1918.

MINA LOY (1882–1966). Born in London, she was closely associated with the American poets of the imagist movement. Lived in France and Spain, and eventually made her home in the United States. BOOKS: *Lunar Baedeker and Time-Tables,* 1958.

LOLA RIDGE (1883–1941). Born in Dublin, Ireland, spent her childhood and youth in Australia. Came to the United States in 1907. Earned her living by working in factories, writing and drawing, until her long poem

"The Ghetto" was published in *The New Republic* in 1918. Was founder and later editor of *Others* and an editor of *Broom.* Through the twenties, her work invoked social justice and attacked the social system. Her later work is mystical. BOOKS: *The Ghetto and Other Poems,* 1919; *Sun-up,* 1920; *Red Flag and Other Poems,* 1927; *Firehead,* 1929; *Dance of Fire,* 1935.

ETHEL ANDERSON (1883–1958) Born in Leamington, Warwickshire, Australia, and spent most of her childhood near Picton, New South Wales. Educated at the Sydney Church of England Girls' Grammar School. Married Brigadier-General Austin Anderson and lived some years on the Indian frontier, returning to Australia in 1924. She wrote essays and short stories as well as poetry. BOOKS: *Squatter's Luck,* 1942; *Sunday at Yarralumla,* 1947; *The Song of Hagar,* 1957.

ELIZABETH MADOX ROBERTS (1885–1941). Born in Perrysville, Kentucky, and lived most of her life there, making the lives and often archaic dialects of Kentuckians the subject of her novels. She attended the University of Chicago (Ph. B. 1921) after reeciving a small legacy. There she won the Fiske prize for poems which later became her first volume of poetry. BOOKS: *Under the Tree,* 1922; *Song in the Meadow,* 1940. Novels: *The Time of Man,* 1926; *My Heart and My Flesh,* 1927; *Jingling in the Wind,* 1928; *The Great Meadow,* 1930; *A Buried Treasure,* 1931; *He Sent Forth a Raven,* 1935; *Black Is My Truelove's Hair,* 1938; *Not by Strange Gods,* 1941. Short stories: *The Haunted Mirror,* 1932.

ELINOR WYLIE (1885–1928). Born in Somerville, New Jersey, of a family long associated with Pennsylvania. Educated in private schools in Bryn Mawr. Lived in England for several years after 1910, and moved to New York in 1921. In 1924, after a divorce from Horace Wylie, she married the poet William Rose Benét. Most of her literary production was concentrated in the last nine years of her life, during which she wrote four volumes of verse, four novels, and a number of short stories and essays. BOOKS: *Collected Poems,* 1932; *Last Poems,* 1943. Novels, etc.: *Collected Prose of Elinor Wylie,* 1933.

H. D. (1886–1961) pseudonym of Hilda Doolittle, born in Bethlehem, Pennsylvania, daughter of a professor of mathematics and astronomy. Educated in private schools and at Bryn Mawr College. Went to London in 1911 and became one of the leaders in the imagist group. Married the poet Richard Aldington, took over his editorship of *The Egoist* during World War I. Separated from Aldington in 1919. From 1918 on her life was closely linked to that of Bryher, the historical novelist, who became her friend and benefactor. In 1923 she settled in Switzerland, remaining for the rest of her life except for brief periods spent in London. BOOKS: *Collected Poems,* 1925; *Red Roses for Bronze,* 1931; *The Walls Do Not Fall,* 1944; *Tribute to the Angels,* 1945; *The Flowering of the Rod,* 1946; *By Avon River,* 1949; *Selected Poems of H.D.,* 1957; *Helen in Egypt,* 1961. Drama: *Hippolytus Temporizes,* 1927. Novels: *Palimpsest,* 1926; *Hedylus,* 1928; *Bid Me to Live,* 1960. Translations: *Choruses from the Iphigenia in*

Aulis and the Hippolytus, 1919; *Euripides' Ion,* 1937. Other: *Tribute to Freud,* 1956.

EDITH SITWELL (1887–1964). Member of a famous literary family, sister of Osbert and Sacheverell Sitwell. Born in Scarborough, England. Privately educated. An editor of the anthology *Wheels* 1916–1918, 1921, which protested against the formalities of the Georgian school of poets. Created Dame, Commander Order of the British Empire (the first poet so honored), 1954. Anthologist, critic, and biographer. BOOKS: *Collected Poems,* 1954. *The Outcasts,* 1962; *Music and Ceremonies,* 1963. Novel: *I Live Under a Black Sun,* 1937. Biography and criticism: *Alexander Pope,* 1930; *The English Eccentrics,* 1933; *Victoria of England,* 1936; *English Women,* 1942; *A Notebook on William Shakespeare,* 1948. Autobiography: *Taken Care Of,* 1965.

MARIANNE MOORE (1887–1972). Born in St. Louis, Missouri. Graduated from Bryn Mawr College. Taught in Carlisle Indian School, Carlisle, Pennsylvania, 1911–1915; assistant in New York Public Library, 1921–1925; acting editor of *The Dial,* 1925–1929. In 1915 began contributing poems to *The Egoist* in London, and to *Poetry,* Chicago. She was associated with members of the imagist group, though she developed her own style of syllabic verse combined with a mosaic of eclectic bits of knowledge. Her *Collected Poems* (1952) received the National Book Award, the Pulitzer Prize, and the Bollingen Award. BOOKS: *Collected Poems,* 1952; *Like a Bulwark,* 1956; *O to Be a Dragon,* 1959; *The Arctic Ox,* 1964; *Tell Me, Tell Me,* 1966; *Complete Poems,* 1967. Translations: *The Fables of La Fontaine,* 1954. Criticism: *Predilections,* 1955; *Idiosyncracy and Technique,* 1958. Play: *The Absentee,* 1962.

DOROTHY WELLESLEY (1889–1956). Born at Heywood Lodge, White Waltham, Berkshire, daughter of Robert Ashton. Educated at home mostly by foreign governesses. In 1914 married Lord Gerald Wellesley, who became Duke of Wellington in 1943. Selections of her poems were published from 1913 on. Yeats admired her work; his letters to her were published in 1940 under the title *Letters on Poetry.* BOOKS: *Early Light: The Collected Poems of Dorothy Wellesley,* 1955. Autobiography: *Far Have I Traveled,* 1952.

EDNA ST. VINCENT MILLAY (1892–1950). Born in Rockland, Maine. Educated at Barnard and Vassar. Lived in Greenwich Village, later joined the Provincetown Players. After her marriage in 1923, lived in the Berkshires, except for occasional travel. Noted especially for her sonnets. Her collection *The Harp Weaver* (1923) received the Pulitzer Prize. BOOKS: *Collected Poems,* 1956. Plays: *Aria da Capo,* 1921; *The Lamp and the Bell,* 1921; *Two Slatterns and a King,* 1921; *The King's Henchman,* 1927. Translation (with George Dillon): *Flowers of Evil* (Charles Baudelaire), 1936.

VICTORIA SACKVILLE-WEST (1892–1962). Born at historic Knole Castle, daughter of Baron Sackville. Educated at home. In 1913

351

married Harold Nicolson, author and diplomat, and spent many years abroad, notably in Persia. Her volume of "British Georgics," *The Land* (1926), received the Hawthornden Prize. BOOKS: *Collected Poems*, 1933; *Some Flowers*, 1937; *Solitude*, 1938; *Selected Poems*, 1941. Fiction: *Heritage*, 1918; *The Dragon in Shallow Waters*, 1920; *The Heir and Other Stories*, 1922; *Challenge*, 1923; *Grey Wethers*, 1928; *Seducers in Ecuador*, 1924; *Twelve Days*, 1928; *The Edwardians*, 1930; *All Passion Spent*, 1931; *Family History*, 1932; *Thirty Clocks Strike the Hour and Other Stories*, 1932; *The Dark Island*, 1934; *Grand Canyon*, 1942. Other prose: *Knole and the Sackvilles*, 1923; *Passenger to Teheran*, 1926; *Aphra Behn*, 1927; *Andrew Marvell*, 1929; *Sissinghurst*, 1933; *Joan of Arc*, 1936; *Pepita*, 1937; *Country Notes*, 1939; *Country Notes in Wartime*, 1940; *English Country Houses*, 1941. Editor: *Diary of the Lady Anne Clifford*, 1923.

GENEVIEVE TAGGARD (1894–1948). Born in Waitsburgh, Washington, spent youth in Hawaii. Educated at the University of California, Berkeley. Worked in a publishing house in New York and in 1920 helped found the poetry magazine, *The Measure*. Taught at Mount Holyoke, Bennington, and Sarah Lawrence. BOOKS: *Collected Poems: 1918–1938*, 1938; *Long View*, 1942; *Slow Music*, 1946. Biography: *The Life and Mind of Emily Dickinson*, 1930.

ELIZABETH DARYUSH. Daughter of the poet Robert Bridges. Educated at home, married in 1923, and went to Persia for several years. Has since lived at Boar's Hill, Oxford, England. Her experiments with syllabic verse are described by Yvor Winters in the Introduction to her *Selected Poems*, 1948. BOOKS: *Verse*, 1916; *Verses*, 1930; *Verses, Second Book*, 1932, *Third Book*, 1933, *Fourth Book*, 1934; *Poems*, 1935; *The Last Man and Other Verses*, 1936; *Verses, Sixth Book*, 1938.

BABETTE DEUTSCH. Born in New York City. Educated at Barnard College. Taught at the New School for Social Research, 1933–1935, and since 1944, at the School of General Studies, Columbia University. Honorary Consultant in Poetry to the Library of Congress, 1960–1966. Married to Avrahm Yarmolinsky, with whom she has done translations from German and Russian. BOOKS: *The Collected Poems of Babette Deutsch*, 1969. Novels: *A Brittle Heaven*, 1926; *In Such a Night*, 1927; *Mask of Silenus*, 1933; *Rogue's Legacy*, 1942. Verse translations: *The Twelve* (Alexander Blok); *Modern Russian Poetry*, 1921; *Contemporary German Poetry*, 1923; *Crocodile* (K. I. Chukovsky), 1931; *Poems from the Book of Hours* (Rainer Maria Rilke), 1941, 1969; *Eugene Onegin* (Alexander Pushkin), 1943; *Selected Writings of Boris Pasternak*, 1949; *Jean Sans Terre* (Yvan Goll), 1958. Criticism: *Potable Gold: Some Notes on Poetry and This Age*, 1929; *This Modern Poetry*, 1936; *Poetry in Our Time*, revised 1956, 1963; *Poetry Handbook: A Dictionary of Terms*, 1956, revised 1964, 1969.

RUTH PITTER. Born at Ilford, Essex. Educated at Coborn School, London. Worked for two years in the War Office, then for a pottery company in Suffolk and later London, doing painting. Became a working partner in the firm of Deane & Forester, Chelsea, London, in 1930, painting gift goods and furniture. Received the Hawthornden Prize for *A Trophy of Arms* (1936) and the Queen's Gold Medal for Poetry in 1955. BOOKS: *Poems 1926–1966,* 1968.

LOUISE BOGAN (1897–1970). Born at Livermore Falls, Maine. Educated at the Boston Girls' Latin School and at Boston University. Served as Consultant in Poetry to the Library of Congress, 1945–1946, and for over twenty years as poetry critic for *The New Yorker*. Taught, as Visiting Professor, at a number of universities in the United States and Austria. Her *Collected Poems,* 1954, received the Bollingen Prize. BOOKS: *The Blue Estuaries: Poems 1923–1968,* 1968. Criticism: *Achievement in American Poetry, 1900–1950,* 1951; *Selected Criticism* (1955).

LÉONIE ADAMS. Born in Brooklyn. Educated at Barnard College. Worked on the editorial staff of the Metropolitan Museum. Taught at New York University, Sarah Lawrence, Bennington, and New Jersey College for Women. Consultant in Poetry to the Library of Congress, 1948–1949, and Library of Congress Fellow in Letters, 1949–1955. Lecturer at Columbia University, 1946–1968. Has been Fulbright Professor in France and Visiting Professor at Trinity College, Hartford, Connecticut, and at the University of Washington, Seattle. She received the Bollingen Prize, 1955. BOOKS: *Those Not Elect,* 1925; *High Falcon and Other Poems,* 1929; *Poems: A Selection,* 1959. *This Measure,* 1933. *Poems: A Selection,* 1954. Translation: *Lyrics of François Villon,* 1931.

JANET LEWIS. Born in Chicago, Illinois, daughter of novelist, poet, and teacher Edwin Herbert Lewis. Educated at the University of Chicago, where she was a member of the Poetry Club with Elizabeth Madox Roberts and Glenway Wescott. Worked at the American Consulate in Paris, as proofreader for *Redbook,* and as teacher at Lewis Institute, Chicago. Lived in Santa Fe, New Mexico, 1923–1927. Married the poet and critic Yvor Winters in 1926. Has been visiting lecturer at Stanford University, and lecturer at writers' workshops at the University of Missouri and the University of Denver. BOOKS: *The Indians in the Woods,* 1922; *Poems 1924–1944,* 1950. Prose: *The Invasion,* 1932; *The Wife of Martin Guerre,* 1941; *Against the Darkening Sky,* 1943; *Good-bye, Son, and Other Stories,* 1946; *The Trial of Soren Qvist,* 1947; *The Ghost of Monsieur Scarron,* 1959. Opera libretto: *The Wife of Martin Guerre.*

HILDEGARDE FLANNER. Born near Indianapolis, Indiana. Educated at Sweet Briar College and the University of California, Berkeley, where she studied with Witter Bynner. Married the artist and architect Frederick Monhoff in 1926 and has lived since that time in California. Her sister is the author Janet Flanner (Genêt). BOOKS: *Young Girl,* 1920; *This Morning,* 1921; *A Tree in Bloom,* 1925; *Time's Profile,* 1929; *If There Is Time,* 1942; *In Native Light,* 1970. Editor (with others): Borestone Mountain Poetry Awards annual volume of *Best Poems.*

MARYA ZATURENSKA. Born in Russia, came to New York in 1909, naturalized in 1912. Worked in a factory at fourteen, became interested in poetry, and had her first poems published at eighteen. Educated at Valparaiso University, Indiana, and the University of Wisconsin. Married the poet and critic Horace Gregory in 1925. Her second book, *Cold Morning Sky,* 1938, received the Pulitzer Prize. BOOKS: *Collected Poems,* 1965. Other: *A History of American Poetry, 1900–1940* (with Horace Gregory), 1946; *Christina Rossetti,* 1949. Editor: *The Mentor Book of Religious Verse* (with Horace Gregory), 1957; *The Crystal Cabinet: An Invitation to Poetry* (with Horace Gregory), 1962; *Collected Poems of Sara Teasdale,* 1966.

STEVIE SMITH (1902–1971). Born in Hull, Yorkshire, England. Attended high school in Palmers Green, London, and North London Collegiate School. Prior to 1953, worked in a publisher's office in London; afterwards gave poetry readings for British Broadcasting Corporation and read and sang poems set to music at festivals in London, Edinburgh, Stratford on Avon, and elsewhere. Illustrated each volume of her poems. Has edited anthologies for children. In 1969 received the Queen's Gold Medal for Poetry. BOOKS: *A Good Time Was Had By All,* 1937; *Tender Only to One,* 1938; *Mother, What Is Man?* 1942; *Harold's Leap,* 1950; *Not Waving But Drowning,* 1957; *Selected Poems,* 1962; *The Frog Prince and Other Poems,* 1966; *The Best Beast,* 1969. Novels: *Novel on Yellow Paper,* 1936; *Over the Frontier,* 1938; *The Holiday,* 1949. Other: *Some Are More Human Than Others,* 1958.

KAY BOYLE. Born in St. Paul, Minnesota. Attended Cincinnati Conservatory of Music and Ohio Mechanics Institute. Her first poems were published in *Broom,* and she worked with Lola Ridge on that magazine. Has lived much of her life abroad, especially in France. Has since taught at San Francisco State College. Received the O. Henry Memorial Prize for her short stories in 1935 and 1941. BOOKS: *Collected Poems,* 1962; *Testament for My Students,* 1970. Novels: *Plagued by the Nightingale,* 1931; *Year Before Last,* 1932; *Death of a Man,* 1936; *Avalanche,* 1944; *A Frenchman Must Die,* 1946; *The Seagull on the Step,* 1955; *Generation Without Farewell,* 1960. Stories: *Wedding Day,* 1930; *The First Lover,* 1933; *The White Horses of Vienna,* 1936; *Thirty Stories,* 1946; *The Smoking Mountain,* 1951; *Nothing Ever Breaks Except the Heart,* 1966. Memoirs: *Being Geniuses Together* (with Robert McAlmon), 1968.

PHYLLIS McGINLEY. Born in Ontario, Oregon. Educated at University of Utah, and University of California, Berkeley. Taught school in Utah and New York, wrote copy for an advertising agency, and was a staff writer for *Town and Country.* Wrote lyrics for "Small Wonder," a Broadway revue, and narration for film "The Emperor's Nightingale." Also has written for juveniles. Her selected poems, *Times Three,* (1960), received the Pulitzer Prize. BOOKS: *On the Contrary,* 1934; *One More Manhattan,* 1937; *A Pocketful of Wry,* 1940; *Husbands Are Difficult, or, The Book of Oliver Ames,* 1941; *Stones From a Glass House,* 1946; *A Short Walk From the Station*, 1951; *The Love Letters of Phyllis McGinley*, 1954; *Merry Christmas, Happy New Year*, 1958. Essays: *The Province of the Heart*, 1959; *Sixpence in Her Shoe*, 1964.

ROBIN HYDE (1906–1939). Pseudonym for Iris Guiver Wilkinson. Born in Capetown, South Africa, a few months before her parents settled in Wellington, New Zealand. Became a journalist, working on women's pages in Wellington, Christchurch, Wanganui, and Auckland. Left for England in 1938, visited China on the way, and for a month was reported missing in the war area. Her last year was spent in England, where she wrote *Dragon Rampant*, her book on China. BOOKS: *The Desolate Star*, 1929; *Persephone in Winter*, 1937; *Houses by the Sea and Later Poems*, 1952.

EVE LANGLEY. Born in Forbes, New South Wales. Worked on the land in Gippsland, Victoria. Went to New Zealand in 1932 and there wrote *The Pea Pickers*, her prize-winning novel. Returned to Australia where her second novel, *White Topee*, was published in 1954. Lives in the Blue Mountains, New South Wales.

CELESTE TURNER WRIGHT. Born in Saint John, New Brunswick, Canada. Educated at the University of California, Berkeley (Ph.D.). Since 1928 a member of the English Faculty, University of California, Davis; Chairman of the Department, 1928–55. BOOKS: *Etruscan Princess and Other Poems*, 1946. Biography: *Anthony Mundy: An Elizabethan Man of Letters*, 1928.

KATHLEEN RAINE. Born in London, but lived as a child in Northumberland. Educated at Cambridge, M.A. in Natural Sciences, 1929, one of a generation of Cambridge poets which included William Empson, Ronald Bottrall, John Cornford, Julian Bell, and Charles Madge. Research Fellow of Girton College, Cambridge, 1955–1961. Andrew Mellon Lecturer, National Gallery of Art, Washington, D.C. Recipient, Bollingen Fellowship and Arts Council Prize for Poetry. She is especially noted for her studies of William Blake. BOOKS: *The Collected Poems of Kathleen Raine*, 1956; *The Hollow Hill and Other Poems*, 1960–1964, 1964; *Six Dreams and Other Poems*, 1968; *Ninfa Revisited*, 1968. Other: *William Blake*, 1951; *Coleridge*, 1953; *Blake and England*, 1960; *Defending Ancient Springs; William Blake and Traditional Mythology*, 1969. Translations: *Talk of the Devil* (D. de Rougemont), 1945; *Cousin Bette* (Honoré de Balzac), 1948; *Lost Illusions* (Honoré de Balzac), 1951. Editor: *Letters of Samuel Taylor Coleridge*, 1950; *Thomas Taylor the Platonist: Selected Writings* (with George Mills Harper), 1969.

HELEN SORRELLS. Born in Stafford, Kansas. Educated at Kansas State University. Reporter for the Hutchinson, Kansas, *Herald*. Wrote radio scripts, and occasional news stories for the Kansas City *Star*. Has lived in Pacific Palisades, California, since 1945. BOOK: *Seeds as They Fall*, 1971.

355

The Women Poets in English

CONSTANCE CARRIER. Born in Connecticut. Educated at Smith College and M.A. from Trinity College, Hartford, Connecticut. Formerly Latin instructor, Senior High School, New Britain, Connecticut. Instructor, Classics Workshop, Tufts University Summer Sessions 1969, 1970. Received the Lamont Poetry Prize for her first book, 1954. BOOKS: *The Middle Voice*, 1954. Translations: *The Poems of Propertius*, 1963; *The Poems of Tibullus*, 1968.

GENE DERWOOD (1909–1954). Born in Illinois. Lived in midwest and south, and in New York, where she painted portraits of poets and artists, among them W. H. Auden, George Barker, Richard Eberhart, Oscar Williams, Max Ernst, Dunstan Thompson, and Yvan Goll. Married the poet and anthologist Oscar Williams. BOOK: *The Poems of Gene Derwood*, 1955.

MARGUERITE YOUNG. Born in Indianapolis, Indiana. Educated at Indiana University, Butler University, University of Chicago (M.A.), and University of Iowa. Has taught at Indiana University, the New School for Social Research, and Fordham University. BOOKS: *Prismatic Ground*, 1937; *Moderate Fable*, 1944. Novels: *Angel in the Forest*, 1945; *Miss MacIntosh, My Darling*, 1965.

FRANCES MINTURN HOWARD. Born in New York City. Educated at Friend's School, Art Students' League, Academy of Design, all in New York. Has worked as a medical secretary, nurse's aid, editor. For the past twenty years has lived in Boston. BOOKS: *All Keys Are Glass*, 1950; *Sleep Without Armor*, 1953. Editor (with others): Borestone Mountain Poetry Awards annual volume of *Best Poems*.

JOSEPHINE JACOBSEN. Born in Canada. Consultant in Poetry to the Library of Congress, 1971–1972. Lives in Baltimore, Maryland. BOOKS: *For the Unlost*, 1946. *The Human Climate*, 1953. *The Animal Inside*, 1966. Other: *Testament of Samuel Beckett*, 1964. *Playwrights of Silence* (Ionesco and Genet), with William R. Mueller, 1968.

JOSEPHINE MILES. Born in Chicago, Illinois. Educated at the University of California, Los Angeles, and the University of California, Berkeley (Ph.D.). Since 1940, Professor of English at the University of California, Berkeley. She has published extensively on the language of poetry. BOOKS: *Poems, 1930–1960*, 1960; *Kinds of Affection*, 1967. Literary Criticism: *Wordsworth and the Vocabulary of Fiction*, 1942; *Pathetic Fallacy in the 19th Century*, 1942; *The Vocabulary of Poetry: Three Studies*, 1946. *The Continuity of Poetic Language: Studies in English Poetry from the 1540's to the 1940's*, 1951; *Eras and Modes in English Poetry*, 1957; *Renaissance, Eighteenth Century and Modern Language in English Poetry: A Tabular View*, 1960; *Style and Proportion*, 1967. Editor: *Criticism: The Foundations of Modern Literary Judgment* (with Mark Schorer and G. McKenzie), 1948, revised 1958; *The Poem: A Critical Anthology*, 1959; *Classic Essays in English*, 1961.

BRENDA CHAMBERLAIN (1912–1971). Born in Bangor, Caernarvonshire, Wales. Educated at Royal Academy Schools, Burlington House, London. Received the Arts Council (Welsh Committee) Poetry Award, 1956. Was a painter as well as a poet. BOOKS: *The Green Heart,* 1958. *Poems with Drawings,* 1969. Other: *Tide-Race,* 1962; *The Water Castle,* 1964; *A Rope of Vines,* 1965; *Alun Lewis and the Making of the Caseg Broadsheets* (edited letters), 1969.

MAY SARTON. Born in Wondelgem, Belgium, daughter of George Sarton, historian of science. Educated at Shady Hill School, Cambridge, Massachusetts, Institut Belge de Culture Francaise, Brussels; Cambridge High and Latin School. Emigrated to the United States, 1916, naturalized, 1924. Script-writer for Overseas Film Unit, New York, 1941–1942; taught or lectured at Harvard University, University of Chicago, University of Kansas, University of Iowa, Colorado State College, Beloit College, Wellesley College, and Lindenwood College, and at Bread Loaf Writers Conference. Phi Beta Kappa Visiting Scholar, 1960. Lives in New Hampshire. BOOKS: *Encounter in April,* 1937; *Inner Landscape,* 1939; *The Lion and the Rose,* 1948; *The Land of Silence,* 1953; *In Time Like Air,* 1958; *Cloud Stone Sun Vine,* 1961; *A Private Mythology: New Poems,* 1966; *As Does New Hampshire and Other Poems,* 1967. Novels: *The Single Hound,* 1938; *Shadow of a Man,* 1950; *The Small Room,* 1961; *Mrs. Stevens Hears the Mermaids Singing,* 1965; *The Poet and The Donkey,* 1969. Autobiography: *I Knew a Phoenix,* 1959; *Plant Dreaming Deep,* 1968.

ANNE RIDLER. Born in Rugby, Warwickshire, England. Educated at King's College, University of London, diploma in journalism. An influential teacher was Olive Willis of Downe House School. Married to Vivian Ridler, printer to Oxford University. Worked in the editorial department of Faber & Faber Ltd., 1935–1940. BOOKS: *Poems,* 1939; *A Dream Observed,* 1941; *The Nine Bright Shiners,* 1943; *The Golden Bird,* 1951; *A Matter of Life and Death,* 1959; *Selected Poems,* 1961. Plays: *Cain,* 1943; *The Shadow Factory: A Nativity Play,* 1946; *Henry Bly and Other Plays,* 1950; *The Trial of Thomas Cranmer,* 1956; *Who Is My Neighbor?* 1963. Biography: *Olive Willis and Downe House,* 1967. Editor: *Best Ghost Stories,* 1967. *The Faber Book of Modern Verse,* 1951, revised 1960. *Shakespeare Criticism, 1919–1935,* 1936. *The Image of the City and Other Essays, by Charles Williams,* 1958; *Shakespeare Criticism, 1935–1960; Poems and Some Letters of James Thomson,* 1963. *Thomas Traherne: Poems, Centuries and Three Thanksgivings,* 1966; (with Christopher Bradley) *Best Stories of Church and Clergy,* 1966.

MURIEL RUKEYSER. Born in New York City. Educated at Vassar College and Columbia University. Arrested during the second Scottsboro trial in Alabama. On assignment to report the People's Olympics in Barcelona when the Spanish Civil War began. In 1941 joined staff of *Decision.* Vice President, House of Photography, since 1946; on faculty of Sarah

Lawrence College since 1956. Received the Yale Younger Poets Award for her first book *Theory of Flight*, 1935. BOOKS: *Waterlily Fire: Poems 1932–1962*, 1962; *The Speed of Darkness*, 1968; *29 Poems*, 1970. Novel: *The Orgy*, 1966. Other: *Willard Gibbs*, 1964; *The Life of Poetry*, 1949, 1968; *One Life*, 1958; *The Traces of Thomas Hariot*, 1970. Translation: *Sun Stone* (Octavio Paz), 1962.

JEAN GARRIGUE. Born in Evansville, Indiana. Educated at the University of Chicago and the University of Iowa, Iowa City (M.F.A.). Has spent a year as lecturer or poet-in-residence at several colleges and universities, including the University of Iowa, Bard College, Queens College, the New School for Social Research, the University of Connecticut, Smith College, and the University of Washington. Since 1965, poetry editor of *The New Leader*. She lives in New York City. BOOKS: *The Ego and the Centaur*, 1947; *The Monument Rose*, 1953; *A Water Walk by Villa d'Este*, 1959; *Country Without Maps*, 1964; *New and Selected Poems*, 1967. *Chartres and Prose Poems*, 1971. Novel: *The Animal Hotel*, 1966. Criticism: *Marianne Moore*, 1965. Editor: *Translations by American Poets*, 1970.

JEAN BURDEN. Born in Waukegan, Illinois. Educated at the University of Chicago; influenced by Thornton Wilder. Worked in advertising and insurance offices and as an editor. Public relations executive for Meals for Millions foundation, Los Angeles, 1956–1966. Now has her own public relations business. Has taught poetry workshops. Since 1954, poetry editor of *Yankee* magazine. BOOKS: *Naked as the Glass*, 1963. Essays: *Journey Toward Poetry*, 1966.

BARBARA HOWES. Born in New York City. Educated at Bennington College; studied with Genevieve Taggard and William Troy. Founded the literary magazine *Chimera* in 1943 and edited it until 1947. Formerly married to the author William Jay Smith. Lived for long periods of time in Italy and France. BOOKS: *The Undersea Farmer*, 1948; *In the Cold Country*, 1954; *Light and Dark*, 1959. *Looking Up at Leaves*, 1966. Editor: *23 Modern Stories*, 1963; *From the Green Antilles: Writings of the Caribbean*, 1966; with Gregory Jay Smith, *The Sea-Green Horse: Short Stories for Young People*, 1970.

ISABELLA GARDNER. Born in Newton, Massachusetts. Educated at Foxcroft School and the Embassy Theatre School of Acting, Hampstead, London. Acted professionally for several years. Formerly married to the poet and critic Allen Tate. Associate Editor of *Poetry*, 1952–1956. Has given poetry readings in London, Italy, and Ireland, as well as the United States. Now lives in New York. BOOKS: *Birthdays From the Ocean*, 1955; *West of Childhood: Poems 1950–1965*, 1965.

BARBARA GUEST. Born in North Carolina, spent youth in Florida and California. Educated at the University of California, Berkeley. Settled in New York City, where she became identified with a group of young abstract

painters. Has written articles on painters and was a reviewer for *Art News*.
BOOKS: *Poems*, 1962; *The Blue Stairs*, 1968.

RUTH STONE. Born in Roanoke, Virginia, grew up in Indianapolis, Indiana. Attended the University of Illinois. Assistant to the literary and dramatic editor of the Indianapolis *Star*. After her marriage to author Walter Stone, she lived in Cambridge, Massachusetts, and in Poughkeepsie, New York, until 1959, when she became an editor for the Wesleyan University Press. BOOKS: *In an Iridescent Time*, 1959; *Topography and Other Poems*, 1971.

BERNICE AMES. Born in Pennsylvania. Educated at Wilson College, Chambersburg, Pennsylvania. Has lived in Los Angeles since 1950. BOOKS: *Where the Light Bends*, 1955; *In Syllables of Stars*, 1958; *Antelope Bread*, 1966.

JUDITH WRIGHT. Born in Armidale, New South Wales, Australia. Educated at New South Wales Correspondence School, New England Girl's School, and the University of Sydney. Was Commonwealth Literary Fund Lecturer in Australian universities. Since 1967, Honours Tutor in English, University of Queensland, Brisbane. Was President of the Wildlife Preservation Society of Queensland, 1962–1965. Received the *Encyclopaedia Britannica* award, 1964. BOOKS: *Collected Poems, 1942–1970*, 1971. Novel: *The Generations of Men*, 1959. Short stories: *The Nature of Love*, 1966. Criticism: *Charles Harpur*, 1963; *Preoccupations in Australian Poetry*, 1965; *Henry Lawson*, 1967. Editor: *A Book of Australian Verse*, 1956, 1968; *New Land, New Language*, 1957; with A. K. Thomson, *The Poet's Pen*, 1965.

ANN STANFORD. Born in La Habra, California. Educated at Stanford University and the University of California, Los Angeles. Since 1962 on the faculty of California State University, Northridge. BOOKS: *In Narrow Bound*, 1943; *The White Bird*, 1949; *Magellan: A Poem to Be Read by Several Voices*, 1958; *The Weathercock*, 1966; *The Descent*, 1970; *The Bhagavad Gita: A New Verse Translation*, 1970.

NANCY CATO. Born in Adelaide, South Australia. Educated at Adelaide University, and studied for a short time at South Australia School of Arts. Has been a journalist and art critic, has traveled in Europe, Russia, and Asia, and explored the Australian outback by jeep to collect material for historical novels. Was advisory editor of *Poetry* (Australia) and *Overland*. BOOKS: *The Darkened Window*, 1950; *The Dancing Bough*, 1957. Novels: *All the Rivers Run*, 1958; *Green Grows the Vine*, 1961; *Time Flow Softly*, 1959; *Northwest by South*, 1965. Short stories: *The Sea Ants*, 1964. Editor: *Jindyworobak Anthology*, 1950.

EDITH MARCOMBE SHIFFERT. Born in Toronto, Ontario, Canada. Educated at the University of Washington, specializing in Far

Eastern Studies. Has worked as a secretary in Los Angeles, for the U.S. Weather Bureau in Anchorage, and briefly as a policewoman in Hawaii. Co-director of a series of public poetry programs broadcast on radio and television 1958–62. A founder and former Far Eastern editor of *Poetry Northwest*. Since 1963 has taught in Japan, formerly at Doshisha University, Kyoto, now as Professor of English at Kyoto Seika College. BOOKS: *In Open Woods*, 1961; *For a Return to Kona*, 1964; *The Kyoto Years*, 1971. Translation: (with Yūki Sawa) *Anthology of Modern Japanese Poetry*, 1971.

GWENDOLYN BROOKS. Born in Topeka, Kansas. Educated at Wilson College, Chicago. Her second book of poetry received the Pulitzer Prize for 1949. Has taught and lectured at colleges and universities across the United States. Poet Laureate of Illinois, succeeding Carl Sandburg. BOOKS: *A Street in Bronzeville*, 1945; *Annie Allen*, 1949; *Bronzeville Boys and Girls*, 1956; *The Bean Eaters*, 1960; *Selected Poems*, 1963; *In the Mecca*, 1968. Novel: *Maud Martha*, 1953.

RUTH HERSCHBERGER. Born in Philipse Manor, New York. Educated at the University of Chicago, Black Mountain College, and the University of Michigan, where she received a Hopwood Award in 1941, and in the Dramatic Workshop of the New School for Social Research, New York. Has written plays for radio and stage. BOOKS: *A Way of Happening*, 1948. *Nature & Love Poems*, 1969. Other: *Adam's Rib*, 1948.

MAY SWENSON. Born in Logan, Utah. Educated at Utah State University. Has since lived in New York. Formerly editor for a publishing firm. Has been poet-in-residence at Purdue University; the University of North Carolina, Greensboro; and the University of Lethbridge, Alberta, Canada. Four of her volumes of poetry were final contenders for the National Book Award. BOOKS: *Another Animal*, 1954; *A Cage of Spines*, 1958; *To Mix With Time: New and Selected Poems*, 1963; *Poems to Solve*, 1966; *Half Sun, Half Sleep*, 1967; *Iconographs*, 1970; *More Poems to Solve*, 1971.

GWEN HARWOOD. Born in Taringa, Queensland, Australia. Educated at Brisbane Girls' Grammar School. Formerly music teacher and organist at All Saints' Church. Her opera libretto, *The Fall of the House of Usher*, was performed at the Theatre Royal in Hobart, Tasmania, 1965. BOOKS: *Poems*, 1963; *Poems*, Volume II, 1968.

MARCIA LEE MASTERS. Born in Chicago, Illinois, daughter of the poet Edgar Lee Masters. Educated at the University of Chicago and Northwestern University. Taught creative writing in Los Angeles and worked on newspapers in that city and in Chicago. Currently, editor of *Today's Poets*, a weekly feature in the *Chicago Tribune Magazine*. Received the Midland Poetry award for her first book of poems. BOOK: *Intent on Earth*, 1965.

JOAN FINNIGAN. Born in Ottawa, Ontario, Canada. Educated at Carleton University, Ottawa, and Queen's University, Kingston, Ontario. Has been a teacher and a reporter for the *Ottawa Journal*. Received Canada

Council Grants, 1965, 1968, 1969; Canada Council Senior Arts Grant, 1967. Now a free-lance writer, doing film and radio scripts. Lives in Kingston, Ontario, Canada. BOOKS: *Through the Glass, Darkly*, 1957; *A Dream of Lilies*, 1965. *Entrance to the Green-House*, 1968; *It Was Warm and Sunny When I Set Out*, 1970.

MONA VAN DUYN. Born in Waterloo, Iowa. Educated at Iowa State Teachers College and the State University of Iowa (M.A.). Has taught English at the State University of Iowa, Iowa City; the University of Louisville, Kentucky; and since 1950 has been a lecturer at University College, Washington University, St. Louis, Missouri. With her husband Jarvis Thurston has edited *Perspective: A Quarterly of Literature* since 1947. Received the National Book Award and the Bollingen Award in 1970 for *To See, To Take*. BOOKS: *Valentines to the Wide World*, 1959; *A Time of Bees*, 1964; *To See, To Take*, 1970.

DENISE LEVERTOV. Born in Ilford, Essex, England. Educated privately. Served as a nurse during World War II. In 1947 married the writer Mitchell Goodman; has lived in the United States since 1948, naturalized 1955. Has been visiting professor at colleges and universities, including the University of California, Berkeley, and the Massachusetts Institute of Technology. Poetry editor of the *Nation*, 1961. BOOKS: *The Double Image*, 1946; *Here and Now*, 1957; *Overland to the Islands*, 1958; *With Eyes at the Back of Our Heads*, 1960; *The Jacob's Ladder*, 1962; *O Taste and See*, 1964; *The Sorrow Dance*, 1968; *Relearning the Alphabet*, 1970. *To Stay Alive*, 1971. Translations: *In Praise of Krishna: Songs from the Bengali* (with Edward C. Dimock, Jr.), 1967; *Selected Poems of Guillevic*, 1969. Editor: *Out of the War Shadow*, 1967.

JULIA RANDALL. Educated at Bennington College and Johns Hopkins University (M.A.). Lived in Paris, 1952–54. On English Faculty at Hollins College, Virginia, since 1962. BOOKS: *The Solstice Tree*, 1952; *Mimic August*, 1960; *The Puritan Carpenter*, 1965; *Adam's Dream*, 1969.

JANET FRAME. Born in New Zealand. Educated at Dunedin Teachers Training College and Otago University in New Zealand. Received the Hubert Church Memorial Award, New Zealand, for *The Lagoon*, 1951; and a Literary Fund Award, New Zealand, for *Owls Do Cry*. Better known as a novelist, she has published one volume of poetry. BOOKS: *The Pocket Mirror*, 1967. Novels: *Owls Do Cry*, 1960; *Faces in the Water*, 1961; *The Edge of the Alphabet*, 1962; *The Adaptable Man*, 1965; *A State of Siege*, 1966. Stories: *The Reservoir and Other Stories*, 1963; *Scented Gardens for the Blind*, 1964.

VASSAR MILLER. Born in Houston, Texas. Educated at the University of Houston (M.A.). Teacher of creative writing at St. John's School, Houston, since 1964. BOOKS: *Adam's Footprint*, 1956; *Wage War on Silence*, 1960; *My Bones Being Wiser*, 1963; *Onions and Roses*, 1968.

The Women Poets in English

MAXINE KUMIN. Born in Philadelphia, Pennsylvania. Educated at Radcliffe College (M.A.). Has taught at various colleges and universities including Tufts University, Medford, Massachusetts. Besides poetry and fiction, writes books for children. BOOKS: *Halfway*, 1961; *The Privilege*, 1965; *The Nightmare Factory*, 1970. Novels: *Through Dooms of Love*, 1965; *Passions of Uxport*, 1968.

CAROLYN KIZER. Born in Spokane, Washington. Founder and formerly editor of *Poetry Northwest.* Spent a year in Pakistan as poet-in-residence for the United States State Department. Director of literary programs for the National Endowment for the Arts during the Johnson administration. Poet-in-residence at the University of North Carolina, Chapel Hill, since 1970. BOOKS: *The Ungrateful Garden*, 1962; *Knock Upon Silence*, 1965; *Midnight Was My Cry: New and Selected Poems*, 1971.

ELIZABETH JENNINGS. Born in Boston, Lincolnshire, England. Educated at Oxford University (M.A.). Librarian and publisher's reader, 1950–1961. Received the Somerset Maugham Award in 1956. Since 1961, freelance writer. Lives in Oxford. BOOKS: *Collected Poems 1967*, 1967, *The Animals' Arrival*, 1969. *A Translation of Michelangelo's Sonnets*, 1961. Other: *Every Changing Shape*, 1959; *Let's Have Some Poetry*, 1960; *Robert Frost*, 1964; *Christianity and Poetry*, 1965. Editor: *An Anthology of Modern Verse 1940–60*, 1961; *A Choice of Christina Rossetti's Verse*, 1970.

ANNE SEXTON. Born in Newton, grew up in Wellesley, and now lives in Weston, Massachusetts. Has taught at Wayland High School and lectured on creative writing at Boston University. Her third collection of poetry received the Pulitzer Prize for 1966. BOOKS: *To Bedlam and Part Way Back*, 1960; *All My Pretty Ones*, 1962; *Live or Die*, 1966; *Love Poems*, 1969; *Transformations*, 1971.

SYLVIA PLATH (1932–1963). Born in Boston, Massachusetts. Educated at Smith College, Harvard University, and Newnham College, Cambridge University, as a Fulbright scholar, 1955–1957 (M.A.). Married the English poet Ted Hughes in 1956. Taught English at Smith College, 1957–1958; lived in Boston, 1958–1959, settled in London, later in Devon, England, where she ended her own life in 1963. BOOKS: *The Colossus*, 1960; *Ariel*, 1965; *Uncollected Poems*, 1965. Novel: *The Bell Jar*, 1963.

ADRIENNE RICH. Born in Baltimore, Maryland. Educated at Radcliffe College. Received the Yale Series of Younger Poets award for her first book, 1951. Lived in the Netherlands, 1961–1962. Taught at Swarthmore College, Pennsylvania, 1966–1968; in the Graduate School of the Arts, Columbia University 1967–1969; and in the SEEK Program, City College of New York, since 1968. BOOKS: *A Change of World*, 1951; *The Diamond Cutters*, 1955; *Snapshots of a Daughter-in-Law*, 1962; *Necessities of Life*, 1966; *Selected Poems*, 1967; *Leaflets*, 1969; *The Will to Change: Poems 1968–1970*.

MARGE PIERCY. Born in Detroit, Michigan. Educated at the University of Michigan, where she received a Hopwood Award for Poetry, and Northwestern University (M.A.). BOOKS: *Breaking Camp*, 1968. *Hard Loving*, 1969. Novel: *Going Down Fast*, 1969.

LUCILLE CLIFTON. Born in Depew, New York. Educated at Howard University and Fredonia State Teachers College. Participated in the YW–YMHA Poetry Center's Discovery Series, 1969. Now lives in Baltimore, Maryland. BOOK: *Good Times*, 1969.

SHIRLEY KAUFMAN. In 1969 received the United States Award of the International Poetry Forum for her first book. Has translated from the work of the Hebrew poet Abba Kovner. Lives in San Francisco. BOOK: *The Floor Keeps Turning*, 1970.

MARGARET ATWOOD. Born in Ottawa, Ontario, Canada. Educated at the University of Toronto and Radcliffe College (M.A:). Has taught at the University of British Columbia, Vancouver, 1964–1965; Sir George Williams University, Montreal, 1967–1968. Her book *The Circle Game* received the Governor-General's Award, 1966. Lives in Edmonton, Alberta. BOOKS: *Double Persephone*, 1961; *The Circle Game*, 1966; *The Animals in That Country*, 1968; *The Journals of Susanna Moodie*, 1970. Novel: *The Edible Woman*, 1969.

MARY OLIVER. Born in Cleveland, Ohio. Attended Ohio State University and Vassar College. Was secretary to Norma Millay Ellis, the poet's sister, at Steepletop. In England, worked as a writer for the Unicorn Theatre for Children. Lives in Provincetown, Massachusetts. BOOKS: *No Voyage and Other Poems*, 1963; new edition, with additional poems, 1965.

Index of Authors

Index of Titles

373